Cake & Loaf

GATHERINGS

Sweet and Savoury Recipes
to Celebrate Every Occasion

NICKEY MILLER & JOSIE RUDDERHAM

PENGUIN

an imprint of Penguin Canada, a division of Penguin Random House Canada Limited

Canada • USA • UK • Ireland • Australia • New Zealand • India • South Africa • China

First published 2023

www.penguinrandomhouse.ca

LIBRARY AND ARCHIVES CANADA CATALOGUING IN PUBLICATION

Title: Cake & Loaf gatherings : sweet and savoury recipes to celebrate every occasion / Nickey Miller and Josie Rudderham.
Other titles: Cake and Loaf gatherings
Names: Miller, Nickey, author. | Rudderham, Josie, author.
Identifiers: Canadiana (print) 20220142874 | Canadiana (ebook) 20220142882 | ISBN 9780735239852 (softcover) | ISBN 9780735239869 (EPUB)
Subjects: LCSH: Baking. | LCSH: Baked products. | LCSH: Entertaining. | LCGFT: Cookbooks.
Classification: LCC TX765 .M55 2023 | DDC 641.81/5—dc23

Cover and interior design by Kate Sinclair
Food and Prop Styling by Nickey Miller and Josie Rudderham
Photography and Illustrations by Nickey Miller
Photo on page 209 by Tamara Campbell

Manufactured in China

10 9 8 7 6 5 4 3 2 1

Penguin
Random House
PENGUIN CANADA

For my kids, Lily and Finn,
all my favourite gatherings include you two.
—Josie

Celebrations would not be the same without friends
and family. Thank you for all the fun, silly, and,
most importantly, delicious memories.
—Nickey

Contents

Introduction

Welcome to *Cake & Loaf Gatherings*, a celebration of our favourite sweet and savoury recipes for sharing. We are Nickey Miller and Josie Rudderham, co-owners of Cake & Loaf Bakery in Hamilton, Ontario, founded in 2010. Holidays have always been our favourite times of year at the bakery. There's something magical about the energy generated by the hustle and bustle of a well-run kitchen at peak capacity. Especially at Easter and during the winter holidays, we pump out thrice our regular volume of products. In every corner of the bakery there are folks icing cookies, dipping chocolates, or packaging up boxes of treats. Customers line up around the block each holiday to get their favourite pies, cakes, and seasonal treats from our little bake shop. The level of support is always humbling, and it's been a privilege to have our baked goods be the centrepiece of many gatherings over the years. Whether you have tasted these recipes at our bakery or are just now discovering us, we're sure we will have you drooling in no time. Each chapter of this book focuses on a holiday or type of gathering, progressing seasonally through the year from Valentine's Day at the beginning of the year to a New Year's Eve bash. We've always been driven to host gatherings and bring people together with food, and we've been planning and throwing celebrations together for over a decade now. A gathering can be intimate—just your household or a few close friends or family—or as grand as a wedding. It's not the size of the gathering that counts but the connection it creates.

In these pages we'll share all our best party planning and successful gathering advice along with our favourite recipes. Get intimate with Hot Cinnamon Blondies (page 33) from the Valentine's Day chapter or start a cuddle pile with the Sea Salt Brown Butter Pecan Cookies (page 199) in the Fall Feelings chapter. Blow your family away with The Cream Egg Brownies (page 55), an Easter recipe we have been begged to share for years. Get creative and try tempering chocolate with our delightful Halloween treats or plan a kid's party featuring Cheesy Fish Crackers (page 170) and a Raspberry Pop Tart Banner (page 163), both included in our Birthdays chapter. We will help you gain an understanding of how important it is to prepare, not only so you will be ready to host but so you can actually enjoy the celebration too. Let us walk you through timing, preparation, adding a sense of playfulness, and building an environment of connection. If you want to host a gathering, we've got the perfect recipes for you to share.

The Recipes

You will find useful information at the top of each recipe. Vegan recipes contain no animal products and are identified with a "V" symbol. Note the yield for the recipe you are making. This is essential information to make sure you will have enough for your guests. The yield allows you to plan for doubling or tripling recipes, if needed. You also will notice a "Prep" and "Cook" time associated with each recipe. "Prep" indicates the active time involved in a recipe, including any microwaving and most stovetop activities. "Cook" indicates the total bake time. Where appropriate, any extra time needed (such as for cooling or chilling) is indicated. Each recipe also includes "Do Ahead" instructions to clarify timelines and help you plan dishes. When preparing multiple recipes for a gathering, it will help to know what you can make ahead.

How to Host a Gathering

We have a long history of hosting gatherings with our family and friends and have thrown some pretty incredible parties over the years together. In high school and throughout university and college, instead of planning keggers or your average teenage barbecue, Josie hosted elaborate multi-course dinner parties emulating the winery meals she had shared with her family or experimenting with ingredients she had never tried but had seen on the Food Network. Whenever her parents or a friend's parents left a house empty for the weekend, Josie and her friends would hit up the local food stores, the more diverse the better, for new foods and inspiration and then spend hours planning menus, cooking complex dishes, and hosting friends. In the 2000s she would descend on any available house with fresh flowers, an assortment of beverages, and ingredients in hand and then use a last-minute combination of recipes from *Epicurious*, inspiration from the latest *Iron Chef* episode, and everyone's current cravings to create a feast. There was always too much food, lots of deep frying, belly laughs, and a huge mess to clean up the next day, but we always learned something new about the food we were cooking and bonded deeply. For Nickey, hosting has always been a great way to get people together to forget about reality for a little while. Or let's be honest, letting loose and dancing is really what she's here for. When great music and dancing happen, getting lost in the moment is so easy! Halloween parties are a favourite for Nickey, who appreciates an imaginative hands-on approach with all things. Her parties include elaborately staged rooms in a spooky setting with keyed-up lighting, strobe lights, and full-on scene setups from horror movies complete with all the detailed decor that truly transports you into the experience. Freakishly carved pumpkins lit up and lining the walkways to the house, complete with cobwebs, lighting, and eerie music blaring from speakers set up outside. Thoughtful, detailed costumes are an absolute must, and she often has awards for the best costume. These parties are usually a potluck, and the outcome is always an adventure with a variety of interesting cold and hot appetizers. A memorable drink at one of her parties consisted of ice cube hands floating in a deep red spiked punch. The ice cube hands

were created by filling clean plastic gloves with water, tying them off, and freezing them. Creative contributions to the food tables included skeleton-style charcuterie boards complete with a plastic skull coated in prosciutto that you had to peel off and olives for eyeballs.

In the past couple of years, many of us have reinvented what a gathering looks like. We've traded crowded dance floors at large events for cozy family dance parties in our pyjamas and rowdy New Year's Eve extravaganzas for backyard cocktail parties with just two or three special guests. You may even have participated in remote parties over video chat apps, creating meals to be delivered and then consumed together but from afar. All these adaptations taught us important lessons: first, that we will always find a way to connect through food, even when we can't connect in person, and second, that quality connections with the people we love endure and help us navigate the toughest of times.

Planning Multiple Courses

One of the first things they teach you in culinary school is to menu plan, and the key is lots of lists. When preparing multiple recipes for a gathering, you'll want to plan them all out in advance so that nothing gets missed. First, plan a menu that balances impressive centrepieces like our Strawberries and Cream Celebration Cake (page 183) with simpler projects like Ruby Chocolate Chunk Cookies (page 41) or items easily made in advance like Mini Egg Shortbread Cookies (page 62). Each chapter contains some simple recipes that can be made in advance and some that need to be baked fresh that day, like bread products. Read the recipes and create a timeline for yourself that includes shopping for ingredients, any components that can be made in advance, and rough timing for completing each recipe. Create a timeline for the day of the gathering and outline when you think you would like to serve different courses. Think about oven space when considering serving times. All our savoury mains, like Mini Chicken Pot Pies (page 91), can be reheated or assembled earlier in the day and baked fresh for your guests. In the week leading up to your gathering, get to work filling your fridge or pantry as you complete your plan. Two days prior to the event, revisit the recipes and double-check your list to ensure that you have all the ingredients and any compotes, ganaches, and other recipe components made. On the day of your event, rewrite the list one more time with even more detailed items to check off—get as specific as "zest lemons for loaf" or "chop fruit for passion puffs." You'll get the satisfaction of checking off each item as you complete it, but it will also ensure that you don't overlook any recipe components. This list is also helpful if you have any assistants helping you cook, as it will be easy to delegate tasks that need to be done without much thought.

Hosting a Gathering

Gathering to share food is still our favourite way to connect with loved ones and friends. Our parties have evolved over the years, but a few things remain key: invite people worth chatting with and create an environment in which they feel comfortable; pick a reason to celebrate; plan for a variety of foods and drinks and make them accessible; encourage curiosity and discovery with a unique dish, experience, or artistic addition; and don't stress about cleaning up right away. This holds true whether you have 2 or 200 guests. There are times when grand, catered affairs are appropriate, but generally when you are hosting a gathering, it's more about deepening the connections with people you care about. Sometimes the best parties are the mini parties at the beginning and end of the main party. At the beginning, it's just you and a couple of guests united in starting something. There's an electric tension in the air, an excitement about the memories about to be made. Creating something, connecting for a joint purpose, is always powerful. The "after party" has its own special appeal. It is often your best friends who have stuck around till the bitter end, so there's an intimacy to it. Everyone is usually a little tired and ready to just sit, chat, and snack on leftovers. Maybe even cuddle up for a movie. Hosting a successful gathering may seem intimidating at first, but we'll walk you through it step by step, and with all these delicious foods built for sharing, you can't go wrong. Don't get caught up in perfectionism, and have some backup plans for your food if it turns out you're spending more time in the kitchen than hosting. Everyone loves a bag of chips and dip, and your guests won't even realize that your half-finished main course is in the fridge. Eat it later and don't worry about dropping plans that don't serve you mid-party. Your guests are there for you, and if you are too busy rushing around because you overextended yourself or a dish goes awry, they are less likely to enjoy the party.

Creating a Connection

The art of hosting lies in knowing your guests and creating an atmosphere of connection. You would throw a very different party for your best friends than you would for your extended family or a group of co-workers. Connection is about relationships, but it's also about connecting to something larger than ourselves, to the land we inhabit and the food we consume. We all seek to escape the mundane and indulge in something different from our day-to-day. Seek to understand the higher purpose of your gathering and address the needs of the people attending the party to create true connection. A company holiday party superficially may be about celebrating the season and perhaps an upcoming break, but the higher purpose might be to help newer employees feel more comfortable with their co-workers or to build conflict resolution skills in a diverse group. Plan activities that support this purpose, such as *Jeopardy*-style quiz games about the company or ice breakers that allow folks to share details about themselves. One method to create connection in a group is providing space for a united goal. Murder mystery parties are one example of a fantastic way to get a group of strangers united in a task. When a group of people work toward a common goal, it often brings out the best in a group. Plan any gathering to be specific to you by considering the deeper purpose of the event. If the gathering is meant to support someone in an exciting but potentially scary time, such as marriage or parenthood, think about how to incorporate lots of soothing advice or opportunities to record gems of knowledge from your guests. A guest book or creative alternative record will be a meaningful physical reminder of your milestone gathering.

To plan a party that creates connection, first sit down and try to assess: What do these people physically need to create connection? How will the food and drinks help or hinder in creating that connection? Consider accommodations that will help everyone feel welcome. Loud music may be the mainstay of some parties seeking to create atmosphere, but if one of your guests has limited hearing or a tendency to have sensory overload, it can cause a lot of stress. Are there dietary restrictions or physical disabilities to consider? If you don't know, ask! It will be much less awkward to do that in advance than as folks arrive at your party, and you will feel confident that you've done your best to prepare. A great way to do this is to include a note in your invitations: "We want everyone to have a great time at this party; please let us know if you have any dietary restrictions or if there is anything that may affect your enjoyment that you'd like us to know about." Leave space on their RSVP card to write you a short note and make sure you include multiple ways to contact you, such as by email and telephone. If you know your guests well enough, simply ask yourself: "What do they need to feel fully included?" They might need a ride, and you could assist with arranging a carpool or calling taxis at the end of the night. Consider the physical accessibility of your space and washrooms; if it's important to your guests, rent an accessible space that is on ground level with accessible washrooms and accommodations for guide dogs or support animals such as water and an area for toileting. If it's a children's party, decide whether you want parents there and make expectations clear in the invites. Sensory overload at parties is common for a variety of reasons for different folks. Allow for a few quiet spaces where people can go to recover or decompress. Depending on your guests, consider a scent-free party. Strong scents can be overwhelming and may result in allergic reactions in some folks. If a guest is nonverbal or communicates in another way, you can download free software apps to help you communicate. If doing activities, consider teaming people up, such as kids and adults, and using both written and visual instructions to make it easier for everyone. If you know someone has a caregiver, be sure to also invite them to attend so they aren't forced to ask permission.

Before the Party

Planning is key to make your gathering as stress-free as possible and to allow you to enjoy your guests. First and foremost, consider who you want to invite and check their availability. There are great apps that take the hard work out of coordinating a large group of people; just pick a few times that work for you and send out links so that everyone can share their availability. Once you have a time or a few possible times, consider location. Most gatherings are held in the home, but if it's a large event or the guests aren't folks you know well, you may want to rent a venue or set up in a public park or community space. Next, schedule the party roughly into blocks of time to give you an idea of how long a party you want to throw and the direction the food should take. For a tea party, for example, you might want 30 to 45 minutes for guests to arrive and mingle, 60 to 90 minutes of seated eating or passed bite-size foods, and 30 to 45 minutes for circulating and socializing after the food. Therefore, you will need to invite guests for a 2- to 3-hour time block. If the time block includes a standard mealtime like breakfast (7 a.m. to 9 a.m.), lunch (11 a.m. to 2 p.m.), or dinner (5 p.m. to 7 p.m.), you need to serve enough food to act as a full meal. If you choose to hold your party in the afternoon or after dinner, you likely can get away with just snacks. Finalize the menu after you receive the RSVPs so that you can include any dietary restrictions. There's no reason to research a bunch of gluten-free alternatives if no one attending is actually gluten-free. We love a potluck, and it's an excellent alternative if the idea of cooking for a crowd makes your nervous. You can assign recipes directly by hosting a "Cook the Book" party using your favourite cookbook. Or assign invitees a course like main, salad, appetizer, or dessert and let them pick a favourite recipe. Since cooking isn't for everyone, never be snobbish about it and always allow people to purchase their contribution if that makes them more comfortable. If they aren't from the area, suggest small businesses they can order from. Depending on the size of the party, you may want to plan multiple drink stations. Ideally divide your alcoholic drinks, THC/CBD drinks, and virgin offerings into different stations, to make it easy for folks to identify what they are drinking. If you are offering alternatives like THC beverages, make sure that they are clearly labelled and you have potency information readily available. Allow guests the option to label their drinks as theirs with cups they can mark with Sharpies, colour-coded rings, or decorations that attach to the cups.

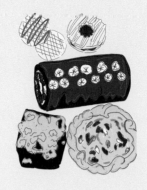

Consider your theme or decor alongside the food. The more you create a temporary alternative world for your guests, the deeper the connections and the more memorable your gathering will be. Use the entire party space as your empty stage and fill it with items that enhance your theme, from the entrance, throughout the home, and in all the small open spaces where you are allowing guests, even in the backyard (weather permitting). Small details really do keep the theme continuous. For example, a summer beach party theme could be assembled from items you likely have at home. Decorate your bathroom with a selection of sunscreens, clean buckets and spades, or decorative shells and driftwood. In the living room, drag out those beach towels and blankets and lay them on the couches. Use sand buckets as drink coolers and set up a beach umbrella over the drink station. Play beachy music or even the sounds of atmospheric waves crashing on the beach. Enhance the feeling of a temporary alternative world with rules for the party. Especially with a diverse group, pop-up rules set a cohesive tone for the group and help unite strangers and harmonize behaviour. Pop-up rules can be formalized and written out, especially if you want to have multiple rules or one as simple as "the first person to check their phone gets penalized and has to sing a childhood song." The more familiar a group of people are with each other, the more complex the fun rules can be. For a group that is used to being together, rules such as a list of banned words that require a penalty are entertaining because people will know the right questions to ask or topics to raise that will bring up the word. The penalty can be taking a shot or losing a privilege (such as cutlery), or each guest can have an item like a clothespin or bracelet distributed at the beginning of the party and they have to forfeit it to their challenger when they are caught. Whoever has the most items at the end of the party wins a prize. For a less familiar group, the fun can be as simple as a few ice-breaking games.

A few practical considerations: It's a good idea to warn your neighbours, or even invite them, if you think your party may be loud or is primarily outside. Make sure you leave time to clean your space. Clean and tidy any areas guests will have access to, empty your garbage and compost, have recycling and waste containers ready for guests, have backup toilet paper within reach in the bathroom, and empty the dishwasher. Designate a space for coats and bags and ensure that you have seating for at least fifty percent of guests. Prepare your entryway and exterior to make them festive and inviting. Communicate with your guests about parking and public transport and make sure that folks have a safe way home so they aren't tempted to drive under the influence. Nickey is the queen of logistics at the bakery and has an incredible eye for efficiency. She also hates the after-party cleanup part of gatherings, so she has perfected making it as easy as possible. She always gets organized before guests arrive by labelling large bins with "to wash," "paper," "plastic," "compost," and "waste" to empower guests to clean up after themselves. Set up these bins close to the food area or in a designated obvious spot so they're easy to access.

Sustainable Hosting

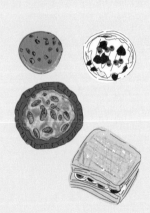

Sustainable parties are generally thrifty parties, and cheaper parties means more parties—so it's a win for everyone! It should be your goal to eliminate plastic and other disposables (even ones that claim to be recyclable) from your gatherings as much as possible. Invest in neutral cloth napkins and tablecloths, reusable fake candles, a set of metal or silicone straws, and reusable decor that's flexible like baskets and neutral platters. Check garage sales or thrift a set, or several sets, of inexpensive plates, glassware, and cutlery and store them in a big rubber tote to avoid buying disposables. Or throw a zero waste–themed party and educate your friends. Have them bring their own place settings and research a fun zero waste project to share, such as making your own laundry detergent or having a visible mending lesson. You can certainly use digital invitations of any variety to invite your guests for the smallest carbon footprint, but we also love cutting the fronts off old greeting cards and using them as postcard invitations. To ensure sustainable menu planning, eat local or grow your own food. Use the food itself and seasonal accents like pumpkins or pussy willows for decorative touches instead of expensive table settings. Shop your own pantry first when menu planning and take a "waste not, want not" attitude. Expand your definition of charcuterie platters to use up as many odds and ends as you can uncover in your pantry; think of it as a black-box culinary challenge. Just taste for freshness to ensure quality and get creative with what you gather.

Avoid plastic-filled goody bags by creating a take-home activity like planting a small plant, or decorate cookies during the party. Every year at the beginning of December, Josie's kids host a "Decorate Your Own Cookies Party" for their friends to ring in the winter season. They source more than a dozen different sprinkles—a cheap but effective way to add colour and personality to your cookies. Josie bakes up a huge batch of sugar cookie snowmen, snowflakes, and mittens. She also makes a huge batch of royal icing, divides it into a rainbow of colours, and sets up piping bags with No. 1 or 2 round tips so that the kids can't load too much icing on their cookies.

Then Josie steps back and watches the imagination flow. Since it has been mostly the same kids for years at a time, it's fascinating to see how the kids evolve their cookie decorating style as they mature, from just piling as much icing and as many sprinkles on a cookie as possible to intricate designs and themes. Each kid heads home with a bakery box full of treats and a great memory.

Getting the Party Started

It can be a little awkward as the first guests arrive at a party. To avoid staring at each other blankly, plan something so your first guests can contribute to the party. You can set up the drink station with a blank display area and ask them to design a signature beverage for the evening or reserve easy food prep like plating cookies or cutting up veggies for crudités. You can leave flower arrangements for the last minute and have your first guests get creative in assembling them. It's a wonderful way to get the first folks to arrive engaged and invested in your gathering by also making it their own. Greet guests as they arrive, give your gathering a brief introduction, and point out where to put coats or bags and where to find beverages. Once most guests have arrived, do a more formal summary. Introduce yourself and your party once people are settled and explain the agenda or provide a written reference. Welcome folks as a group, tell them where the washrooms and quiet areas are, and provide any other details that are key to your party. Creating a mood is important, and something we have found successful is splurging on one big thing that people will be talking about for months to come. For one Cake & Loaf holiday party we hired a glass artist who works with blowtorches to make gorgeous miniature glass animals and plants. He worked away for the whole party, acting as entertainment, and every guest left with a keepsake from the evening. You can hire musicians or another artist to create live art during your party, or you could invest in an adult bouncy castle. Consider your guests and what might wow them and then do some research. Your dream entertainment might be more accessible than you think. Ice breakers at gatherings are optional but a great way to get people talking regardless of how intimately they know each other. Have a couple planned in case the need arises. If it's a competitive group who is not afraid to get loud, have some "Minute to Win It" games ready. For a calmer crowd, try more discussion-based ice breakers like "Path Not Taken," where everyone states what they do now and what their lives would look like if they had engaged a different passion in life or work. "Whose Story Is It?" is another great ice breaker for a crowd. As guests arrive, give each guest a chance to write a true story (the more bizarre, the better) and then place it in a hat; draw a story at random throughout the party and have people guess whose it is.

Keeping Things Rolling

Once everyone is settled in and the agenda is progressing, be flexible. Plans rarely go off without any hitches, so don't be surprised if there are a few bumps. It's okay! There's no such thing as perfect. To keep the party rolling, it's always nice to have music. Make or find a couple of playlists in advance for different moods throughout the party. If any of your guests are musical, you could invite them to bring their instruments along to the party and play a few songs or start a spontaneous jam

session. Nothing gets people moving their bodies better than live music, even if it's just some basic acoustic guitar skills. Add to the mood by preparing various lighting levels for the different areas or activities of your gathering. You can hang fairy lights and turn off the main lights as the party goes on to switch moods. Or you can hang scarves over lamps to change the lighting colour (just make sure the lights don't get hot for safety). It may seem cheesy, but prepare a few talking points for conversations with people you don't know well to keep discussions rolling effortlessly: safe and fluffy topics like some interesting facts about the food or ingredients you've chosen or a discussion about hobbies. If you are really nervous, research a couple of jokes or funny stories to tell that work with your theme. Laughing makes everyone relax a little and helps with connection.

Have a couple of activities planned into the evening, such as "Build Your Own" foods like cheesecakes or trifle cups or organized group games. Keep people's interest by having activities in different areas of the gathering and space them throughout the party with breaks in between so folks don't feel overscheduled. Every party at Nickey's house involves at least one game; if you don't own any games yourself, ask a few close friends if they can bring some. It will keep the night going as people break into smaller groups and the mood shifts as people get to know each other better. If you have a pet and safety isn't an issue, let it roam the party. Some people are happiest at a party if they can just find the resident cat and chill; we know Josie's cats are always the most popular guests at the Cake & Loaf holiday parties. Most importantly, try to relax into your gathering and have fun! You have done a lot of work to organize and prepare, and it's time to appreciate your efforts.

Packaging Take Home-Treats and Favours

Everyone loves a little gift, and there are lots of fun and sustainable ways to package up take-home treats for your guests. Whatever you are packaging, try to make it as airtight as possible to keep your baked goods fresh longer. Plastic bags or poly bags are ideal for keeping out air and will allow a great view of your gift, but we believe most folks will appreciate you skipping the plastic. Sandwich cookies, like White Chocolate Marshmallow Surprise Sandwich Cookies (page 159), can be individually wrapped in parchment paper and closed with baker's twine or a sticker. To make your job easier, let the cookies chill in the refrigerator for an hour before packaging so that the buttercream is firm while you work. Cookies or Cheesy Fish Crackers (page 170) are best packaged in rigid reusable containers like tins, jars, or recycled takeout containers. You can use parchment paper or wax paper as a stuffing to fill out the container and make sure your baked goods are protected for their journey home. Alternatively, cookies or bars can be arranged on paper plates and wrapped in butcher paper or wax paper and decorated with ribbon or natural elements like sprigs of rosemary or a piece of cedar. If budget allows, purchase or make your own beeswax wraps and wrap your baking in a useful gift. You can find recyclable bakery boxes at most party stores or baking supply stores. They are relatively cheap and easy to dress up with small details like paper flowers or washi tape. Make your take-home gifts part of your decor by arranging them on a table by the entrance.

Sharing Platters

Sharing platters are a beautiful and easy way to round out a party spread or provide the perfect snacks for a small group. Choose a beautiful platter, cutting board, piece of wood, or unique surface to display your spread. It doesn't have to be a real plate, just a clean and food-safe surface. You can even line a surface with wax paper or brown butcher paper to create a food-safe surface on any material. Consider using something interesting to highlight your theme, such as aged lumber, old tiles, or a bed of greenery.

Cheese Platters

Cheese platters are wonderful crowd-pleasers and relatively easy to throw together for last-minute guests. Select a variety of cheese colours and textures to add visual appeal to your platter. Dried fruits (think dates, cranberries, goji berries, figs, apples, and pears), savoury jellies (like spicy red pepper jelly, chutneys, or wine jellies), and nuts (simply roasted, candied, or spiced) are natural pairings for cheese and allow you to add colour or texture pops to your platter. To start, consider a cheese from each of the following categories and then purchase one ounce of cheese per person as part of a buffet or appetizer spread or two to three ounces per person if it's a main dish. We like to include a soft ripened cheese like brie or camembert, an aged cheddar or other slightly sharp and firm cheese, a creamy cheese like goat cheese or boursin, a Swiss-style cheese or a Gruyère, and finally something unique that you enjoy. Any good cheese shop should allow you to taste samples of their cheese, so follow your senses to something you think your guests will love. A unique cheese can be visually stunning (there are some gorgeous layered cheeses and fruit cheeses with beautiful wax exteriors). It might be a strong blue cheese if you know your guests tastes run that way. Or think about a cheese that's unique to you or your cultural background; maybe you could share something new with your guests. You can serve the cheeses whole and provide appropriate knives or spreaders or cut them into single-serving pieces to facilitate serving. For larger crowds we always pre-cut the servings. Add a twist to the platter by adding something unexpected, such as freeze-dried cheese snacks or your favourite hard candy. If you are hosting vegan or dairy-free guests, there are excellent nut cheeses and alternatives like fermented tofu or halva. Finish off the spread with something to enjoy the cheese with, like our Flatbread Seed Crackers (page 95), Cheesy Fish Crackers (page 170), or your favourite store-bought crackers or bread. Cheese tastes best at room temperature, so be sure to assemble your platter at least an hour before it will be eaten; you can prepare the cheese platter up to six hours in advance and store it in the refrigerator, covered, until an hour before you serve it.

Charcuterie Platter

Charcuterie is a broad category encompassing many prepared meat products, but for this purpose we mean cured meat products that are best served at room temperature. Cured meats are excellent for platters, as they keep well at room temperature for several hours. If possible, seek out locally cured, nitrate-free products. We love to include something from each of these categories: a prosciutto or another raw-cured pork like guanciale, a spicy salami like calabrese or chorizo, a smoked meat like speck or Landjäger or a good-quality ham, something spreadable like rillettes or liverwurst, and something interesting your guests might not have tried before. Mix it up with a trip to your local Chinese BBQ for smoked duck or BBQ pork and serve it cold and sliced thinly. Explore the unique cultural offerings your community presents, and visit a small grocery store or deli you've never shopped at to try something new. Every culinary tradition has its own spin on charcuterie, so be a little adventurous and maybe you'll discover a new favourite food. Make sure the meats are cut into bite-size pieces. Try to purchase any sliced meats on the day you serve them, as their quality declines quickly. Soft Pretzels (page 129) or some breadsticks go nicely with charcuterie, and you'll want to round out your platter with some colourful pickles, nuts, or dried fruits. Cured meats tend to be salty, so you will want something sweet or vinegary to balance that out. You can even add chocolate or other sweets to the platter. Take a look deep into your pantry and get creative. Maybe you have something like candied ginger to add a little sparkle or chocolate covered pretzels for a sweet bite. Purchase two ounces of meat per person as an appetizer or up to four ounces per person if this is the main dish. You can assemble the platter up to two hours in advance and store it, covered, in the refrigerator.

Veggie Platter

Lean into the season to make the most of your vegetable platter. In summer, show off those gorgeous tomatoes, beans, peas, baby carrots, cucumbers, and maybe some grilled eggplant or zucchini. You can add interest by making some mini skewers from cherry tomatoes and basil leaves (even add a mini bocconcini), or roast baby carrots and roll them in a spice mix like za'atar. Later in the year, go for carrots, peppers, roasted sweet potato, broccoli, and cauliflower. Remember to include a variety of textures and colours to entice your guests. Prepare the vegetables by washing them well and cutting them into easy-to-eat sizes that only require a bite or two. If you grow the vegetables yourself or have bought them fresh locally and know you are serving vegetable lovers, you may be able to skip a dip and just focus on the natural amazingness, but most guests will appreciate a dip or two. It's nice to have something creamy and simple like ranch or hummus and something more complex like a Romesco dip, freshly made guacamole, or a beet and walnut dip. Add visual interest to your platter by adding some edible flowers or herbs. Don't be afraid to add some pickled vegetables for a little sour or spicy kick! If this is a main dish, you can serve the platter with Flatbread Seed Crackers (page 95) or Pull-Apart Garlic Cheese Buns (page 277) to round out the meal. It's best to cut up the vegetables right before serving, although the platter can be made up to six hours in advance and stored, covered, in the refrigerator.

Fruit Platter

We love adding fruit platters to morning events or to longer parties where people will be grazing for a while and will be looking for something sweet without necessarily being ready for dessert. The same basics for the veggie platter apply here: source the freshest local produce you can and stay seasonal for more delicious results. Raspberries may seem like a beautiful addition, but if it's January in North America, you are better off focusing on citrus fruits and firm tree fruits like apples and pears over out-of-season berries that have travelled halfway across the world. We love sneaking a few cookies onto a fruit platter for those who really can't wait for dessert (we understand). Mini Egg Shortbread Cookies (page 62) add nice colour, and you can use other candies like M&Ms if it's not mini egg season. Scottish Shortbread Cookies (page 239) are a simple and universally popular cookie that also work well with any fruit. Sweet yogurt dips, Dreamy Cream Cheese Icing (page 295), or thinned Chocolate Ganache (pages 307 to 308, just add an extra tablespoon or two of whipping cream to warm ganache to thin it) make excellent dips for fruit. Fruit platters are best made right before serving, although they can be made up to four hours in advance and stored, covered, in the refrigerator.

Equipment and Tools

Having the right tools and equipment makes cooking and baking a breeze. Collect the following pieces over time and add your own favourites. We love shopping at small restaurant supply stores for our smallwares. They usually have the best prices, they offer items meant to stand up to daily use, and you can develop a relationship with the staff that allows you to learn something new every time you shop.

Baking Sheets: 13- × 18-inch aluminum pans bake evenly and are easy to find. Pick one style and stick with it for easy stacking storage.

Bar Pans: 9- × 13-inch aluminum cake pans with nice straight sides.

Beeswax Wraps: A lovely alternative to plastic wrap, these wraps stick to themselves and can be moulded around bowls and pans to create a seal.

Bench Scraper: A metal rectangle, usually with a wooden handle, perfect for scraping the counter clean or lifting dough.

Bowl Scraper: Rounded on one side and generally made of hard plastic for scraping out bowls and scraping down counters.

Cake Pans: We always use 3-inch-deep round aluminum cake pans to allow for nice tall cake layers and even baking.

Cake Turntable: A metal stand that rotates effortlessly on ball bearings to make it a snap to ice cakes and top cream pies.

Circle Cookie Cutters: It's nice to have a variety of cookie cutters, but a circle set in various sizes is a great start to your collection.

Digital Kitchen Scale: Measure to 1 gram increments and often can be picked up on sale at kitchen stores for less than 15 dollars. Keep a few extra batteries on hand.

Glass Liquid Measuring Cups: We like to use these to microwave ingredients and measure liquids. We suggest a set of 1-, 2-, 4-, and 8-cup sizes.

Infrared (Laser) Thermometer: The cleanest and easiest way to assess temperature for chocolate tempering or candy making.

Kitchen Torch: For finishing meringue and heating pans to release product or to toast marshmallows.

Knives: A good-quality chef's knife, bread knife, and paring knife are essentials.

Measuring Cups: Stainless steel is our favourite; look for a set of ¼-, ⅓-, ½-, and 1-cup sizes that stack into each other for easy storage.

Measuring Spoons: Look for spoons that fit into your spice jars. We prefer stainless steel, round measuring spoons.

Microplane Grater: Essential for zesting citrus fruit effortlessly. It creates lovely tiny curls and makes it easy to avoid the white pith of the fruit.

Mixing Bowls: A set of four or five bowls in different sizes ranging from 1 cup to 28 cups in an easy-to-clean, non-reactive material like stainless steel or glass is ideal.

Muffin and Doughnut Pans: Look for nonstick and always avoid cleaning them with anything abrasive—just use hot water and a soft cloth to maintain the nonstick surface.

Offset Palette Knife (also called an Offset Spatula): Essential for spreading batters, lifting baked goods, and icing cakes.

Parchment Paper: Perfect for lining baking dishes or making paper cones. Look for silicone alternatives to line baking sheets without waste.

Pastry Brushes: Look for firmly affixed boar hair pastry brushes with wooden handles and always clean these very well, as it's easy for debris to get in between the bristles and mould over time.

Pastry Cutter: This classic tool makes cutting fats into flour without warming the fat easy-peasy.

Pie Plates: Pottery, metal, glass, and ceramic all work. Look for a sturdy pan that will conduct heat slowly and evenly.

Piping Bags: Look for 12- to 16-inch featherweight polyester bags for comfort and longevity.

Piping Tips: Invest in a set and proper storage for these easy-to-lose pieces. Start with a small and large star tip and small and large round tips.

Pots and Pans: Invest in good-quality pots and pans to last a lifetime. Every cook should own at least a small and a large heavy-bottomed pot, a shallow saucepan, and a frying pan.

Rolling Pins: Our rolling pins of choice at the bakery are marble— their weight does most of the work for you and they remain cold at room temperature to keep your dough chilled.

Scissors: Buy good-quality kitchen scissors that can cut bones and herbs and don't let your kids anywhere near them.

Scoops: Make portioning cookies and cupcakes easy-peasy. Invest in two or three sizes that work for you.

Silicone Spatula: Heat resistant and easy to clean. Perfect for stirring or scraping out the bowl.

Stainless Steel Mesh Sieve: For sifting dry ingredients and custards or curds to sift out any eggy bits. Look for a smaller size for dusting icing sugar or cocoa.

Stainless Steel Ruler: Perfect for cutting bars, lifting pastry off your counter, releasing the dough from the counter while rolling cookies, or measuring cookies.

Stand Mixer: We like a 6-quart or bigger mixer and ideally a brand that allows you to order parts and repair the mixer as it ages.

Vegetable Peeler: We prefer the Y-shaped peelers with horizontal blades for more control while peeling.

Whisks: Look for stainless steel whisks that don't have any nooks and crannies in which dirt can hide. Silicone whisks are also great for pastry creams and curds.

Wire Cooling Racks: Look for stainless steel racks that can double as icing grates.

Wooden Spoon: Find a spoon that feels like an extension of your hand when you use it. Every baker has a favourite wooden spoon.

Pantry Staples

Keeping these ingredients on hand in your pantry, freezer, or refrigerator will ensure that you are always ready to whip up something to satisfy a sudden craving or last-minute guests.

Almond Flour: Buy this fresh as you need it from bulk stores or make your own by finely grinding blanched almonds.

Bacon: Seek out naturally smoked bacon from a butcher or deli counter and keep ½-pound packages ready to defrost in the freezer.

Butter: Baking requires unsalted butter, and we do not recommend swapping out for salted. Salted butter is a condiment, not an ingredient, in our kitchens.

Buttermilk: Use full-fat buttermilk. In a pinch you can add 1 tablespoon vinegar or lemon juice to 1 cup milk and let it stand at room temperature for 15 minutes.

Canned Crushed Tomatoes: The best tomatoes are the ones you can yourself but seek out good-quality brands in your community.

Canola Oil: This is our neutral oil of choice at the bakery for baking and frying.

Cheese: Check out your local farmers market for a variety of local cheeses and don't be afraid to ask for samples.

Chili Flakes, Red: Buy these in small amounts to ensure freshness.

Chocolate: Good-quality milk, dark, white, or ruby chocolate can be found at most bulk stores or good grocery stores. Seek out couverture chocolate for tempering.

Chocolate Hazelnut Spread: We love Nutella, but many alternative brands are available.

Citrus Fruits: It's always a good idea to have a few lemons or oranges on hand to enrich your baking. Limes, grapefruit, and any number of orange varieties can be used too.

Cocoa Powder: We use 22% to 24% royal Dutch processed cocoa for all our recipes.

Cookie Butter: This speculoos spiced cookie–flavoured spread is a fun nut-free alternative to Nutella and something your guests may not have tried before.

Cornstarch: Always good to have on hand to adjust the thickness of fillings or to lighten up baked goods.

Cream: Full-fat cream should be 35% butterfat or higher and as fresh as possible.

Cream Cheese: Use full fat. Cream cheese is an ingredient to have on hand to whip up icing or mini cheesecakes.

Crisp Pearls: These are little balls of puffed rice coated in various types of chocolate. Usually can be found at bulk stores.

Dairy: Whole milk is our go-to for baking. Two percent is an acceptable substitute, but we would avoid baking or cooking with skim milk.

Edible Flowers: Look for food grade or grow your own violets, nasturtiums, borage, lavender, chive flowers, pansies, or honeysuckle to add to salads and platters.

Eggs: Seek out eggs laid by locally raised chickens you can visit yourself if possible. Meeting your farmer is rewarding and can help you understand your food better.

Extracts and Oils: Look for natural oils over extracts when possible and buy high quality in small amounts so it's fresh.

Flour: Do some research in your community and see if you can find local flour, locally ground. We love a stone ground flour for great flavour and a little texture.

Fondant: Fondant icing is a rollable, malleable coating for confections and cakes made with sugar, gelatin, and usually vegetable fat. You can purchase it at most bulk stores and colour it yourself with gel food colouring or purchase pre-coloured fondant.

Fresh Fruit: We like to keep apples and some citrus fruit on hand for last-minute baking needs, but berries or other soft fruit should be purchased as needed.

Fresh Herbs: It's easier than you might think to grow your own herbs, and many grocery stores even sell baby herb plants. Find a sunny window and you'll always have fresh flavour and a beautiful garnish available.

Fresh Meats: Ideally we like to purchase fresh meat on the day it is being cooked. Look for a butcher in your community that works directly with farmers.

Fresh Vegetables: We always like to have at least the mirepoix trio available in our fridges and pantries—carrots, celery, and onions.

Frozen Fruit: Very convenient for last-minute pies or cakes. Frozen fruit is a wonderful alternative if fresh fruit is hard to source or out of season.

Frozen Vegetables: Often flash frozen right after picking, frozen vegetables are excellent for fillings or soups.

Garlic: Garlic keeps well, so please skip the jarred garlic and always use fresh garlic (which is also packed with health benefits).

Gel Food Colouring: Essential for vibrant colours, gel food colouring is significantly more concentrated than liquid food colouring. Widely available at bulk food stores.

Goat Cheese (Chèvre): This creamy, slightly crumbly mild cheese is delicious on salads, in quiche, or as part of a cheese platter.

Graham Crumbs: These keep well and are great to have on hand to make a last-minute pie shell or to add a little flavour and texture to cookies.

Honey: Consuming local honey is known to help with seasonal allergies; it has a lower glycemic index than sugar, and it's delicious!

Jam: Keep a jar or two of your favourite jams on hand for sandwiching cookies or filling tarts. Or take advantage of summer's bounty and make a couple of batches of jam to last the year.

Leaveners: Baking soda and baking powder are both examples of chemical leaveners, and yeast is a biological leavener. Leaveners are the key ingredient in adding air to your baked goods.

Maple Syrup: We love grade A dark maple syrup for its intense maple flavour.

Milk Chocolate Candy Mini Eggs: We like to use a 50/50 mix of Cadbury Mini Eggs and Hershey's Eggies, but any chocolate candied eggs you enjoy can be used.

Mixed Candied Peel: We love making our own (page 318), but there's nothing wrong with a high-quality store-bought version. They keep well and can stay in your pantry for more than a year if needed.

Non-Dairy Milk: Generally we use unsweetened soy or almond milk at the bakery, but any unsweetened non-dairy milk meant for drinking should work in these recipes.

Nuts: It's nice to have small amounts of almonds, pecans, and walnuts available for baking but don't over-purchase them, as they can go rancid after a few months.

Olive Oil: Quality olive oil is a fresh product and shouldn't be stored for long, especially if you are using it as a condiment or for salad dressings.

Panko Bread Crumbs: Crispier and larger than traditional bread crumbs, panko bread crumbs are made from a crustless white bread that is grated to create lighter, crunchier crumbs.

Peanut Butter: We have tested all our recipes with smooth Kraft brand peanut butter. Other sweetened peanut butters may work, but we don't recommend using unsweetened peanut butter.

Pickles: We love having a few pickles in the fridge for last-minute guests or garnishes. Cucumber pickles like dill or gherkins are wonderful, as are pickled vegetables like beans, beets, zucchini, or cherry tomatoes.

Pumpkin Purée: It's best to buy a pumpkin and roast it, then purée and sieve it to make your own pumpkin purée, but there are some good-quality canned pumpkin purées, and any leftovers freeze well.

Pure Vanilla Extract: Although pure vanilla extract is expensive, it's worth every drop for that real vanilla flavour.

Seeds: Keep some of your favourite seeds (we like pumpkin, sunflower, sesame, and flaxseed) on hand to top salads, add to bread or crackers, and add visual interest to platters.

Spice Mixes: A few house spice mixes will become your go-to and are a great launching pad for new combinations. See our basic dry spice mixes for inspiration (pages 311 to 313).

Spices: Keep your pantry stocked with warm spices like cinnamon, ginger, allspice, nutmeg, and cloves and savoury dried herbs like thyme, rosemary, oregano, bay leaves, and black peppercorns.

Sprinkles: It's always nice to have a few sprinkles in the pantry to pretty up a dessert. Buy them fresh in small amounts from your local bulk store and look for seasonal specials.

Sugar: You will want to have at least dark brown sugar and white granulated sugar on hand in your pantry, but turbinado (large crystals of brown sugar) or sanding sugar (large crystals of clear sugar) are a nice addition to add sparkle to baked goods.

Vanilla Bean Paste: Generally a mixture of glucose and suspended vanilla beans, more intense in flavour than pure vanilla extract; since it has a glucose base instead of a liquid base, it is great to use in icings or drier products like shortbread.

Vegan Margarine: We like Crystal soft margarine. We prefer a soft margarine for baking and icings but a firmer margarine like Earth Balance for pastry.

Vinegar: White or apple cider vinegar is great to have on hand for cleaning or as an acid in baking.

Worcestershire Sauce: A fermented English condiment that adds umami flavour to dishes.

Yeast: We use instant dried yeast for all our recipes because it keeps well and is the easiest to activate.

Valentine's Day is all about spreading the love! Whether it's for an intimate evening for you and your partner(s), a family party, or a gathering of friends, take the time to bake everything you can in advance so that you are ready to be present with your guests when they arrive. If possible, clean and decorate the day before so you have the full day of the event to bake anything that's best fresh without rushing, such as Red Velvet Doughnuts with Dreamy Cream Cheese Icing (page 42), Ruby Chocolate Chunk Cookies (page 41), or Nutella Twists (page 47). Plan out any beverages and set up your drinks station with a selection of beverages before guests arrive. Really being present and allowing yourself to relax into your own party is the best form of love you can give any guest. All the recipes in this chapter hold up well at room temperature for three to four hours. You can package up We Belong Together Iced Sugar Cookies (page 35) or Chocolate Heart-Shaped Sandwich Cookies (page 37) in advance for a lovely take-home treat for your guests that will also look stunning as part of the decor. If it's a sensual mood you are looking for, allow your guest(s) to get hands on. They can drizzle their own Nutella on the twists (and anything else that strikes their fancy), or instead of topping the doughnuts, use the icing as a dip and feed each other. For a family-friendly feast for the senses, focus on brightly coloured decor, make a rainbow of love out of different-coloured heart cutouts, and incorporate "build-your-own stations" into your menu. Allow guests to assemble their own personal pizzas, top their own cheesecakes, or build-their-own sandwich cookies. Pick a place that's easily cleaned so it doesn't kill the mood if folks get a little messy with their food and let the sensuality flow.

Valentine's Day

Hot Cinnamon Blondies

DO AHEAD: You can store these baked blondies topped with ganache, covered, at room temperature for up to 3 days. Or make the blondie and ganache ahead, and store the blondie well wrapped at room temperature for up to 5 days and the ganache in an airtight container in the refrigerator for up to 2 weeks. Serve the blondies at room temperature or warm the ganache in the microwave and pour it over plated blondies.

Spiced Sugar Mix

1 tablespoon turbinado or
   sanding sugar
½ teaspoon red chili flakes
½ teaspoon cinnamon
¼ teaspoon cayenne pepper
¼ teaspoon salt

Blondie Batter

1¼ cups all-purpose flour
1 teaspoon baking powder
1 teaspoon cinnamon
½ teaspoon salt
½ cup unsalted butter,
   room temperature
1 cup packed dark brown sugar
1 large egg
1 teaspoon pure vanilla extract

Dark Chocolate Ganache

1 batch Dark Chocolate Ganache
   (page 307)

Just the right amount of spicy heat balanced out beautifully with dark, silky chocolate and a buttery cinnamon blondie. These blondies and their spicy central vein will hit you right in the heart. They are best served warm with ice cream—either classic vanilla or chocolate, depending on your inclinations. These are definitely more adult blondies and would be great with a mature aphrodisiac twist: replace the butter with the same amount of cannabutter and snack responsibly! For a fiery twist, sprinkle the blondies with some thinly sliced fresh chilies or crushed cinnamon hearts while the ganache is still wet.

1. Preheat the oven to 350°F (180°C). Line an 8-inch square cake pan with parchment paper.

2. Make the spiced sugar mix: In a coffee grinder or using a mortar and pestle, grind together the turbinado sugar, chili flakes, cinnamon, cayenne, and salt to a fine powder. Set aside for step 7.

3. Make the blondie batter: Sift the flour, baking powder, cinnamon, and salt into a medium bowl and stir together.

4. In the bowl of a stand mixer fitted with the paddle attachment, beat the butter on medium-high speed until smooth, 2 to 3 minutes. Scrape down the sides and bottom of the bowl. Add the brown sugar and continue to beat on medium-high speed until fluffy, 2 to 3 minutes. Scrape down the sides and bottom of the bowl.

5. Add the egg and vanilla. Beat on high speed for 2 to 3 minutes until the batter is smooth and fluffy. Scrape down the sides and bottom of the bowl.

6. Add the flour mixture and mix on low speed, then increase the speed to medium and mix just until the batter is smooth, 1 to 2 minutes.

7. Assemble and bake: Evenly spread half the batter into the prepared pan. Sprinkle the spiced sugar mix evenly over the batter. Spoon the rest of the batter overtop and gently pat it down with wet hands to form an even layer. (The dough will be stiff.) Bake for 30 to 35 minutes, or until a toothpick inserted into the centre of the blondie comes out clean. Allow the blondie to cool at room temperature for 1 hour before topping.

8. When the baked blondie is cool, pour the dark chocolate ganache evenly overtop and use a small offset palette knife to spread it level to the edges of the pan. Refrigerate the bar for 1 hour before cutting to allow the ganache to firm up.

9. Cut the blondies using a warm chef's knife by dipping it into hot water and drying it on a clean kitchen towel. Wipe the knife between each cut to get nice clean cuts.

netflix + track pants

cats + dogs

nachos + guac

chips + dip

wine + cheese

cake + ice cream

netflix + track pants

an old lady + 27 cats

sour dough + ...

coffee + biscotti

coffee + donuts

milk + cookies

salt + pepper

pizza + garlic dip

We Belong Together Iced Sugar Cookies

Sugar Cookie Dough
1 batch Sugar Cookie Dough
  (page 301)

Royal Icing
2 batches Royal Icing (page 295)
Assorted gel food colouring, 1 to
  3 drops each, depending on
  preferred vibrancy

For more than a decade we have been selling these adorable, romantic cookies iced with royal icing and finished with iconic pairings in flowing hand-piped script. Everything from "Peanut Butter + Jam" to "Netflix + Track Pants." We have offered custom cookies for years so that folks can create their own perfect pairings, and now you can make your own at home. The sugar cookie is buttery and shortbread-like in texture. Not too sweet and with a pronounced vanilla bean flavour. The royal icing changes significantly as it dries and sets, from pillowy clouds to a crispy sweet crust. Once the royal icing is dry, the cookies will last for weeks, which is convenient if you're giving these as gifts. Serve the cookies with tea or milk for dunking.

1. Preheat the oven to 350°F (180°C). Line 3 baking sheets with parchment paper or silicone baking mats.

2. Make the cookies: The sugar cookie dough must be rolled out immediately after making it. On a lightly floured work surface, roll out the dough to about ¼-inch thickness. Move the dough around and check underneath it frequently to make sure it is not sticking, dusting lightly with more flour as needed. Run a floured metal ruler under the dough to release any stuck areas.

3. Using a 4½-inch heart-shaped cookie cutter, cut out 20 hearts of dough. Carefully transfer up to 8 cookies to each prepared baking sheet, leaving a small space between them. Bake one sheet at a time for 18 to 22 minutes, or until the cookies have puffed up and are slightly brown on the bottom and slightly golden on top. Allow the cookies to cool completely on the baking sheets.

4. Start decorating the cookies—flood the cookies: Transfer at least ¾ cup of the white royal icing to a small airtight container and reserve for writing (step 7). Keep at room temperature. (CONTINUES)

DO AHEAD

Make these cookies, pipe the border, and flood them with royal icing at least 2 days ahead. Pipe the royal icing script a day ahead of serving or packaging. You can store the finished cookies in an airtight container at room temperature for up to 1 month. Individually packaged and sealed iced cookies can be stored at room temperature for up to 2 months. Un-iced cookies can be stored in an airtight container at room temperature for 1 month or frozen for up to 3 months. Place the frozen cookies, uncovered, on a baking sheet in a single layer to thaw at room temperature for 30 minutes before icing them.

coffee +
donuts
cats + dogs

5. Divide the remaining white royal icing into as many medium bowls as you would like colours for your heart-shaped cookie bases. Add 1 drop of food colouring to each bowl of icing and stir until fully incorporated. Add another 1 or 2 drops of food colouring, if needed to achieve the desired colour. For each colour of icing, fill a 12-inch piping bag fitted with a No. 4 round tip to create a raised border that will define the icing flooding area. Pipe a heart-shaped border around the edge of each cookie (see Royal Icing Piping Styles, page 288, Stiff Texture H).

6. Return the remaining coloured icings back to their separate bowls. Add 1 to 2 teaspoons of water at a time to each bowl, stirring thoroughly after each addition, to thin the icing to a "flooding consistency" for each colour (see Royal Icing Piping Styles, page 288, Flooding Texture L). Once the icing is runny enough to settle into a smooth, flat surface when piped onto the cookies but still thick enough that it holds its shape briefly before settling, for each colour fill a 12-inch piping bag fitted with a No. 2 round tip (this will give you more control, but you can also use a spoon).

7. Fill the interior of each heart-shaped border. Ensure that the flooding icing meets with the piped border for a seamless finish. You can use the back of a spoon or a small offset palette knife to spread the icing on the cookie. Use a toothpick to pop any air bubbles. Allow the wet icing to dry for at least 4 hours or overnight, uncovered, at room temperature in a dry area before piping the script.

8. Finish decorating the cookies—pipe the icing script: Using a spatula, stir the reserved ¾ cup white royal icing to remove any air bubbles. Fill a 12-inch piping bag fitted with a No. 1 or 2 round tip (depending on the fineness of the desired script) with the white icing. Practice piping your message on clean parchment paper. You can scrape off the icing and use it again. Pipe the message on the cookies (see Royal Icing Piping Styles, page 288, Stiff Texture H).

9. Allow the cookies to set, uncovered, at room temperature in a dry area for at least 24 hours to ensure that the icing is firm to the touch.

Chocolate Heart-Shaped Sandwich Cookies Ⓥ

Vegan Chocolate Sugar Cookies

2 tablespoons cold water

1½ teaspoons Vegan Egg Replacer (page 313)

1½ cups all-purpose flour, more for dusting

1 cup cocoa powder, sifted

½ teaspoon salt

¾ cup soft vegan margarine (we use Crystal)

½ cup granulated sugar

1 teaspoon pure vanilla extract

Pink Vegan Buttercream

1 batch Vegan Vanilla Bean Buttercream (page 294)

1 to 2 drops pink gel food colouring

For assembly

3½ ounces (100 g/½ cup) vegan semi-sweet chocolate callets or good-quality chopped chocolate

2 tablespoons red, pink, or white mini nonpareil sprinkles

The deep chocolate flavour of these cookies is intense. We've paired them here with a vegan icing to keep them plant-based, but they are also incredible sandwiched with our Dreamy Cream Cheese Icing (page 295). This dough is quite delicate to roll, so be extra careful when lifting the cookies from the work surface to the baking sheets. Run an offset palette knife or metal ruler under the dough before lifting to make sure it isn't sticking, then carefully lift each cookie with the offset palette knife and transfer it to your baking sheet. If there is any extra icing, we suggest icing the mini hearts without sandwiching and finishing them with some sprinkles. Otherwise, just serve the mini hearts on the side for little hands or folks not looking for a full dessert.

1. Preheat the oven to 350°F (180°C). Line 3 baking sheets with parchment paper or silicone baking mats.

2. Make the cookies: In a small bowl, stir together the water and vegan egg replacer until dissolved.

3. Sift the flour, cocoa, and salt into a medium bowl and stir together.

4. In the bowl of a stand mixer fitted with the paddle attachment, cream the vegan margarine, sugar, and vanilla on medium speed until just pale in colour and the sugar is starting to dissolve, 1 to 2 minutes. (You don't want this to be too light and fluffy, as it will dry out the dough after baking with too much aeration.) Scrape down the sides and bottom of the bowl.

5. Add the vegan egg replacer and beat on medium-low speed until fully incorporated, 1 to 2 minutes. Scrape down the sides and bottom of the bowl and the paddle.

6. Add the dry mixture and beat on low speed until mostly incorporated, then increase the speed to medium-high and beat just until the dough comes together, about 30 seconds. (CONTINUES)

DO AHEAD

You can store un-iced cookies in an airtight container at room temperature for up to 2 weeks. The vegan vanilla buttercream can be made ahead and stored in an airtight container in the refrigerator for up to 1 month. Store assembled sandwich cookies in an airtight container at room temperature for up to 1 week.

7. On a lightly floured work surface, roll out the dough to about ³⁄₁₆-inch thickness. Move the dough around and check underneath it frequently to make sure it is not sticking to the work surface, dusting lightly with more flour as needed. Run a floured metal ruler under the dough to release any stuck areas. Using a 3-inch heart-shaped cookie cutter, cut out 24 dough hearts. Evenly space 12 cookies each on 2 of the prepared baking sheets, leaving ample space between them. Using a ¾-inch heart-shaped cookie cutter, cut small hearts out of the centre of 12 of the cookies to create a peekaboo for the icing. Place the small heart cutouts on the third prepared baking sheet. Reroll the dough scraps to fill the third baking sheet with mini cookies until you have used all the dough.

8. If there is any flour on top of the cookies, brush it off with a dry pastry brush. Bake the large cookies one sheet at a time for 11 to 14 minutes, or until the cookies have puffed up and appear dry. Bake the smaller cookies for 7 to 10 minutes. Allow the cookies to cool completely on the baking sheets.

9. Heat the chocolate and drizzle the cookies: In a small heat-resistant bowl, heat the semi-sweet chocolate in the microwave for 30 seconds. Vigorously stir for 1 minute until the chocolate is melted. If you see any lumps, heat in the microwave in 15-second intervals, stirring after each interval, for 1 minute, until smooth. Drizzle the melted chocolate in thin diagonal lines over the surface of the 12 cookies with heart cutouts. These will be the tops of the sandwiches.

10. Sprinkle the cookies: While the chocolate is wet, scatter the sprinkles evenly over the chocolate. Allow the cookies to dry, uncovered, at room temperature for 1 hour.

11. Make the pink vegan buttercream: In the bowl of a stand mixer fitted with the paddle attachment, beat the vegan vanilla buttercream on medium-high speed until light and fluffy, 3 to 5 minutes. Add the food colouring and beat on medium speed just until evenly distributed throughout the icing, 2 to 3 minutes. (Use the buttercream immediately or it will crust quickly.)

12. Assemble the sandwich cookies: Place the 12 large heart cookies without cutouts, bottom side up, on a baking sheet. Fill a piping bag fitted with a No. 802 round tip with the pink vegan buttercream. Pipe a thick layer of buttercream onto each cookie by zig-zagging back and forth, leaving a ⅛-inch border of exposed cookie around the edge. Place a decorated cookie with a heart cutout on top of a filled cookie to form a sandwich. Using even pressure, gently push down on the top to form a bond with the filling. Continue until all the sandwiches are filled.

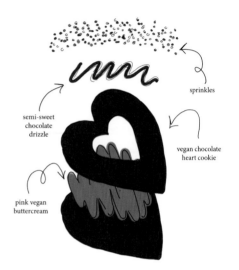

sprinkles

semi-sweet
chocolate
drizzle

vegan chocolate
heart cookie

pink vegan
buttercream

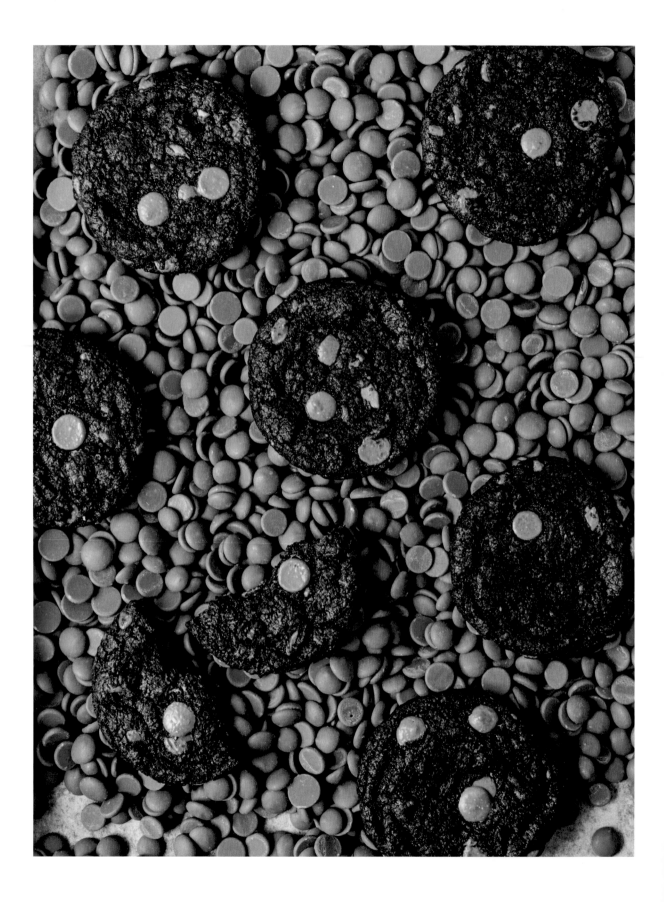

Ruby Chocolate Chunk Cookies

1¼ cups all-purpose flour

¼ cup cocoa powder

¾ teaspoon baking soda

½ cup unsalted butter, melted and warm

½ cup granulated sugar

½ cup packed dark brown sugar

½ teaspoon salt

1 large egg

1 teaspoon pure vanilla extract

⅔ pound (300 g/1½ cups) ruby chocolate callets or chopped ruby chocolate

This is the ultimate mood-elevating cookie and is best shared with loved ones. Especially if you can't connect in person, baking is a great way to share the love from afar. Introduced a few years ago, ruby chocolate is not a flavoured or dyed chocolate but a completely new form of base chocolate like white, milk, or dark chocolate. Ruby chocolate is made with a secret patented process and specific cocoa beans that lend themselves to the beautiful rose pink colour and unique sweet and sour flavour. We think it has a wonderful raspberry-like flavour that is quite creamy, and we couldn't help showing off its beauty in these simple cookies. These cookies are quick to make and perfect for any chocolate lover. If you cannot find ruby chocolate, you can easily swap it out for any other chocolate. Make sure you taste these luscious beauties warm from the oven or reheat them for thirty seconds in the microwave. You'll want to capture their ooey-gooey warm chocolate heaven, which just isn't the same at room temperature.

1. Preheat the oven to 350°F (180°C). Line 2 baking sheets with parchment paper or silicone baking mats.

2. Sift the flour, cocoa, and baking soda into a small bowl and stir together.

3. In a large bowl, whisk together the melted butter, granulated sugar, brown sugar, and salt until the mixture is smooth and no oily film remains around the edges. Whisk in the egg and vanilla until the mixture is smooth and light in colour.

4. Stir in the flour mixture and ruby chocolate until no dry flour remains. The dough may look a little wet, but it will firm up as the butter cools.

5. Scoop thirteen 1½-tablespoon portions of cookie dough onto each prepared baking sheet, leaving ample space between them. Bake one sheet at a time for 12 to 15 minutes, or until the cookies are puffy and their tops look dry. For chewier, gooey cookies, bake until the centre has risen but is a little shiny and wet looking. Allow the cookies to cool completely on the baking sheets.

DO AHEAD

These cookies are best enjoyed on the day of baking but can be stored in an airtight container at room temperature for up to 1 week. You can scoop and chill the dough in an airtight container in the refrigerator for up to 3 days.

Place the chilled cookies, uncovered, on a lined baking sheet with ample space between them. Let them come to room temperature for 30 minutes before baking.

Red Velvet Doughnuts with Dreamy Cream Cheese Icing

Doughnuts

1 cup all-purpose flour

1 tablespoon cocoa powder

1 teaspoon baking powder

½ teaspoon baking soda

½ teaspoon salt

½ cup granulated sugar

2 large eggs, room temperature

3 tablespoons buttermilk,
room temperature

2 tablespoons canola oil

1 teaspoon red gel food colouring

½ teaspoon pure vanilla extract

Dreamy Cream Cheese Icing

½ batch Dreamy Cream Cheese
Icing (page 295)

For assembly

½ cup red, pink, or white sprinkles

We really love the way the dreamy cream cheese icing's delicate tartness plays off these fluffy sweet cake doughnuts. They are just too cute and always fly off our shelves on Valentine's Day. The sprinkles give them the perfect crunchy finish; really any sprinkles will work, but check your local bulk stores for extra-special seasonal sprinkles to give these some added sparkle. These are best served as fresh as possible so you can enjoy their fluffy, milk chocolate-kissed interior at its best. Make your life easier by making the icing a few days in advance so you just have to bake the doughnuts on the day of your gathering.

1. Preheat the oven to 375°F (190°C). Lightly grease two 6-cavity doughnut pans with canola oil cooking spray.

2. Make the doughnuts: Sift the flour, cocoa, baking powder, baking soda, and salt into a medium bowl and stir together.

3. In a small bowl, whisk together the sugar, eggs, buttermilk, canola oil, food colouring, and vanilla until the mixture is smooth, the sugar is dissolved, and the mixture is a consistent red colour throughout.

4. Add the wet ingredients to the dry ingredients and stir just until the ingredients are fully incorporated and no dry flour remains.

5. Using a spoon or a 16-inch piping bag fitted with a No. 806 round tip, fill the wells of the pans about half full with batter. Bake for 10 to 12 minutes, or until a toothpick inserted into the centre of a doughnut comes out clean. Immediately turn the doughnuts out onto a wire rack to cool.

6. Ice the doughnuts: Fill a small heat-resistant bowl with the dreamy cream cheese icing and heat in the microwave in 10-second intervals, stirring after each interval, for 30 seconds, until smooth and softened for dipping. Dip the top of each cooled doughnut halfway into the icing, twisting the doughnut as you lift it to capture as much icing as possible. If the icing does not stick, give the doughnut a bit more wiggle and twist. Immediately decorate the wet doughnuts with sprinkles. Place on a wire rack and allow the doughnuts to set for 30 minutes.

DO AHEAD

These doughnuts are best when baked on the day you wish to serve them. You can make the cream cheese icing ahead and store it in an airtight container in the refrigerator for up to 1 month. Store iced doughnuts in an airtight container at room temperature for up to 2 days.

Mini Chocolate Chili Heat Cheesecakes

Cinnamon Graham Crumb Crust

1 batch Graham Crumb Crust
  (page 299)
1 teaspoon cinnamon

Cheesecake Filling

¾ cup granulated sugar
2 tablespoons all-purpose flour
1 teaspoon cinnamon
⅛ teaspoon cayenne pepper
1½ pounds (675 g/3 cups) cream
  cheese, room temperature
⅔ pound (300 g/1½ cups)
  semi-sweet chocolate callets or
  good-quality chopped chocolate,
  melted and cooled but still liquid
3 large eggs, room temperature
1 teaspoon pure vanilla extract
½ cup whipping (35%) cream,
  room temperature

For assembly

3 batches Milk Chocolate Ganache
  (page 307)
½ cup cinnamon heart candies,
  half crushed and half whole

Perfect for a party, sharing with your friends, a special date, or a solo midday dessert, mini cheesecakes are a wonderful addition to any event. We think they make the perfect little romantic dessert for sharing, as you can easily eat them with your fingers (or lick them off someone else's). The cheesecake bases also can be made and frozen, then topped with whatever you have on hand for last-minute celebrations. In our bakery, mini cheesecakes are sought after for just this reason—you may not want a whole cheesecake, but you'll definitely sign up for a mini or two. This cheesecake only graces our pastry case on Valentine's Day—its sweet, spicy, rich chocolate heat always has people yearning for more.

1. Preheat the oven to 350°F (180°C). Line two 12-cup muffin pans with 20 paper liners.

2. Make the cinnamon graham crumb crust: In a medium bowl, stir together the graham crumb crust mixture and cinnamon. Fill each muffin cup with 1 heaping tablespoon of cinnamon graham crust and press it flat against the bottom of the liner with the back of a spoon. Bake for 5 to 10 minutes until golden brown. Remove from the oven and reduce the temperature to 325°F (160°C).

3. Make the cheesecake filling: Sift the sugar, flour, cinnamon, and cayenne into a small bowl and whisk together.

4. In the bowl of a stand mixer fitted with the paddle attachment, beat the cream cheese on medium-high speed until smooth, 2 to 3 minutes. Scrape down the sides and bottom of the bowl. Add the melted chocolate and beat on low speed until fully combined, 2 to 3 minutes. Scrape down the sides and bottom of the bowl and the paddle.

5. Add the sugar mixture and beat on low speed just until combined, 2 minutes. Keeping air bubbles to a minimum is key. Scrape down the sides and bottom of the bowl. (CONTINUES)

DO AHEAD

The graham crusts can be baked ahead. Let the crusts cook in the pan, then wrap the pan in beeswax or plastic wrap and store at room temperature for up to 1 week. The cheesecake filling (unbaked) and ganache can be made ahead and stored in separate airtight containers for up to 2 weeks. The baked cheesecakes, without toppings, can be stored in an airtight container in the refrigerator for up to 2 weeks or in the freezer for up to 2 months. Thaw frozen cheesecakes overnight in the refrigerator before topping them. Once decorated, store the finished cheesecakes in an airtight container in the refrigerator for up to 3 days.

6. Add the eggs and vanilla and beat on medium-low speed until smooth, 2 to 3 minutes. Scrape down the sides and bottom of the bowl. Add the cream and beat starting on low speed so the cream doesn't splash, increasing the speed to medium until fully incorporated, 1 to 2 minutes.

7. Using an ice cream scoop or ¼-cup measure, scoop the cheesecake batter and fill the muffin cups three-quarters full. Bake for 20 to 26 minutes, or until the cheesecakes have domed slightly but there is still a slight jiggle in the centre. Allow the cheesecakes to cool in the pans to room temperature, then cover the pans with beeswax or plastic wrap and refrigerate for at least 2 hours.

8. Decorate the cheesecakes: When ready to serve, remove the cheesecakes from the muffin pans and keep them in the liners. Pour a heaping tablespoon of milk chocolate ganache on top of each cheesecake and spread it almost to the edges with the back of a spoon or a small offset palette knife. Sprinkle crushed cinnamon hearts and then whole cinnamon hearts on top.

Nutella Twists

Enriched Dough
1 batch Enriched Dough
(page 304)

Filling
1 cup Nutella, divided

Egg wash
1 large egg
1 tablespoon water,
room temperature

Similar to baby chocolate babkas, these buttery Nutella-filled pastries combine layers of creamy hazelnut chocolate with rich, sweet dough. They are best served fresh on the day of baking, but you can prepare the dough the day before to make this recipe easier. The dough can be a little tricky to roll out. If it keeps springing back on you when you roll it out, let the dough rest for 5 to 10 minutes, covered, and then continue rolling the dough. If you would like to keep these nut-free, try speculoos cookie butter as an alternative filling. You can even mix 2 tablespoons of cocoa powder into the cookie butter to make it chocolate flavoured.

1. Make the twists: Line a baking sheet with parchment paper or a silicone baking mat.

2. On a lightly floured work surface, roll out the dough into a 20- × 10-inch rectangle. Move the dough around and check underneath it a couple of times to make sure it is not sticking to the work surface, dusting lightly with more flour as needed. Brush any flour off the top of the dough with a dry pastry brush. Let the dough rest on the counter for 5 minutes.

3. Using an offset palette knife, spread ⅔ cup of the Nutella evenly over half of the dough rectangle to cover a 10-inch square of the dough. Fold the uncovered side of the dough over the Nutella layer to sandwich the Nutella between layers of dough.

4. With the folded side of the dough facing away from you, using a pizza cutter, cut the 10-inch square into 6 even strips of dough. You should have six 10-inch-long strips with a folded side at the end of each.

5. Twist each strip, one at a time, 6 to 8 times to create a twisted rope, 12 to 14 inches long. Hold the unfolded end of the rope still, and with your other hand swirl the dough around the stationary centre, tucking it tightly against itself to create a spiral circle. Lift the twist carefully and tuck 1 inch of the folded end of the dough under the bun as you place it on the baking sheet to rise. (CONTINUES)

DO AHEAD

The dough can be made ahead and stored, covered with beeswax or plastic wrap, in the refrigerator for up to 36 hours or in the freezer for up to 1 month. If frozen, thaw in the refrigerator overnight. Allow refrigerated or previously frozen dough to come up to room temperature for 45 to 60 minutes before rolling out. These pastries are best served immediately, but they can be stored, covered, at room temperature for up to 12 hours or stored in an airtight container in the refrigerator for up to 2 days, then warmed in a 325°F (160°C) oven for 5 minutes.

6. Make the egg wash, brush the twists, and let rise: In a small bowl, thoroughly whisk together the egg and water until combined. Using a pastry brush, brush the tops of the twists generously with egg wash and allow them to rise in a warm, humid area for 30 to 45 minutes or until they increase in size by 50 percent. If the surface of the dough seems to be drying out, spray it with warm water from a spray bottle or brush it with more egg wash.

7. Meanwhile, preheat the oven to 350°F (180°C).

8. Bake the twists: Slide the baking sheet into the oven and bake the twists for 18 to 25 minutes, or until they have puffed up and are golden brown. Allow to cool for 15 minutes.

9. In a small heat-resistant bowl, microwave the remaining ⅓ cup Nutella for 30 to 45 seconds, then stir until evenly melted to make it easier to drizzle. Fill a 12-inch piping bag fitted with a No. 4 round tip with the Nutella and drizzle it over the tops of the twists.

Heart-Shaped Pizzas

Pizza Dough

1 batch Pizza Dough (page 303)

Tomato Sauce

1 cup canned crushed tomatoes
1 tablespoon Italiano seasoning
(we use Club House)

For assembly

2 tablespoons cornmeal, for baking
3 cups (12 ounces/340 g) shredded
mozzarella cheese
12 thin slices Piller's Salami D'Amour
or your favourite salami

Whether you are wishing your best friend, your kid, or your special someone a happy Valentine's Day, everyone will love this fun pizza. Piller's Salami D'Amour is a seasonal heart-shaped salami that not only tastes great but allows you to create your own heart eye emoji pizza faces. If you can't find a heart-shaped salami, use a cookie cutter or kitchen scissors to cut out heart shapes from sliced salami of your choice. Form the pizza heart dough bases earlier in the day and store them, covered, in the refrigerator for up to 8 hours. Prepare the sauce, salami, and grated cheese in advance and add any other pizza toppings your guests might like in a number of small covered bowls. Allow guests to top the pizzas and bake them right away for the freshest party pizza you and your guests have ever experienced.

1. Preheat the oven to 400°F (200°C). Line 2 baking sheets with parchment paper or silicone baking mats.

2. Portion the dough: On a lightly floured work surface, divide the pizza dough into 6 equal portions and form them into balls. Let the dough rest, covered, on the counter for 10 minutes.

3. Meanwhile, make the tomato sauce: In a medium bowl, stir together the crushed tomatoes and Italiano seasoning.

4. Roll out the dough: Using a rolling pin, roll the dough balls, one at a time, into 6-inch circles, using as little flour as possible. Continue to roll the balls into circles, setting them aside to rest, covered.

5. Starting with the first circle you formed, use your thumb and pointer finger to pinch the middle of the top edge of the circle, then lightly pull and fold the top of the dough about 2 inches toward the centre of the circle. Press the dough in firmly to create the dip in the top of the heart and two humps.

6. Using the same fingers, pinch the bottom of the circle and wiggle and drag the pinched dough downward, creating a point. This will be the bottom of your heart. Sprinkle 1 tablespoon of cornmeal evenly over each baking sheet. Place 3 heart-shaped pizzas on each baking sheet, leaving ample room between them.

7. Top the pizzas and bake: Scoop 2 to 3 tablespoons of the tomato sauce into the centre of each pizza and spread it evenly outwards leaving a ¼-inch border of exposed dough around the edge. Sprinkle each pizza with ½ cup of shredded mozzarella. Place 2 heart-shaped salami pieces on top of the cheese for "eyes."

8. Bake for 18 to 25 minutes or until the crusts have puffed up and are golden brown and the cheese is bubbling. Serve hot or at room temperature.

We really love Easter at the bakery. It is by far our busiest season, and the number of pounds of mini eggs we go through is a little obscene. To host a successful party, we suggest embracing your inner child and adding a little whimsy to your normal party planning. Provide a fun activity for kids and kids-at-heart by hiding small bags of cookies or candy-stuffed eggs around the party or preparing a scavenger hunt. If further motivation is required, include a special prize in one of the bags to be revealed at the end of the hunt. Easter time for many also means emerging from a long winter and celebrating the renewal of life all around you, from buds on the trees to the smell of spring in the air. We reflect on the spring equinox and renewal, new life, and fertility. For that reawakening, we love a breakfast party. Serve the Chocolate Mini Egg Scones (page 65) and Hot Cross Buns (page 73) with platters of fresh fruit and a selection of grilled breakfast sausages and bacon or vegan alternatives along with coffee and tea. Include some high-energy activities mid-party, such as an egg hunt or obstacle race, to make room for dessert and then serve The Cream Egg Brownies (page 55), Mini Egg Chocolate Chunk Cookies (page 61), and Mini Egg Cream Pie (page 66). Package Mini Egg Shortbread Cookies (page 62) or Double Chocolate Mini Egg Sandwich Cookies (page 57) as take-home treats.

Easter

The Cream Egg Brownies

Brownie Layer

2 cups granulated sugar

1 cup cocoa powder, sifted

½ teaspoon salt

1 cup unsalted butter, melted

2 large eggs

1 tablespoon pure vanilla extract

½ cup buttermilk

1 cup all-purpose flour, sifted

12 mini Cadbury creme eggs, foil removed

Whipped Ganache Layers

1 batch White Chocolate Whipped Ganache (page 308)

¼ to ½ teaspoon golden yellow gel food colouring

Milk Chocolate Butter Ganache

⅓ cup unsalted butter

14 ounces (400 g/2 cups) milk chocolate callets or good-quality chopped chocolate

Several years ago we introduced our iconic cream egg brownie, and we have been selling more than six thousand of these decadent treats every Easter since then. It's a superhuman effort of logistics and physical endurance, since we make each tray of twelve by hand—that's more than five hundred trays in less than six weeks! We spent quite a long time perfecting the cream layers so that they could be easily cut but still melt in your mouth. Even if white chocolate isn't usually your thing, give this bar a chance. This rich dessert involves a fudge brownie stuffed with a mini Cadbury creme egg, followed by two layers of whipped white chocolate ganache and topped with creamy milk chocolate. We sell these bars in a three-inch square version, but for a party we suggest cutting that size into four to six pieces so that guests can grab a taste and still have room for other treats. This bar does need to set up overnight before you finish it with milk chocolate and cut it, so ensure that you have left yourself enough time. They are easiest to cut chilled just after you've allowed the milk chocolate layer to set, but they taste the best at room temperature, so allow them to lose their chill before serving.

1. Preheat the oven to 350°F (180°C). Line a 9- × 13-inch cake pan with parchment paper, allowing excess paper to hang over each side for easy removal.

2. Make the brownie layer: In a large bowl, whisk together the sugar, cocoa, salt, and melted butter until the mixture is smooth and no oily film remains around the edges.

3. Whisk in the eggs and vanilla, adding a little air, until the mixture is smooth and has lightened slightly in colour. Whisk in the buttermilk until the mixture is smooth.

4. Stir in the flour and mix until no dry flour remains and the batter is smooth.

5. Spread the batter evenly in the prepared pan using a small offset palette knife. Press the mini creme eggs into the batter, evenly spaced so that they will be in the centre of your 12 cut brownies (3 × 4 grid). Cover the tops of the eggs by pulling some batter over them with the offset palette knife. The brownie will level out as it bakes. Bake for 30 to 35 minutes, or until a toothpick inserted into the centre of the brownie comes out clean. Allow to cool at room temperature for 1 to 2 hours. (CONTINUES)

DO AHEAD

These brownies are best enjoyed on the day they are assembled but can be stored in an airtight container at room temperature for up to 5 days. Or make the brownie layer and whipped ganache ahead and store the brownie, well wrapped with beeswax or plastic wrap, at room temperature for up to 3 days and the whipped ganache in an airtight container in the refrigerator for up to 2 weeks. Warm the refrigerated whipped ganache in the microwave for 30 seconds to make it easy to stir in the colour and make it a pourable consistency.

EASTER

55

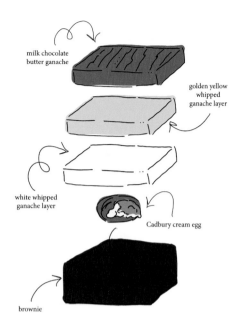

milk chocolate
butter ganache

golden yellow
whipped
ganache layer

white whipped
ganache layer

Cadbury cream egg

brownie

6. Prepare the ganache, assemble and chill the brownie: Place 2½ cups of the whipped ganache in a microwave-safe medium bowl and set it aside, covered, at room temperature. Spread the remaining 3½ cups whipped ganache over the brownie base. It is okay if the brownie is still a little warm but not hot. Refrigerate the brownie for 20 to 30 minutes.

7. Stir ¼ teaspoon of the food colouring into the reserved whipped ganache. If needed, continue to add food colouring, a few drops at a time, to achieve a deep golden yellow yolk colour. If the ganache has already hardened, microwave it for 30 seconds to make it easy to stir in the food colouring and pourable again. Pour the yellow ganache layer carefully over the white layer and spread it out evenly with a small offset palette knife. Wrap the pan in plastic wrap or cover with a tight-fitting silicone cover or lid. Refrigerate overnight or for at least 8 hours.

8. Finish the brownie: In a medium heat-resistant bowl, heat the butter and milk chocolate in the microwave in 30-second intervals, stirring vigorously for 30 to 45 seconds after each interval, until the ganache is smooth and the chocolate is melted. It is very important not to overheat the chocolate or it will bloom after setting. Make sure you vigorously stir the chocolate until all the heat is dissipated between intervals before returning the bowl to the microwave. Stir the ganache until it is smooth and silky. Spread it evenly over the top of the yellow ganache layer. Drag a small offset palette knife horizontally back and forth across the top to form ridges in the chocolate. Refrigerate just until the chocolate has set, 15 to 20 minutes, before cutting. Do not leave the brownie in the fridge any longer before cutting or the milk chocolate layer will tend to crack when sliced.

9. Cut the brownie using a warm chef's knife by dipping it into hot water and drying it on a clean kitchen towel. Wipe the knife between each cut to get nice clean cuts. Trim the edges to get clean sides, then cut into 12 brownies with a cream egg in the centre of each (3 × 4 grid).

Double Chocolate Mini Egg Sandwich Cookies

Double Chocolate Mini Egg Cookies

1 cup all-purpose flour

½ cup cocoa powder

½ teaspoon baking soda

½ cup unsalted butter, melted

½ cup granulated sugar

½ cup packed dark brown sugar

½ teaspoon salt

1 large egg

1 teaspoon pure vanilla extract

3½ ounces (100 g/½ cup) good-quality milk chocolate chunks

4 ounces (115 g/⅔ cup) lightly smashed milk chocolate candy mini eggs

Vanilla Bean Buttercream

¼ batch Vanilla Bean Buttercream (page 293)

Coating

6½ ounces (185 g/1 cup) lightly smashed milk chocolate candy mini eggs

Milk Chocolate Ganache

1½ batches Milk Chocolate Ganache (page 307)

These cookies have a deep chocolate base and are packed with creamy milk chocolate and crunchy candy mini eggs. Adding the fluffy vanilla buttercream, silky milk chocolate ganache, and even more mini eggs takes this dessert to a whole new level. These are beautiful packaged individually as a take-home gift for your guests, and they look stunning piled high on a serving platter. These are sandwich cookies with presence. To make irresistible mini sandwich cookies, scoop 1-tablespoon portions of dough and bake for 10 minutes.

1. Preheat the oven to 350°F (180°C). Line 2 baking sheets with parchment paper or silicone baking mats.

2. **Make the cookies:** Sift the flour, cocoa, and baking soda into a medium bowl.

3. In a large bowl, whisk together the melted butter, granulated sugar, brown sugar, and salt until the mixture is smooth and no oily film remains around the edges. Whisk in the egg and vanilla until the mixture is smooth and light in colour.

4. Using a spatula, stir in the flour mixture, chocolate chunks, and mini eggs and mix until no dry flour remains. The dough may look a little wet, but it will firm up as the butter cools.

5. Scoop six 3-tablespoon portions of cookie dough onto each baking sheet, leaving ample space between them. Bake, one sheet at a time, for 15 to 18 minutes, or until the cookies are puffed up and appear dry on top. Allow the cookies to cool on the baking sheets.

6. **Ice the cookies:** Place half of the cookies, upside down, on a clean baking sheet. Set aside the remaining 6 cookies; these will be the tops. In the bowl of a stand mixer fitted with the paddle attachment, beat the vanilla bean buttercream until light and fluffy, 7 to 10 minutes. Using a small offset palette knife, smooth 1 tablespoon of buttercream on each cookie, leaving a ½-inch border of exposed cookie around the edge. This is to prevent the bottom cookie from getting soggy after you add the filling (see White Chocolate Marshmallow Surprise Sandwich Cookies, page 159, photo A). (CONTINUES)

DO AHEAD

It is best to assemble the sandwich cookies on the day the cookies are baked, but you can store un-iced cookies in an airtight container at room temperature for up to 2 days. The buttercream and ganache can be made ahead. Store the buttercream in an airtight container in the refrigerator for up to 2 months and allow it to come up to room temperature for 4 hours before using. Store the ganache in an airtight container in the refrigerator for up to 2 weeks. Store assembled sandwich cookies in an airtight container in the refrigerator for up to 4 days.

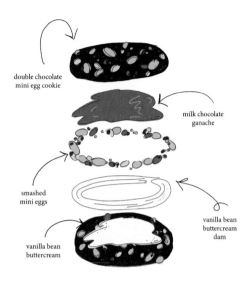

double chocolate
mini egg cookie

milk chocolate
ganache

smashed
mini eggs

vanilla bean
buttercream
dam

vanilla bean
buttercream

7. Pipe the iced cookies: Fill a 16-inch piping bag fitted with a No. 824 star tip with the remaining vanilla bean buttercream. Pipe a thick circle of buttercream onto each iced cookie to create a well for the filling, leaving a ¼-inch border of exposed cookie around the outer edge (see page 286, photo B).

8. Coat the cookies with crushed mini eggs: Fill a medium bowl with the lightly smashed mini eggs for coating. Scoop a palmful of crushed mini eggs in your dominant hand. Hold the cookie in your other hand and, working over the bowl to catch any bits that fall, gently push and coat the sides of the icing with the crushed mini eggs while rotating the cookie. Create an even crust around the buttercream border.

9. Fill the wells with ganache: Place the milk chocolate ganache in a small heat-resistant bowl and heat in the microwave in 15-second intervals, stirring after each interval, until the ganache has a pourable consistency but is not warm enough to melt the buttercream. Fill each well with 2 tablespoons of ganache, being careful not to go above the top of the buttercream border (see page 286, photo C).

10. Top and form the sandwich cookies: Place the remaining cookies on top of the filled cookies to form sandwiches. Using even pressure, gently push down on the tops to form a bond with the filling (see page 286, photo D).

Mini Egg Chocolate Chunk Cookies

1½ cups all-purpose flour

¾ teaspoon baking soda

½ cup granulated sugar

½ cup packed dark brown sugar

½ teaspoon salt

½ cup unsalted butter, melted

1 large egg

1 teaspoon pure vanilla extract

3½ ounces (100 g/½ cup) good-quality semi-sweet chocolate chunks

6½ ounces (185 g/1 cup) lightly smashed milk chocolate candy mini eggs

2 tablespoons pastel rainbow nonpareil sprinkles

This is our favourite version of a chocolate chunk cookie. There's just something about the creamy milk chocolate and crunchy candy shell of mini eggs melted into the cookie that speaks to the child in all of us. The sprinkles add a splash of colour and crunch to the exterior, but you can skip them if you don't have any sprinkles on hand and these cookies will still be delicious. Like all chocolate chunk cookies, these are best eaten warm out of the oven. If you would like to serve your guests freshly baked cookies, you can scoop the cookies and chill them in the refrigerator, covered, on the prepared baking trays, ready to bake on demand.

1. Preheat the oven to 350°F (180°C). Line 2 baking sheets with parchment paper or silicone baking mats.

2. Sift the flour and baking soda into a medium bowl and stir together.

3. In a large bowl, whisk together the granulated sugar, brown sugar, salt, and melted butter until the mixture becomes smooth, the sugars start to dissolve, and no oily film remains around the edges. Whisk in the egg and vanilla, adding a little air, until the mixture is smooth and light in colour.

4. Stir in the flour mixture, chocolate chunks, and mini eggs and mix until no dry flour remains. Do not overmix. The dough may look a little wet, but it will firm up as the butter cools.

5. Scoop six 3-tablespoon portions of cookie dough onto each prepared baking sheet, leaving ample space between them. Decorate the top of each cookie with ½ teaspoon of sprinkles. Bake, one sheet at a time, for 15 to 18 minutes, or until lightly browned all over. For chewier, gooey cookies, bake until the centre is risen but a little shiny and wet looking. Allow the cookies to cool on the baking sheets.

DO AHEAD

These cookies are best enjoyed on the day of baking but can be stored in an airtight container at room temperature for up to 5 days. You can scoop the dough onto prepared baking sheets, cover, and store in the refrigerator, for up to 3 days. Add 1 to 2 minutes to the baking time for chilled cookies and bake them straight from the refrigerator one sheet at a time on demand. Scooped cookie dough can be stored in an airtight container in the freezer for up to 1 month. Place the frozen cookies, uncovered, on a prepared baking sheet with ample space between them. Let them come to room temperature for 30 minutes before baking.

Mini Egg Shortbread Cookies

1 cup unsalted butter,
room temperature

½ cup icing sugar

½ cup cornstarch

1 teaspoon vanilla bean paste

¾ teaspoon salt

1⅓ cups all-purpose flour

10 ounces (285 g/1½ cups) lightly
smashed milk chocolate candy
mini eggs

In an average year our bakery goes through more than seven hundred pounds of chocolate candy mini eggs. That's equivalent to the weight of two full-grown gorillas. Just when we think people are sick of mini eggs, they request more! One customer request led to the creation of these mouth-watering cookies. These melt-in-your-mouth shortbreads last much longer than the Mini Egg Chocolate Chunk Cookies (page 61) and Ruby Chocolate Chunk Cookies (page 41), so you can prepare them up to two weeks in advance for your gathering and they will still taste freshly baked. Because they stay delicious for weeks, they also make a great take-home gift for your guests. Just make sure to bake them thoroughly and that they are dry all the way to the centre if you need them to last; they tend to hang on to moisture in their centres. They are beautiful gems to add to your platters or charcuterie spreads for a little extra colour and an unexpected treat to balance out a cheese tray or other savoury spread.

1. Preheat the oven to 350°F (180°C). Line 2 baking sheets with parchment paper or silicone baking mats.

2. In the bowl of a stand mixer fitted with the paddle attachment, lightly cream the butter on medium-high speed just until it is smooth, 1 to 2 minutes. Do not incorporate air into the butter. Scrape down the sides and bottom of the bowl.

3. Add the icing sugar, cornstarch, vanilla bean paste, and salt and beat on low speed, gradually increasing to medium-high speed, until the mixture is smooth and no chunks remain, 1 to 2 minutes. Scrape down the sides and bottom of the bowl. Add the flour and mini eggs and mix on low speed, gradually increasing to medium-high speed, until the flour is fully incorporated, without whipping air into the dough, 1 to 2 minutes.

4. Scoop twenty-one 1½-tablespoon portions of cookie dough onto each prepared baking sheet, leaving a little space between them. Gently press down on the cookies to flatten them to ¾-inch thickness. Bake, one sheet at a time, for 12 to 16 minutes, or until very lightly browned around the edges. Cool the cookies completely on the baking sheets.

DO AHEAD

You can make these cookies ahead and store them in an airtight container at room temperature for up to 2 weeks. They can be frozen, in an airtight container, for up to 2 months. Thaw them uncovered at room temperature for an hour before serving.

Chocolate Mini Egg Scones

DO AHEAD: These scones are best served immediately, but they can be stored, covered, at room temperature for up to 12 hours or in an airtight container in the refrigerator for up to 2 days, then warmed in a 325°F (160°C) oven for 5 minutes.

Scones

½ cup frozen unsalted butter
2 cups all-purpose flour,
   more for dusting
½ cup cocoa powder
½ cup granulated sugar
2 teaspoons baking powder
1 teaspoon baking soda
¾ teaspoon salt
1 cup buttermilk
1 large egg
2 teaspoons pure vanilla extract
13 ounces (370 g/2 cups) lightly
   smashed milk chocolate candy
   mini eggs

Egg Wash

1 large egg
1 tablespoon water,
   room temperature

We love a scone, and if we had our way, every gathering would feature one! At the bakery we have created hundreds of scone variations over the years, but we rarely do a chocolate base. Cocoa powder can tend to dry out baked goods, and it took us some testing to get the right balance to make this scone super chocolatey but still moist. Mini eggs provide an extra-crunchy exterior and a sweeter flavour than in traditional scones. These scones are almost cake-like in texture. We like them served simply with butter or whipped cream. This recipe is for full-size scones, but if you are serving them alongside other foods, try them at half-size. For sixteen mini scones, reduce the baking time to 15 to 17 minutes.

1. Preheat the oven to 400°F (200°C). Line a baking sheet with parchment paper or a silicone baking mat.

2. Make the scones: Grate the frozen butter on the large holes of a box grater into a small bowl. Store in the refrigerator until needed in step 5.

3. Sift the flour, cocoa, sugar, baking powder, baking soda, and salt into a large bowl.

4. In a small bowl, whisk together the buttermilk, egg, and vanilla.

5. Toss the grated butter into the dry ingredients until evenly distributed. Sift the crushed mini eggs. Reserve the candy dust for step 8. Add the sifted mini eggs to the dry ingredients and stir them in. Create a well in the centre of the dry ingredients, add the wet ingredients, and using a large fork, fold together the dry and wet ingredients. Mix just until all the flour is moist and the dough is still shaggy.

6. Using as little pressure as possible, form a ball with the dough in the bowl. Lightly dust a work surface with flour. Turn the dough out onto the work surface. Working quickly and with as little kneading as possible, shape the dough into a 6- to 7-inch disc, 1 to 2 inches thick.

7. Using a large sharp knife or bench scraper, cut the dough into 8 equal wedges and place on the prepared baking sheet 2 to 3 inches apart.

8. Make the egg wash, brush, and dust the scones: In a small bowl, thoroughly whisk the egg and water until combined. Using a pastry brush, brush the tops of the scones evenly with the egg wash. Sprinkle the candy dust over the scones.

9. Bake for 18 to 22 minutes, or until the scones are puffy and dry and the edges look crispy.

Mini Egg Cream Pie

DO AHEAD: The graham crust, ganache, and caramel can be made ahead. Let the graham crust cool in the pie plate, then wrap the pie plate in beeswax or plastic wrap and store at room temperature for up to 1 week. Store the ganache in an airtight container in the refrigerator for up to 2 weeks. Store the caramel in an airtight container at room temperature for up to 1 month. The assembled pie can be stored, covered, in the refrigerator for up to 3 days.

Graham Crumb Crust
1 batch Graham Crumb Crust (page 299)

White Chocolate Cream Cheese Filling
2 ounces (50 g/⅓ cup) white chocolate callets or good-quality chopped chocolate
2 tablespoons whipping (35%) cream
8 ounces (225 g/1 cup) cream cheese, room temperature
⅓ cup icing sugar

Dark Chocolate Ganache
1 batch Dark Chocolate Ganache (page 307), room temperature

Whipped Cream
½ batch Whipped Cream (page 300)

For assembly
6 tablespoons Caramel (page 317), divided
3 ounces (85 g/½ cup) lightly smashed milk chocolate candy mini eggs

Kate was a wonderful night baker who came to us as a co-op student during her pastry school placement and stayed with us for years before leaving to start her own bakery. She helped us create several delicious desserts, but this might be our favourite. The white chocolate layers are similar to chocolate mousse: silky smooth but also fluffy and creamy. The vein of dark chocolate running right through the centre balances out the sweetness of the white chocolate. This beauty is finished with caramel and mini eggs to give it a nutty flavour and crunch factor. The trick for cutting this pie is to use a hot, clean knife on every cut, wiping down the knife between cuts. Cut the first slice and remove it before you cut the next slice to make serving easy.

1. Preheat the oven to 350°F (180°C).

2. Bake the graham crumb crust: Firmly and evenly press the graham crumb crust mixture into the bottom and all the way up the sides of a 9-inch pie plate. Bake for 10 to 15 minutes until light golden brown.

3. Make the white chocolate cream cheese filling: In a small heat-resistant bowl, melt the white chocolate and cream in the microwave in 30-second intervals, stirring vigorously after each interval, until smooth and the chocolate is melted. Stir the ganache until silky smooth.

4. In the bowl of a stand mixer fitted with the paddle attachment, beat the cream cheese and icing sugar on medium-high speed for 2 to 3 minutes until smooth. Add the white chocolate ganache. Beat on medium-high speed until smooth, 3 to 4 minutes.

5. Layer the pie crust with white chocolate cream cheese filling and dark chocolate ganache: Spoon two-thirds of the white chocolate cream cheese filling into the baked pie shell and smooth it flat with a small offset palette knife or the back of a spoon. Set aside the remaining cream cheese filling at room temperature until needed in step 7.

6. Pour the dark chocolate ganache evenly over the cream cheese layer and smooth it flat with a small offset palette knife or the back of a spoon. Allow the pie to set in the refrigerator for 20 to 25 minutes.

7. Top with the whipped cream and caramel mixture: Fold the whipped cream and 2 tablespoons of the caramel into the reserved white chocolate cream cheese filling and spread it evenly over the ganache layer. Allow the pie to firm up in the refrigerator, uncovered, for 1 hour.

8. Assemble: Using a spoon or small piping bag, drizzle the remaining 4 tablespoons caramel over the top of the pie in a crosshatch design. Sprinkle the smashed mini eggs over the caramel, forming a 2-inch border around the edge of the pie.

Carrot Whoopie Pies

DO AHEAD: The cake batter can be made up to 24 hours ahead. Chill the batter in the refrigerator, covered with beeswax or plastic wrap, until you are ready to scoop and bake. Un-iced baked cakes can be stored in an airtight container at room temperature for up to 2 days. The cream cheese icing can be stored in an airtight container in the refrigerator for up to 1 month or in the freezer for up to 2 months. If refrigerated, let soften at room temperature. If frozen, thaw in the refrigerator overnight. Store assembled whoopie pies in an airtight container in the refrigerator for up to 3 days.

Carrot Whoopie Pies

2 cups all-purpose flour
1½ teaspoons Pumpkin Spice Mix (page 312)
1½ teaspoons baking soda
1 teaspoon baking powder
½ teaspoon salt
½ cup unsalted butter, room temperature
½ cup granulated sugar
½ cup packed dark brown sugar
2 large eggs, room temperature
1 teaspoon pure vanilla extract
1½ cups grated peeled carrots

Dreamy Cream Cheese Icing

½ batch Dreamy Cream Cheese Icing (page 295)

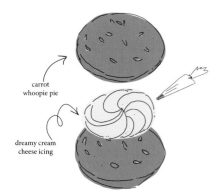

carrot whoopie pie

dreamy cream cheese icing

Carrot cake and all its varieties are one of our favourites at the bakery. We love it as macarons, cookies, cupcakes, and more, but this handheld portable version is one of the best. We've kept them simple here with no fillings, just icing, but if you like you can add ½ cup raisins, flaked coconut, or chopped pecans to the cake batter or even stick these additions to the sides of the icing once the whoopie cakes are sandwiched. The carrots keep the whoopie pies super moist and tender, and they have just the right balance of spice and sweetness.

1. Make the batter: Sift the flour, pumpkin spice mix, baking soda, baking powder, and salt into a medium bowl and stir together.

2. In the bowl of a stand mixer fitted with the paddle attachment, beat the butter on medium-high speed until smooth, 3 to 5 minutes. Scrape down the sides and bottom of the bowl. Add the granulated sugar and brown sugar and continue to cream on medium-high speed until fluffy, 3 to 4 minutes. Scrape down the sides and bottom of the bowl.

3. Add the eggs and vanilla. Beat on high speed for 3 to 4 minutes until the batter is smooth and fluffy. Scrape down the sides and bottom of the bowl.

4. Add the flour mixture and carrots and mix on low speed just until combined, 1 minute. Chill the batter in the refrigerator, covered with beeswax wrap or plastic wrap, for at least 1 hour before scooping.

5. Meanwhile, preheat the oven to 350°F (180°C). Line 3 baking sheets with parchment paper or silicone baking mats.

6. Bake the whoopie pies: When the batter has chilled, scoop ten 2-tablespoon portions of the batter onto each baking sheet, leaving ample space between them. Bake, one sheet at a time, for 14 to 16 minutes, or until the cakes are puffed up and appear dry on top. Allow the cakes to cool on the baking sheets.

7. Assemble the whoopie pies: Place half of the cakes, bottom side up, on a baking sheet. Set aside the remaining cakes; these will be the tops. In the bowl of a stand mixer fitted with the paddle attachment, beat the dreamy cream cheese icing until light and fluffy, 4 to 6 minutes.

8. Fill a piping bag fitted with a No. 824 star tip with the cream cheese icing. Pipe a thick layer of icing onto each cake, forming a rosette (see Buttercream and Whipped Cream Piping Styles, page 286, C), and leaving a ¼-inch border of exposed cookie around the edge. Place the remaining cakes on top of the filled cakes to form whoopie pies. Using even pressure, gently push down on the tops to form a bond with the filling.

EASTER

69

Mini Egg Cake

Vanilla Mini Egg Cake

1 batch Vanilla Cake Batter
(page 282)
6 ounces (170 g/1 cup) lightly
smashed milk chocolate candy
mini eggs, sifted, mini egg dust
and small bits of candy shells
reserved for assembly

Simple Syrup

1 batch Simple Syrup (page 293)

Vanilla Bean Buttercream

1 batch Vanilla Bean Buttercream
(page 293), ½ cup reserved
for Chocolate Buttercream
(see below)

Chocolate Buttercream

½ cup Vanilla Bean Buttercream,
reserved (see above)
2 ounces (50 g/½ cup) bittersweet
chocolate callets or good-quality
chopped chocolate, melted and
room temperature
1 teaspoon cocoa powder, sifted

(INGREDIENTS CONTINUE)

Your guests will all be drooling over this stunning cake. We sell more than a hundred of these decadent centrepieces each Easter season because people just really love mini eggs! The beauty of taking popular commercial products and adding them to your baked goods is to draw folks into something familiar and approachable so that they can try something new. We've switched up our standard version of this cake and added mini eggs baked right into the vanilla cake to add texture and that distinct mini egg flavour throughout. Not only are the mini eggs inside the vanilla cake layers, but that sweet milk chocolate with crunchy shell can be found inside the buttercream layers and on top too. Layer all that scrumptious flavour with the richness of the chocolate buttercream—it's truly irresistible.

1. Preheat the oven to 350°F (180°C). Grease four 6-inch round cake pans with canola oil cooking spray and line the bottoms with parchment paper circles.

2. Make the cake layers: Divide the vanilla cake batter evenly between the 4 prepared pans. Sprinkle ¼ cup of the crushed mini eggs over the batter in each pan. Using a small offset palette knife, swirl the mini eggs into the batter and smooth out the top of the batter. Bake for 25 to 40 minutes, or until a toothpick inserted into the centres of the cakes comes out clean. Allow the cakes to cool in the pans on a wire rack for 20 minutes. Remove the cakes from the pans, leaving the parchment paper circles on the bottoms, and cool completely on the wire rack.

3. Assemble and decorate the cake—prepare the cake layers: Trim the domes off the tops of the 4 baked cake layers, moistening each cake layer with simple syrup (follow instructions on page 283, step 1, photo A).

4. Prepare the buttercreams: Make the vanilla bean buttercream or re-beat premade buttercream to make it light and fluffy again (follow instructions on page 293, step 2). To make the chocolate buttercream, transfer ½ cup of the buttercream to a small bowl. Add the melted chocolate and sift the cocoa on top, then use a whisk to combine and whip until light and fluffy, about 2 minutes. (CONTINUES)

DO AHEAD

The finished cake is best enjoyed at room temperature on the day it is made but can be stored, covered, in the refrigerator for up to 4 days. Remove the cake from the refrigerator and let sit at room temperature for 5 to 8 hours before serving. All the components of the layered cake can be made ahead to simplify assembly. Fully cool the baked cake layers, then wrap them tightly in plastic wrap and store at room temperature for up to 3 days. The simple syrup can be stored in an airtight container in the refrigerator for up to 3 weeks. Store the vanilla bean buttercream in an airtight container in the refrigerator for up to 2 months and allow it to come up to room temperature for 4 hours before using. Store the ganache in an airtight container in the refrigerator for up to 2 weeks.

EASTER

71

Robin Egg Blue Ganache

1 batch White Chocolate Ganache (page 308)
2 drops white gel food colouring
2 drops sky blue gel food colouring
1 drop teal gel food colouring

For assembly

¾ cup lightly smashed milk chocolate candy mini eggs, divided
Reserved mini egg dust and candy shells

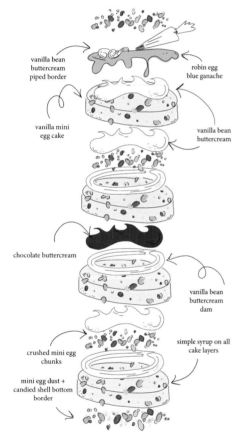

vanilla bean buttercream piped border
robin egg blue ganache
vanilla mini egg cake
vanilla bean buttercream
chocolate buttercream
vanilla bean buttercream dam
crushed mini egg chunks
simple syrup on all cake layers
mini egg dust + candied shell bottom border

5. Stack the cake: Stack the vanilla mini egg cake with vanilla bean buttercream on an 8-inch cake board or serving plate, adding ¼ cup of crushed mini eggs topped with ½ cup vanilla bean buttercream to each of the first and third filling layers with a dam of vanilla buttercream. For the second filling layer, fill the vanilla bean buttercream dam with all the chocolate buttercream. Moisten each layer with 4 tablespoons of simple syrup (follow instructions on page 283, step 2, photos B to E).

6. Crumb coat the cake: Crumb coat the top and sides of the stacked cake with a thin layer of the vanilla bean buttercream and place the cake, uncovered, in the refrigerator for 15 minutes (follow instructions on page 284, step 3, photos F and G).

7. Mask the cake: Mask the cake with the vanilla bean buttercream using a rustic finish or horizontal lines by starting at the bottom edge of the cake, placing the tip of the pallet knife against the cake horizontally. Slowly turn the turntable, pulling the palette knife up the cake to create horizontal lines on the side of the cake (follow instructions on page 284, step 4, photos H and I).

8. Using your hand, gently pat the reserved mini egg dust and candy shells into the soft vanilla bean buttercream around the bottom edge of the cake to create a decorative border. Place the cake, uncovered, in the refrigerator for 30 minutes.

9. Make the robin egg blue ganache: Place the white chocolate ganache in a small heat-resistant bowl and heat in the microwave in 15-second intervals, stirring after each interval, until the ganache has a pourable consistency but is not warm enough to melt the buttercream. Add the white food colouring and stir until fully combined. (The white food colouring cuts out the yellow undertone and provides a more opaque base to give the ganache a vibrant final colour.) Add the sky blue and teal food colouring and stir until completely combined. Pour the ganache in the centre of the cake, spreading it outward with a palette knife to the edges of the cake and allowing it to overflow onto the sides. Place the cake, uncovered, in the refrigerator for 10 minutes, or until the ganache is firm to the touch.

10. Finish the cake: Pipe a border of vanilla bean buttercream around the edge of the cake top in a reverse swirl using a No. 804 round tip (see Buttercream and Whipped Cream Piping Styles, page 286, B), leaving ½ inch of exposed ganache around the outer edge. Sprinkle the piped buttercream border with the remaining ¼ cup crushed mini eggs.

Hot Cross Buns

Soaker

⅔ cup sultana raisins or golden raisins (or a combination)

⅓ cup currants

1 batch (⅓ cup) finely chopped Mixed Candied Peel (page 318) or store-bought (if using store-bought, add the zest of 1 lemon and 1 orange)

1½ teaspoons cinnamon

½ teaspoon ground ginger

½ teaspoon freshly grated or ground nutmeg

½ teaspoon ground allspice

¼ teaspoon ground cloves

2 tablespoons hot water

1 tablespoon dark rum

1 tablespoon pure vanilla extract

Dough

3 cups all-purpose flour

2 tablespoons granulated sugar

2 tablespoons packed dark brown sugar

1 tablespoon instant dry yeast

1 teaspoon salt

¾ cup whole milk, warm

1 large egg

¼ cup unsalted butter

2 tablespoons canola oil

(INGREDIENTS CONTINUE)

Originally developed by Josie for her husband, Luke, this is our pastry chef Kyle's baby now. Kyle put in more than a half-decade of recipe tweaks and perfections to bring you this version. His easy candied citrus peel is the crowning touch; it adds intense citrus flavour that you just can't get from store-bought peel. Kyle came to us as a co-op student during his chef training program, and he loved the bakery so much he ended up as our bread baker instead of a chef. He spent years heading up our bread department before switching to our pastry and savoury department. He's a very talented baker and one of the nicest, most interesting folks you could ever meet. These hot cross buns have a buttery base packed with warm spices and layers of citrus flavour. The crosses have a sweet pastry/shortbread-like texture, and you can make them thinner or thicker depending on your preference. We always provide cream cheese icing with our hot cross buns at the bakery because that's how we like them best—cut in half, toasted, and slathered in fluffy icing.

1. Make the soaker: In a medium bowl, stir together the raisins, currants, mixed candied peel, cinnamon, ginger, nutmeg, allspice, and cloves until the dried fruit is covered in spices. Add the hot water, dark rum, and vanilla and stir to coat well. Set aside, covered with beeswax or plastic wrap, to soak at room temperature for 24 to 48 hours or in the refrigerator for up to 4 days.

2. Make the dough: In the bowl of a stand mixer fitted with the dough hook attachment, add the flour, granulated sugar, brown sugar, instant yeast, and salt and mix on low speed for 1 minute to evenly distribute the yeast.

3. Add the milk, egg, butter, and canola oil and mix on medium speed until no dry flour remains, about 2 minutes. Decrease the speed to medium-low and mix for 8 to 10 minutes, or until the dough has pulled away from the sides and bottom of the bowl and is silky smooth. It will be quite a stiff dough. Allow the dough to rest in the bowl, covered with beeswax or plastic wrap, for 10 minutes. (CONTINUES)

DO AHEAD

These buns are best served immediately but can be stored, covered, at room temperature for up to 12 hours or in an airtight container at room temperature for up to 2 days, then warmed in a 325°F (160°C) oven for 5 minutes. Make the soaker at least 8 or up to 48 hours before you mix the dough to give it time to develop flavour and infuse the spices into the fruit. You can mix the dough ahead and store it covered in the refrigerator for up to 36 hours. Let the dough rise, covered, for just 30 minutes at room temperature in step 5 before transferring it to the refrigerator. If using chilled dough, remove from the refrigerator 45 to 60 minutes before step 6. The cross batter can be made and stored in an airtight container at room temperature up to 2 days ahead.

Cross Batter

¾ cup all-purpose flour
¼ cup granulated sugar
⅓ cup canola oil
¼ cup water

To finish

¼ cup unsalted butter, melted
½ batch Dreamy Cream Cheese
    Icing (page 295)

4. Mix in the soaker and proof the dough: Add the soaker, and any liquid that has not been absorbed by the fruit, to the bowl with the dough and mix on medium-low speed until all the fruit has been evenly distributed and the dough has absorbed any liquid, 2 to 3 minutes.

5. Lightly grease a large bowl with canola oil. Gather the dough into a ball and place it in the bowl. Let the dough rise, covered with beeswax or plastic wrap, for 1 hour at room temperature or until it has doubled in size.

6. Portion and shape the buns: Turn the dough out onto a lightly floured work surface. Divide the dough into 15 equal pieces weighing about 3 ounces (85 g) each. Working with one piece of dough at a time and keeping the other pieces covered with beeswax or plastic wrap, shape it into a smooth ball. Place the buns on a baking sheet lined with parchment paper, spacing them evenly in a 3 × 5 grid.

7. Let the buns rise, uncovered, in a humid and warm area until doubled in size, about 1 hour. If you don't have a humid area, you can mist the buns with warm water in a spray bottle every 10 to 15 minutes. After 30 to 45 minutes, preheat the oven to 375°F (190°C).

8. Meanwhile, make the cross batter: In a small bowl, whisk together the flour, sugar, canola oil, and water until the mixture is smooth.

9. Pipe the crosses and bake the buns: When the oven is preheated and the buns are fully risen, fill a 12-inch piping bag fitted with a No. 804 round tip with the cross batter. Pipe a line across the centre of the buns from one side of the baking sheet to the other, for all three lines of buns. Rotate the pan 90 degrees and pipe lines in the opposite direction to create a cross in the centre of each bun. Bake for 20 to 30 minutes until the tops are golden brown.

10. As soon as the buns come out of the oven, using a pastry brush, brush them with melted butter, covering the tops and sides of the buns with a thin layer. This will give the buns a lovely shiny glow. Allow the buns to cool on the baking sheet for 30 minutes and then serve them warm with the dreamy cream cheese icing.

We love the idea of gathering for Mother's Day with anyone you consider maternal in your life. Moms come in all shapes and sizes, and we celebrate that diversity! The best way to celebrate moms is to give them your undivided attention, so make sure you take the time to plan and bake your menu choices in advance. Creating the appropriate atmosphere will really depend on your moms and their personal preferences. Anything that celebrates mom is perfect—whether they prefer beer over tea or modern touches over frilly doilies, celebrate the moms you have. If possible, we recommend an outdoor Mother's Day party since the weather in May usually cooperates. All the recipes in this chapter hold up well at room temperature except for the chicken pot pies and tarts, but luckily they both are easily reheated at the last minute. We love this menu for brunch: add a cheese platter to go with the Flatbread Seed Crackers (page 95) and serve the Mini Raspberry Vanilla Bean Scones with Clotted Cream (page 83), Creamy Garlic Kale and Prosciutto Tarts (page 89), and Mini Chicken Pot Pies (page 91) as the main course with a green salad, family-style. The Raspberry Lemon Poke Cake (page 85) or a spread of Rhubarb Custard Bars (page 79) and Citrus Spice Biscotti (page 80) make the perfect dessert with some fresh fruit.

Mother's Day

Rhubarb Custard Bars 79

(V) Citrus Spice Biscotti 80

Mini Raspberry Vanilla Bean Scones
with Clotted Cream 83

Raspberry Lemon Poke Cake 85

Creamy Garlic Kale
and Prosciutto Tarts 89

Mini Chicken Pot Pies 91

(V) Flatbread Seed Crackers 95

Rhubarb Custard Bars

Shortbread Base
1 cup all-purpose flour
2 tablespoons granulated sugar
½ cup unsalted butter

Custard Filling
1¼ cups granulated sugar
6 tablespoons all-purpose flour
1 cup whipping (35%) cream
3 large eggs
2 teaspoons pure vanilla extract
1 pound (450 g) rhubarb, thick stalks
halved lengthwise, cut crosswise
into 1½-inch pieces (3½ cups)

Fluffy Cream Cheese Icing
½ cup whipping (35%) cream
1½ cups Dreamy Cream Cheese
Icing (page 295)

To finish
1 teaspoon strawberry crisp pearls
1 teaspoon white chocolate crisp
pearls

Rhubarb is just starting to come into season in May and featuring this underused fruit is easy with these bars. The shortbread crust and creamy custard balance out the rhubarb's sourness perfectly. We make this custard bar at the bakery with many different fruits throughout the seasons. Peach and strawberry are two other fruits that work well, and you can switch out the same amount of those fruits in these bars.

1. Preheat the oven to 350°F (180°C). Grease an 8-inch square baking pan with canola oil cooking spray and line it with parchment paper.

2. Make the shortbread base: In a medium bowl, stir together the flour and sugar. Using a pastry cutter, cut in the butter until the mixture resembles coarse crumbs.

3. Press the shortbread mixture evenly into the bottom of the prepared pan. Bake for 12 to 15 minutes, or until the top of the shortbread looks dry but not brown. Allow to cool while you prepare the filling.

4. Make the custard filling: In a medium bowl, whisk together the sugar and flour until combined. Whisk in the cream until smooth. Whisk in the eggs and vanilla and mix until smooth. Set aside.

5. Evenly spread the rhubarb over the cooled shortbread base. Pour the custard filling over the rhubarb. Bake for 40 to 45 minutes, or until the custard is firm and lightly browned. Allow to cool to room temperature and then cover the pan with beeswax or plastic wrap and place in the refrigerator for 2 hours before icing.

6. Ice and finish the bars: In the bowl of a stand mixer fitted with the whisk attachment, whip the whipping cream on medium-high speed until it forms stiff peaks, 2 to 3 minutes. Transfer the whipped cream to a small bowl.

7. Return the bowl to the stand mixer (you don't need to wipe the bowl or whisk clean). Add the dreamy cream cheese icing to the bowl and whip for 2 to 3 minutes on medium-high speed to fluff up the icing. Gently fold the whipped cream into the fluffy icing. Using a small offset palette knife, spread the icing evenly over the top of the cooled bar. Evenly sprinkle the strawberry and white chocolate crisp pearls over the bar.

8. Cut the bars using a warm chef's knife by dipping it into hot water and drying it on a clean kitchen towel. Wipe the knife between each cut to get nice clean cuts.

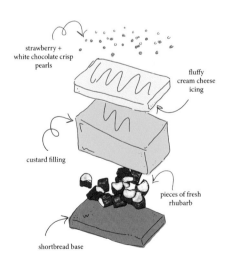

strawberry +
white chocolate crisp
pearls

fluffy
cream cheese
icing

custard filling

pieces of fresh
rhubarb

shortbread base

DO AHEAD

These bars can be baked and stored un-iced, covered, in the refrigerator for up to 2 days. You can make the cream cheese icing ahead and store it in an airtight container in the refrigerator for up to 1 month, but don't fold it with the whipped cream until you are ready to ice and serve the bars. Iced bars can be stored in an airtight container in the refrigerator for up to 4 days.

Citrus Spice Biscotti ⓥ

½ cup + 2 tablespoons granulated
    sugar
⅓ cup canola oil
6 tablespoons warm water
1 tablespoon ground flaxseed
1½ teaspoons pure vanilla extract
Zest of 1 lemon
Zest of 1 orange
2 cups all-purpose flour
1 cup almond flour
2 teaspoons baking powder
1 teaspoon dried lavender flowers
½ teaspoon salt
¼ teaspoon freshly grated or
    ground nutmeg
¼ cup almond milk
3 tablespoons turbinado sugar

There's something special about snuggling up with a perfectly made tea or coffee in your favourite mug, wrapped in a warm blanket in your most comfy spot, and dipping crunchy sweet biscotti into your hot drink. Sounds like the perfect moment of comfort to share with your moms. Over the years we have created many different flavour variations of biscotti, but this bright and spicy biscotti pulls on all your heartstrings with a comforting, familiar flavour. You would not guess it given the ingredients, but the flavour profile of these biscotti is similar to animal crackers, so it is a very approachable cookie. The turbinado sugar crunch on top makes this a complete texture and flavour experience.

1. Preheat the oven to 350°F (180°C). Line 2 baking sheets with parchment paper or silicone baking mats.

2. In a large bowl, whisk together the granulated sugar, canola oil, water, flaxseed, vanilla, and lemon and orange zest until the mixture is smooth, no oily film remains around the edges, and the mixture has thickened slightly.

3. Stir in the all-purpose flour, almond flour, baking powder, lavender flowers, salt, and nutmeg until the mixture comes together as a dough and no dry flour remains.

4. Turn out the cookie dough onto a lightly floured work surface and knead the dough gently into a ball. Divide the ball into 2 portions and roll each into a thick rope, about 17 inches in length. Place both ropes on one of the prepared baking sheets and press down gently so that they are about 2 inches wide and ¾ inch thick.

5. Using a pastry brush, brush each log with the almond milk. Sprinkle each log with 1½ tablespoons of turbinado sugar. Bake the logs for 30 to 35 minutes until they crack along the top, appear dry, and are a light golden brown. Allow the logs to cool on the baking sheet for 25 to 30 minutes. Reduce the oven temperature to 300°F (150°C).

6. When the logs are cool enough to handle, cut them crosswise into ¾-inch-thick slices using a bread knife. Arrange the cookies evenly on the prepared cookie sheets, 21 cookies per sheet, and bake them again for 25 to 30 minutes or until they look completely dry and are slightly brown around the edges. Allow the cookies to cool completely on a cooling rack.

DO AHEAD ────────────────

These cookies can be made ahead and stored in an airtight container at room temperature for up to 1 month.

Mini Raspberry Vanilla Bean Scones with Clotted Cream

Clotted Cream (makes 2 cups)

4 cups whipping (35%) cream
  (local grass-fed preferred;
  not ultra-pasteurized)

Raspberry Scones

½ cup unsalted butter, frozen
2¾ cups all-purpose flour
⅓ cup granulated sugar
2 teaspoons baking powder
1 teaspoon baking soda
½ teaspoon salt
1 cup buttermilk or liquid reserved
  from the clotted cream
1 large egg
2 teaspoons pure vanilla extract
1 cup frozen raspberries

Egg Wash

1 large egg
1 tablespoon water,
  room temperature

Glaze

½ cup icing sugar
1 to 1½ tablespoons warm water

These adorable bite-size scones are a cute crowd-pleasing staple for any brunch party. The tart raspberry flavour pops against the buttery sweet scone just perfectly. Drizzle these with icing or leave them plain so that they can be reheated easily. Be careful, though—Nickey can eat six in one sitting with no problem, so make sure you control your taste-testing before guests arrive. Don't be intimidated by the clotted cream. It is so easy and satisfying to make—you'll feel like a genuine cheesemaker! It has a unique nutty flavour and incredibly creamy texture. The clotted cream does take some planning, so start it at least two full days in advance of your event. In a pinch, you can buy clotted cream, so don't worry if you miss your deadline.

1. Make the clotted cream: Preheat the oven to 200°F (100°C). Pour the cream into an 8-inch square glass or stainless steel baking dish. Bake, uncovered, for 12 hours. When done, there will be a golden-brown crust floating on top of the cream. Allow the cream to cool, uncovered, for 2 hours at room temperature. Cover the pan with beeswax or plastic wrap and place it in the refrigerator for 12 to 24 hours to continue setting.

2. Pour off the liquid and reserve 1 cup for the scones (if you would like to use it instead of buttermilk). Stir the golden-brown crust into the thickened cream to finish the clotted cream. Scoop the clotted cream into a serving dish, and store, covered, in the refrigerator for up to 1 week.

3. Make the scones: Preheat the oven to 400°F (200°C). Line 2 large baking sheets with parchment paper or silicone baking mats.

4. Grate the frozen butter on the large holes of a box grater into a small bowl. Store in the refrigerator until needed in step 7.

5. Sift the flour, sugar, baking powder, baking soda, and salt into a large bowl and stir together.

6. In a small bowl, whisk together the buttermilk (or reserved clotted cream liquid), egg, and vanilla. (CONTINUES)

DO AHEAD

The clotted cream can be made ahead and stored in an airtight container in the refrigerator for up to 1 week. The scones are best served immediately but can be stored un-glazed, covered, at room temperature for up to 12 hours or in an airtight container in the refrigerator for up to 2 days, then warmed in a 325°F (160°C) oven for 5 minutes and glazed.

MOTHER'S DAY

7. Toss the frozen grated butter into the dry ingredients until evenly distributed. Create a well in the centre of the dry ingredients, add the wet ingredients, and using a large fork, fold the dry and wet ingredients together. When half the flour looks mixed in, add the frozen raspberries and continue mixing until all the flour is moist and the dough is still a bit shaggy. The dough should be fairly dry but workable.

8. Using as little pressure as possible, form a ball with the dough in the bowl. Lightly dust a work surface with flour. Turn the dough out onto the work surface and cut into 3 portions. Working quickly and with as little kneading as possible, shape each portion of dough into a 3- to 4-inch disc, 1 to 1½ inches thick.

9. Using a large sharp knife or bench scraper, cut each disc into 8 equal wedges and place 12 wedges on each prepared baking sheet, 1 to 2 inches apart.

10. Make the egg wash and bake the scones: In a small bowl, thoroughly whisk together the egg and water until combined. Using a pastry brush, brush the tops of the scones evenly with egg wash. Bake for 10 to 12 minutes, or until the scones are evenly browned and the edges look crispy.

11. Meanwhile, make the glaze: In a small bowl, whisk together the icing sugar and warm water. Glaze the scones as soon as they come out of the oven by spooning the glaze over the scones. Serve warm with the clotted cream.

Raspberry Lemon Poke Cake

Vanilla Lemon Cake
½ batch Vanilla Cake Batter
   (page 282)
Zest of ½ lemon

Raspberry Simple Syrup
1 batch Simple Syrup (page 316)
2 tablespoons Raspberry Jam
   (page 310) or store-bought

Lemon Curd
½ batch Lemon Curd (page 316)

Vanilla Bean Buttercream
1 batch Vanilla Bean Buttercream
   (page 293)

For assembly
2 pints fresh raspberries, washed
   and dried, divided
1 to 2 drops of two different colours
   of gel food colourings

Gifting a creative and edible present to your special person can be a lovely alternative to purchasing a material gift. By baking, you get the opportunity to showcase your delicious talents, as well as to customize flavour and appearance to please the person you are gifting. For this Mother's Day creation, sweet and sour raspberry takes centre stage with a bright, pucker-up lemon curd to complement the vanilla cake perfectly. Poke as many holes in the cake as you wish for slices, the goal is to have everyone experience that pop of flavour in the centre of their slice.

This cake can be decorated as simply or elegantly as you wish. Play with fresh fruit and floral garnishes, use different star and round tip sizes for piping, or try Russian floral piping tips to create buttercream flowers. We went for a rustic buttercream finish and focused on a corner of the cake with floral tip piping, kisses, and flourishes finished with some fresh berries.

1. Preheat the oven to 325°F (160°C). Grease an 8-inch square cake pan with canola oil cooking spray and line the bottom with a parchment paper square.

2. Make the vanilla lemon cake: Stir the lemon zest into the cake batter until evenly distributed. Pour the cake batter into the prepared pan and, using a small offset palette knife, smooth out the top. Bake for 35 to 45 minutes, or until a toothpick inserted into the centre of the cake comes out clean. Allow the cake to cool in the pan on a wire rack for 20 minutes. Remove the cake from the pan, leaving the parchment paper square on the bottom, and cool completely on the wire rack.

3. Place the cake on a 10-inch square cake board or serving plate. Using an apple corer or a No. 806 round tip, poke ¾-inch-deep holes, evenly spaced, in the cake (4 × 4 grid). Use a skewer or the end of a wooden spoon to push the cake in the holes downward to ensure that the hole is clear and ready for filling. (CONTINUES)

DO AHEAD

The finished cake is best enjoyed at room temperature on the day it is made but can be stored, covered, in the refrigerator for up to 4 days. Remove the cake from the refrigerator and let sit at room temperature for 5 to 8 hours before serving. All the components of the finished cake can be made ahead to simplify assembly. Fully cool the baked cake, then wrap it tightly in plastic wrap and store at room temperature for up to 3 days. The raspberry simple syrup can be stored in an airtight container in the refrigerator for up to 3 weeks. Store the vanilla bean buttercream in an airtight container in the refrigerator for up to 2 months and allow it to sit at room temperature for 4 hours before using. Store the lemon curd in an airtight container in the refrigerator for up to 1 month or in the freezer for up to 6 months. If frozen, thaw in the refrigerator overnight before using.

4. Make the raspberry simple syrup and fill the cake: In a small bowl, stir together the simple syrup and raspberry jam. Moisten the cake surface with the raspberry simple syrup. Using a spoon or piping bag, fill the holes three-quarters full with lemon curd, leaving enough headspace for a single raspberry. Poke a raspberry into each hole, top side down so it fills with curd.

5. Crumb coat the cake: Set aside 1 cup of the vanilla bean buttercream to finish the cake in step 9. Crumb coat the top and sides of the cake with a thin layer of the buttercream and place the cake, uncovered, in the refrigerator for 15 minutes.

6. Mask the cake: Place ½ cup of the buttercream on top of the cake. Using a step palette knife, spread and smooth the icing ¼ inch thick over the top surface of the cake. Cover the sides of the cake with additional buttercream, flattening it to ¼ inch thick while turning the turntable to create smooth sides. The icing from the sides will peak and push over the top of your cake, creating a wall.

7. To create perfectly square corners, continue adding to the buttercream walls, focusing on the corners. The more icing, the better, as this allows for a sharper level corner (sides and top) when smoothing the top out. Before removing the built-up icing wall, complete the sides by first flattening out the corner by pulling the palette knife vertically away from the corners, creating a sharp flat side surface. Create a rustic finish on the sides only (follow instructions on page 284, step 4, photos H to J).

8. Finish the top of the cake by flattening the wall of buttercream, creating a sharp edge by pulling a clean palette knife from the outside in toward the centre of the cake. Continue with this technique until you have a smooth, level top and sharp corners, cleaning the palette knife between each pass. Continue with the rustic finish technique for the top.

9. Decorate the cake: Use the reserved buttercream to prepare two different buttercream colours using ½ cup of buttercream for each. In small bowls, mix in the food colourings using a whisk until fully incorporated. Fill separate 12-inch piping bags with different tips (No. 804 large star tip, No. 820 tight star tip, No. 199 fine star tip, and different Russian floral tips). Decorate the cake by piping different styles and sizes (see Buttercream and Whipped Cream Piping Styles, page 286, G), focusing on framing the top left corner and coming down the sides a bit. Start with larger piped flourishes in both colours and fill the gaps with smaller rosettes and kisses in both colours. Finish with the placement of the remaining raspberries on top.

Creamy Garlic Kale and Prosciutto Tarts

Butter Pastry
1 batch Butter Pastry (page 296)

Filling
1 tablespoon olive oil
1 small Vidalia onion, thinly sliced
2 cloves garlic, crushed
6 cups roughly chopped curly kale
    leaves, stems trimmed
¾ cup whipping (35%) cream
½ teaspoon Ranch Spice Mix
    (page 312)
Salt and freshly ground black pepper

Egg Wash
1 large egg
1 tablespoon water,
    room temperature

To finish
⅔ pound (300 g) thinly sliced
    prosciutto

When you are a professional baker and a busy mom, you develop some interesting late-night snacking habits. Often when we are doing big holiday overnight bakes, we order takeout feasts for midnight snacking to keep us going through the night. But sometimes you get home from a shift starving, and you are so sick of smelling sweetness and sticky sugar that you need something deeply savoury and a departure from your regular kid-friendly meals. This creamy garlic kale sauté served with a lightly fried egg was Josie's go-to midnight snack for years whenever there was kale in the garden. We've paired that garlicky, creamy goodness with crispy pastry and salty-sweet prosciutto to balance out the cream. We hope this will be your new go-to late-night munch, and we are sure that your guests will appreciate this tart as part of a meal or as a midnight buffet dish.

1. Line a baking sheet with parchment paper. Set aside a second sheet of parchment paper.

2. Roll out the butter pastry: On a lightly floured work surface, roll out the butter pastry to about ³⁄₁₆-inch thickness. Cut the pastry into twelve 3- × 4-inch rectangles using a metal ruler and pizza cutter. Place 6 pastry rectangles on the prepared baking sheet, cover with the second sheet of parchment paper to keep them flat. Place the remaining 6 pastry rectangles on top of the parchment paper. Store in the refrigerator, for at least 30 minutes to firm up the pastry.

3. Make the filling: In a large, heavy skillet, heat the olive oil over medium heat. When the oil is hot, add the onions and garlic and cook, stirring frequently, until the onions are soft and translucent, 3 to 4 minutes. Add the kale and cook, stirring frequently, until wilted, about 2 minutes.

4. Add the cream and ranch spice mix to the pan. Increase the heat to high and bring the cream to a boil, stirring frequently, until all the liquid has evaporated and you are left with a thick, creamy coating on the kale, about 5 minutes. Add salt and pepper to taste. Using a silicone spatula, transfer and spread the kale mixture out on a large plate and allow it to cool, uncovered, in the fridge until room temperature, about 15 minutes. (CONTINUES)

DO AHEAD

These tarts are best enjoyed on the day they are baked, but you can store the baked tarts (without prosciutto) in an airtight container in the refrigerator for up to 2 days and then warm them in a 325°F (160°C) oven for 5 minutes before topping with the prosciutto.

The butter pastry can be made ahead, wrapped tightly in plastic wrap, and stored in the refrigerator for up to 1 week or in the freezer for up to 6 months. If frozen, thaw in the refrigerator overnight before using. The pastry rectangles can be rolled,

cut, and stored in the refrigerator, covered with beeswax or plastic wrap, for up to 2 days. The kale filling can be made ahead and stored in an airtight container in the refrigerator for up to 3 days.

5. Meanwhile, preheat the oven to 400°F (200°C). Line 2 baking sheets with parchment paper or silicone baking mats.

6. Make the egg wash, assemble, and bake the tarts: In a small bowl, thoroughly whisk together the egg and water until combined. Place 6 pastry rectangles on each prepared baking sheet and, using a pastry brush, lightly brush egg wash over the entire surface of each rectangle, all the way to the edges. Scoop ¼ cup of the cooked kale mixture into the centre of each egg-washed rectangle. Spread out the kale with the back of a spoon so it covers most of the surface, leaving a ⅛-inch border of exposed pastry around the edge.

7. Bake the tarts for 20 to 25 minutes, or until the pastry is a deep golden brown. Remove from the oven and transfer the tarts to a wire rack to cool for 5 to 10 minutes. Evenly divide the prosciutto and scatter it on top of the tarts. Serve warm or at room temperature.

Mini Chicken Pot Pies

Chicken Filling
1 (3- to 3½-pound/1.35 to 1.6 kg)
   chicken (3 cups chopped
   cooked chicken)
1 tablespoon olive oil
1 teaspoon salt, more for seasoning
1 teaspoon freshly ground black
   pepper, more for seasoning
3 tablespoons unsalted butter
1 cup sliced cremini mushrooms
½ cup chopped white onion
½ cup chopped leeks (white and
   light green parts only)
½ cup chopped celery
½ cup peeled and chopped carrots
2 cups Poultry Stock (page 319)
   or store-bought chicken stock
1 cup cubed russet potatoes
   (about 1 large potato)
1 tablespoon chopped fresh thyme
2 tablespoons chopped fresh sage
1 cup whipping (35%) cream
2 tablespoons cornstarch
½ cup frozen corn kernels
½ cup frozen peas

Butter Pastry
1½ batches Butter Pastry (page 296)

Egg Wash
1 large egg
1 tablespoon water,
   room temperature

First introduced years ago by our former chef Sara, our classic creamy chicken pot pie has been popular ever since. The recipe underwent a rewrite when Erin took over the savoury department's leadership, but the essentials remained. Each week, Erin makes a scenic drive into the country to pick up whole fresh chickens from a local farm. She roasts the chickens and makes fresh stock with the bones. When creating the filling, she adds lots of local vegetables, cream, and fresh herbs and just the right seasoning to consistently achieve the taste our customers have grown to crave. Once this hearty savoury filling cools, it is wrapped in a buttery, golden brown pastry hug. A lot of love and time goes into these pot pies, and we think that's fitting for celebrating mom. If you are making the stock fresh from your roasted chicken, remove the meat from the bones and store the cooked meat, unchopped, in an airtight container in the refrigerator for up to 2 days. Prepare the filling a day in advance of baking the pie to allow the flavours to mingle and so that the filling is cold when you fill the pastry shell.

1. Preheat the oven to 375°F (190°C). Line a baking sheet with parchment paper.

2. Make the chicken filling: Place the chicken on the prepared baking sheet. Rub the chicken all over with the olive oil, salt, and pepper to evenly coat. Roast the chicken until it reaches an internal temperature of at least 170°F (77°C) and the juices from the meat run clear, 60 to 75 minutes. Allow the chicken to cool to room temperature. Remove all the meat from the bones and cube the chicken meat. Discard the skin but reserve the bones for Poultry Stock (page 319).

3. In a large, heavy pot, heat the butter over medium heat. When the butter is bubbly, add the mushrooms, onions, leeks, celery, and carrots and cook, stirring frequently, until the onions are soft and translucent, 3 to 4 minutes. Add the stock, potatoes, thyme, and sage, then increase the heat to high and bring to a boil, stirring occasionally. Once boiling, reduce the heat to medium-low to maintain a gentle boil and cook, covered, for 15 to 20 minutes or until the potatoes are fork-tender. (CONTINUES)

DO AHEAD

You can make these pies up to 3 days ahead and store them, covered, in the refrigerator. To serve, warm them in a 325°F (160°C) oven for 20 to 25 minutes. The butter pastry can be made ahead, wrapped tightly in plastic wrap, and stored in the refrigerator for up to 1 week or in the freezer for up to 6 months. If frozen, thaw in the refrigerator overnight before using. The pastry circles can be rolled, cut, and stored, covered with beeswax or plastic wrap, in the refrigerator for up to 2 days. The chicken filling can be made ahead and stored in an airtight container in the refrigerator for up to 3 days.

4. In a small bowl, stir together the cream and cornstarch until the cornstarch is dissolved. Add this slurry to the filling and, stirring constantly, bring the filling back to a boil over high heat. Cook until the mixture has thickened, 2 to 3 minutes.

5. Remove the filling from the heat and stir in the cubed chicken, corn, and peas. Season with salt and pepper to taste. You should slightly overseason the filling, as the pastry tends to absorb the salt in the filling as the pie bakes. Allow the filling to cool to room temperature, then cover and store in the refrigerator overnight to allow the flavours to meld.

6. Roll out and chill the butter pastry: Preheat the oven to 400°F (200°C). Generously grease a 12-cup muffin pan with canola oil cooking spray.

7. On a lightly floured work surface, roll out the butter pastry dough to about ⅛-inch thickness. Cut out twelve 5-inch circles and twelve 2-inch circles of dough. Gently press the 5-inch circles into the muffin cups, making sure not to stretch the dough. Place the muffin pan in the refrigerator for 15 to 20 minutes to allow the pastry to relax and firm up a bit. Place the 2-inch circles on a baking sheet or plate lined with parchment paper and store in the refrigerator, covered with parchment or plastic wrap, until needed.

8. Make the egg wash, fill, and bake the mini pot pies: In a small bowl, thoroughly whisk together the egg and water until combined. Scoop the cooled chicken filling into the mini pie shells to the rim of the muffin cups. Place a 2-inch pastry circle on top of the filling and brush it gently with egg wash. Egg-wash the edges of any exposed pastry. Place the muffin pan on a baking sheet to catch any juices that overflow and bake until the pastry is a deep golden brown and the filling is bubbling around the edges, 35 to 40 minutes. Remove the pies from the muffin pan immediately and serve hot.

Flatbread Seed Crackers Ⓥ

DO AHEAD: These crackers are best enjoyed on the day they are baked. The pizza dough can be made ahead and stored, covered with beeswax or plastic wrap, in the refrigerator for up to 36 hours. Allow the chilled dough to come to room temperature, covered, for 45 to 60 minutes before rolling it out. Store baked crackers in an airtight container at room temperature for up to 3 days.

Pizza Dough
½ batch Pizza Dough (page 303), room temperature

Seed Mix
3 tablespoons raw pumpkin seeds
3 tablespoons raw sunflower seeds
1 tablespoon flax seeds
1 tablespoon sesame seeds

To finish
2 tablespoons olive oil
2 teaspoons flaky sea salt (we use Maldon)

These crackers are as addictive as potato chips on their own, but really shine dipped into a hummus or your favourite dip. Elevate any soup by serving these as dippers on the side or use them to garnish larger platters with some texture and colour from the seeds. If you ever find yourself with leftover bread or pretzel dough, you can use this same sandwiching and rolling technique to create a small batch of seeded crackers. If you would like, you can even add in chopped dried fruit, like cranberries, for jewel-like additions to the crackers. Your mom(s) will certainly be impressed by these deceptively simple crackers; they look beautiful on a table, and their nutty, salty crunch is universally popular.

1. Preheat the oven to 400°F (200°C). Line 2 baking sheets with parchment paper or silicone baking mats.

2. Roll out the dough: If using refrigerated pizza dough, make sure it has come to room temperature before rolling it out. Divide the dough into 4 equal portions. Lightly flour a work surface. Working with one piece of dough at a time and keeping the other portions covered with beeswax or plastic wrap, roll it out into an 8-inch circle. Set each circle aside, covered, as you roll out the remaining dough.

4. Make the seed mix: In a small bowl, stir together the pumpkin seeds, sunflower seeds, flax seeds, and sesame seeds.

5. Place one dough circle on the work surface and, using a dry pastry brush, brush any flour off the surface of the dough. Sprinkle the dough circle evenly with ¼ cup of the seed mix. Place a second dough circle on top and line up the edges with the bottom circle, pinching the edges together. Repeat with the remaining circles.

6. Gently roll out one of the sandwiched circles, as flat as you can, turning and moving the dough frequently to make sure it is not sticking to the work surface. Keep rolling out the dough from the centre of the circle, giving the dough time to rest if it's pulling back. Continue rolling until you have a rectangle about 13 x 18 inches. Gently lift the cracker onto one of the prepared baking sheets and spread it out as flat as possible. Brush any flour off the surface and dock the dough with a fork or rolling docker. This will prevent the cracker from puffing up too much during baking. Repeat with the second sandwiched circle and place it on the second baking sheet.

7. Finish and bake: Using a pastry brush, lightly brush the surface of each cracker with 1 tablespoon of olive oil and sprinkle with 1 teaspoon of flaky sea salt. Bake for 12 to 15 minutes, or until the crackers puff up off the baking tray and are crisp and golden brown. Transfer the crackers to a wire rack to cool to room temperature and then break them into desired size for serving.

Embrace your delicate side by hosting a fancy tea party. Tea parties should be sophisticated but relaxed affairs with seating or comfortable standing tables for all your guests. You want them to enjoy the food you have spent your energy creating, and it should be able to shine as the centrepiece of your gathering. For a large group, keeping tea hot can be a challenge, so try sourcing a large kettle or borrow a few electric kettles to create multiple tea stations, and keep them going with a bottle of water placed under the table so that people can make their own fresh tea. Do a little tea research so that you are comfortable preparing a variety of teas, and prepare some iced teas in advance of your tea party. Most herbal teas make great iced tea just by brewing as usual and chilling them, but you can add some honey, maple syrup, or sugar to sweeten them to your taste. There are also several different ways to make overnight cold brewed iced tea with a little research. A cute way to display a selection of teas is in glass mason jars or decorative canisters with paper labels tied on or folded in front; include the name, tasting notes, how long to steep, and what sweet or savoury item to pair it with. We love an eclectic mix of decor for a tea party: handsewn bunting, a mix of vintage tablecloths, wildflower bouquets, and light and airy decor. Thrift some china cups and teapots or serving platters and towers; they don't have to match. Keep all the food bite-size so that folks can indulge in a variety of sweet and savoury treats to complement their tea. Cut the Raspberry Lemon OMG Bars (page 99) and Black and White Coffee Cake (page 109) into bite-size pieces and serve them alongside the Lavender Earl Grey Shorties (page 100) and Belgium Cookies (page 103) as your sweet offerings. Pair them with mini Quiche Two Ways (page 111) and tea sandwiches or crudités as your savoury component. After some musical entertainment or party games, close the party with the Chocolate Sour Cherry Whipped Cream Jelly Roll (page 105) and send your guests home with a few Mini-Cinny Buns (page 113) for late-night snacking.

Tea Party

Raspberry Lemon OMG Bars

These bars can be baked and stored un-iced, covered, in the refrigerator for up to 2 days. You can make the cream cheese icing ahead and store it in an airtight container in the refrigerator for up to 1 month. Iced bars can be stored in an airtight container in the refrigerator for up to 5 days.

Raspberry Purée
5 ounces (140 g/½ cup) frozen
   raspberries

Lemon Cake Batter
½ batch Vanilla Cake Batter
   (page 282)
Zest of 2 lemons

Raspberry Cheesecake Filling
4 ounces (115 g/½ cup) cream
   cheese, room temperature
2 tablespoons granulated sugar
1 tablespoon all-purpose flour
1 large egg yolk

Dreamy Cream Cheese Icing
¼ batch Dreamy Cream Cheese
   Icing (page 295)

For assembly
1 cup fresh raspberries, cut in half
Zest of 1 lemon
2 tablespoons granulated sugar

These bars have stunning deep raspberry–coloured swirls throughout, which contrast beautifully against the bright white icing and golden cake. We make several versions of our OMG bars at the bakery, from the classic Chocolate Cream Cheese OMG to our Orange Gingerbread OMG. They are all variations on fluffy cake paired with dense cheesecake, and each is delicious but this one might be the most beautiful. Any extra purée you don't use for baking can be mixed into lemonade to make pink lemonade or added to iced teas to add flavour and colour. If you prefer, these bars are delicious and still beautiful plain, without the icing and garnishes.

1. Preheat the oven to 350°F (180°C). Grease an 8-inch square cake pan with canola oil cooking spray and line with parchment paper.

2. Make the raspberry purée: Allow the berries to thaw in the refrigerator overnight or at room temperature for 1 hour. Once thawed, using a silicone spatula, press the raspberries through a fine-mesh sieve into a small bowl. (Freezing and defrosting the berries causes them to break down so that they are easy to push through the sieve.) You should end up with a thick raspberry juice with maybe a few seeds. You will need ¼ cup of purée. Set aside for step 4.

3. Make the lemon cake batter: Mix the lemon zest into the vanilla cake batter. Pour the batter into the prepared pan and, using a small offset palette knife, smooth out the top. Set aside.

4. Make the raspberry cheesecake filling: In the bowl of a stand mixer fitted with the paddle attachment, beat the cream cheese on high speed for 2 to 3 minutes until smooth. Scrape down the sides and bottom of the bowl. Add the sugar, flour, and egg yolk and beat on medium-high speed for 2 to 3 minutes until smooth. Scrape down the sides and bottom of the bowl. Add the ¼ cup raspberry purée and mix until the raspberry is evenly distributed and the mixture is smooth.

5. Combine the batter and filling: Drop large spoonfuls of the raspberry cheesecake filling into the lemon cake batter. Using a butter knife, swirl the two batters together a little. You want to leave distinct areas of cheesecake and lemon cake batter. Bake for 35 to 45 minutes, or until a toothpick inserted into the centre of the lemon cake area comes out clean. Allow to cool at room temperature for 1 to 2 hours before icing.

6. Ice and finish the bars: Using a small offset palette knife, spread the dreamy cream cheese icing evenly over the baked bar. Place the raspberry halves on top of the icing, distributing them evenly over the surface.

7. In a small bowl, rub together the lemon zest and sugar and sprinkle it over the bar for a little sparkle.

8. Cut the bars using a warm chef's knife by dipping it into hot water and drying it on a clean kitchen towel. Wipe the knife between each cut to get nice clean cuts.

TEA PARTY

Lavender Earl Grey Shorties

1 cup unsalted butter,
    room temperature
½ cup icing sugar
½ cup cornstarch
1 tablespoon finely ground
    lavender Earl Grey tea
    (or your favourite Earl Grey tea)
½ teaspoon salt
1½ cups all-purpose flour

You can use any high-quality tea in these shortbread cookies, so grab your favourite loose leaf tea and a clean coffee grinder and experiment. Finely grind the tea just like you would coffee, in an old school coffee grinder with a spinning blade; unfortunately, fancy burr grinders aren't useful here. Sift the ground tea through a fine-mesh metal sieve to get rid of any larger pieces and you are ready to bake! You can make a few different batches with various teas and use a unique pattern on top of the cookies to differentiate them. Try using your fingers to form ridges on top of the cookies or a fork to create a crosshatch pattern, or even use a cookie press to stamp the tops. You want to make sure that the cookies are fully cooked through and are dry all the way to the centre, so if you aren't sure, it's better to overbake these cookies a little instead of risking a raw centre. As a variation, use the chocolate tempering instructions on page 305 with 1 pound, 9 ounces (700 g / 3½ cups) milk chocolate couverture callets. Drizzle the tops of the cookies with tempered milk chocolate.

1. Preheat the oven to 350°F (180°C). Line 2 baking sheets with parchment paper or silicone baking mats.

2. In the bowl of a stand mixer fitted with the paddle attachment, lightly cream the butter on medium-high speed just until the butter is smooth, 1 to 2 minutes. Do not incorporate air into the butter. Scrape down the sides and bottom of the bowl.

3. Add the icing sugar, cornstarch, ground tea, and salt and mix on low speed until the dry ingredients are fully incorporated into the butter. Increase the speed to medium-high and continue to mix until smooth, 2 to 3 minutes. Add the flour and mix on low speed until most of the flour has been incorporated. Increase the speed to medium-high and continue to mix until the dough is smooth, without whipping air into the dough, 1 to 2 minutes.

4. Scoop thirteen 1½-tablespoon portions of cookie dough onto each prepared baking sheet, leaving ample space between them. Gently press down on the cookies to flatten them to ½-inch thickness. Using a lightly floured fork or other metal utensil, press a pattern into the tops of the cookies. Bake, one sheet at a time, for 13 to 15 minutes, or until very lightly browned around the edges. Allow the cookies to cool to room temperature on the baking sheets.

DO AHEAD

You can make these cookies ahead and store them in an airtight container at room temperature for up to 2 weeks or in the freezer for up to 2 months.

Thaw the cookies, uncovered, at room temperature for 1 hour before serving.

Belgium Cookies

Sugar Cookie Dough
1 batch Sugar Cookie Dough
  (page 301)

Icing
1 cup icing sugar
3 to 6 teaspoons water, warm
¼ teaspoon vanilla bean paste

Raspberry Jam
2 cups Raspberry Jam (page 310)
  or store-bought

Belgium or Empire, the official name of these cookies is up for much debate, but we prefer Belgium because the rise of any empire makes us shudder. Whatever you call them, these ruby jewel-toned cookies will become a fast favourite. After your first bite, you'll be making up new holidays just to get these cookies on the menu. The not-too-sweet vanilla sugar cookie perfectly sandwiches your most prized raspberry jam, and the sweet drizzle adds that perfect finishing touch. For a more traditional look found throughout the Commonwealth and European bakeries, omit the peekaboo window, flood the entire top of the cookie with icing, and finish with glacé cherries for that classic look. Alternatively, fill them with different jams or preserves to personalize them to your taste.

1. Preheat the oven to 350°F (180°C). Line 3 baking sheets with parchment paper or silicone baking mats.

2. **Make the cookies:** On a lightly floured work surface, roll out the sugar cookie dough to about ¼-inch thickness. Move the dough around and check underneath frequently to make sure it is not sticking to the work surface, dusting lightly with more flour if needed. Using a 2½-inch round cookie cutter, cut out 60 rounds and place 20 on each of the prepared baking sheets, evenly spaced. Use a small round scalloped cookie cutter or small decorative shaped cutter to cut out the centre of 30 of the cookie rounds to create a peekaboo for the top cookies.

3. If there is any flour on top of the cookies, brush it off with a dry pastry brush before baking. Bake, one sheet at a time, for 14 to 18 minutes, or until the cookies have puffed up, there is light browning on the bottoms, and the tops are just lightly browned. Allow the cookies to cool completely on the baking sheets.

4. **Make the icing:** In a medium bowl, whisk together the icing sugar, 3 teaspoons of the water, and the vanilla bean paste until smooth. Adjust by adding 1 teaspoon of water at a time until desired drizzling consistency has been achieved. (CONTINUES)

DO AHEAD

It is best to assemble these cookies a day ahead of serving to ensure that the sandwiches are stable, especially if you are travelling with them. If stability isn't an issue, you can serve them immediately after assembling.

You can store un-iced cookies in an airtight container at room temperature for up to 1 month. The raspberry jam can be made ahead and stored in an airtight container in the refrigerator for up to 1 month or in the freezer for up to 4 months. If frozen, thaw in the refrigerator overnight before using. Store assembled sandwich cookies in an airtight container at room temperature for up to 2 days.

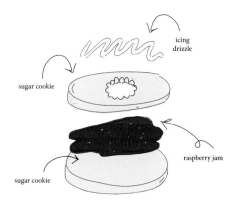

icing drizzle

sugar cookie

raspberry jam

sugar cookie

5. Decorate and assemble the sandwich cookies: Collect the cookies with holes in the centre and place them right side up on a baking sheet lined with parchment paper. Using a spoon, drizzle the icing over the cookies. Allow to dry for at least 2 hours, or until dry to the touch.

6. Arrange the cookies with no holes in the centre upside down on a work surface. Place a 12-inch piping bag fitted with a No. 805 round tip in an empty tall cup for extra stability. Fold the top edge of the piping bag over the lip of the cup to form a pocket and fill it with the raspberry jam. Pipe a layer of raspberry jam onto each cookie, leaving a ½-inch border of exposed cookie around the edge. Alternatively, use a spoon to place a tablespoon of jam into the centre of each cookie and use the back of the spoon to spread the jam into a circle, leaving a ½-inch border of exposed cookie.

7. Place the iced cookies on top of the cookies that have jam on them to form sandwiches. Using even, light pressure, gently push down on the tops to form a bond with the jam. You will see the jam starting to come to the edge. Allow the cookies to set, undisturbed and uncovered, at room temperature, for at least 6 to 12 hours to ensure that the jam has settled and the cookies will stay sandwiched.

Chocolate Sour Cherry Whipped Cream Jelly Roll

Chocolate Chiffon Cake

1 cup all-purpose flour
½ teaspoon baking powder
½ teaspoon baking soda
¼ teaspoon salt
6 large egg yolks, room temperature
1 large whole egg, room temperature
⅓ cup + ¼ cup granulated sugar,
    divided
¼ cup canola oil
1 tablespoon water,
    room temperature
1 teaspoon pure vanilla extract
1 teaspoon vanilla bean paste
6 large egg whites,
    room temperature
½ cup icing sugar

Sour Cherry Compote

1 batch Sour Cherry Compote
    (page 310)

Whipped Cream

1 batch Whipped Cream (page 300)

Dark Chocolate Ganache

1 batch Dark Chocolate Ganache
    (page 307)

As a child, Nickey's family on her mother's Italian side would always celebrate birthdays with Black Forest Cake. The grocery-store version was well soaked in rum flavouring with industrial whipped topping, layered with cherry filling, and finished with shaved chocolate and a crown of maraschino cherries. You knew it was a birthday celebration when this cake came out to party, and there was absolutely no shame in this store-bought delight. For our version, we focus on from-scratch sour cherry compote with a pop of orange juice and zest to complement and bring out the cherry flavour, paired with fresh whipped cream and a light and fluffy chocolate chiffon roll. The dark chocolate ganache and whipped cream to finish are truly optional, but we think it adds just that little bit of extra pizzazz!

1. Preheat the oven to 350°F (180°C). Grease a 13- × 18-inch baking sheet only on the bottom with canola oil cooking spray and line with parchment paper. Try to avoid the sides of the pan while spraying the canola oil, as the cake needs something to grip as it rises to achieve full volume.

2. Make the cake: Sift the flour, baking powder, baking soda, and salt into a medium bowl 3 times and whisk until thoroughly combined. This will help make the cake light and airy.

3. In the bowl of a stand mixer fitted with the whisk attachment, combine the egg yolks, whole egg, and the ⅓ cup granulated sugar. Whisk on high speed until the mixture is pale in colour and has reached the ribbon stage, 12 to 15 minutes. You will know the mixture has reached the ribbon stage when you lift the whisk and the mixture drops back into the bowl in long ribbons. Add the canola oil, water, and vanilla extract and paste. Whip until combined, 1 to 2 minutes. Transfer the mixture to a medium bowl and set aside.

4. Wash the bowl of the stand mixer and the whisk attachment thoroughly with soap and water, ensuring that all oil and soap residue is gone. It's important to completely dry the bowl and whisk.

5. In the bowl of a stand mixer fitted with the whisk attachment, beat the egg whites to soft peaks on medium-high speed, about 2 or 3 minutes. Slowly add the remaining ¼ cup granulated sugar and continue beating until stiff peaks form and the egg whites are glossy but not dry, 2 to 3 minutes. (CONTINUES)

DO AHEAD

The finished jelly roll is best enjoyed from the refrigerator on the day it is made, but it can be stored, covered, in the refrigerator for up to 2 days. Remove the cake from the refrigerator and let sit at room temperature for 20 to 30 minutes before serving.

The baked cake can be left rolled in the kitchen towel in step 8 for up to 24 hours. The sour cherry compote and ganache can be made ahead. Store the cherry compote in an airtight container in the refrigerator for up to 1 month or in the freezer for up to

6 months. Store the ganache in an airtight container in the refrigerator for up to 2 weeks or in the freezer for up to 6 months. If frozen, thaw the compote or ganache in the refrigerator overnight before using.

6. Using a spatula, fold half of the whipped egg whites gently into the egg yolk mixture, until just combined. Gently fold in the remaining whipped egg whites into the mixture. Add and fold the dry ingredients into the mixture to create a light and fluffy batter.

7. Gently scrape the batter into the prepared pan and, using an offset palette knife, evenly smooth out the top. Bake for 15 to 20 minutes, or until the centre bounces back slightly when pressed lightly. Allow the cake to cool in the pans on a wire rack for 10 minutes.

8. Roll the cake: Run a paring knife around the edges of the cake to loosen it from the pan. Sift the icing sugar over the entire surface of a clean, lint-free kitchen towel. Invert the pan onto the towel and tap the bottom to release the cake. Gently remove the parchment paper.

9. With a short side facing you, roll up the cake with the kitchen towel, away from you, and allow the rolled cake to cool completely, 3 to 4 hours. This trains the cake to roll and decreases any tears during the final rolling process.

10. Assemble the jelly roll: Unroll the cake in the towel. With a short side facing you, use an offset palette knife to evenly spread the sour cherry compote over the entire surface, leaving a ½-inch border of exposed cake on the short side farthest from you. Evenly spread 1½ cups of whipped cream over the entire surface, including the ½-inch border of exposed cake. Reserve the remaining whipped cream for step 13.

11. Using the kitchen towel as support, begin to roll up the cake, jelly roll style. Once it starts to roll, use the towel as a guide to lift the cake and continue rolling it all the way to the other end. Place the jelly roll seam down on a serving plate.

12. Reheat the dark chocolate ganache to a pourable consistency in the microwave. Pour the ganache along the centre of the jelly roll, spreading it outward with a palette knife and allowing it to overflow and drip down the sides. Place the jelly roll, uncovered, in the refrigerator for 10 minutes, or until the ganache is firm to the touch.

13. Fill a 12-inch piping bag fitted with a No. 825 star tip with the remaining whipped cream and pipe a decorative flourish of kisses or rosettes on top, zig-zagging back and forth (see Buttercream and Whipped Cream Piping Styles, page 286, C). For kisses (as shown in the photo), using even pressure, attach the whipped cream to the cake, pull up and away from the cake slightly to build a wide bottom, and continue pulling up, releasing pressure completely to create a point. (For rosettes, using even pressure, attach the whipped cream to the cake and begin to move the tip counter-clockwise in a tight circle. End the rosette once you have closed the circle, begin to release pressure, and with a flick of the wrist end pressure completely to create a point ending on the starting point lying down.)

14. Chill the cake for 1 hour before serving. Cut the jelly roll using a warm chef's knife by dipping it into hot water and drying it on a clean kitchen towel. Wipe the knife between each cut to get nice clean cuts.

Black and White Coffee Cake

DO AHEAD: This cake is best enjoyed at room temperature on the day it is made, but it can be stored in an airtight container at room temperature for up to 3 days.

Shortbread Crumble
¾ cup all-purpose flour
½ cup unsalted butter, cold and cut into ½-inch cubes
½ cup icing sugar

Chocolate Cake Batter
1 cup buttermilk
1 teaspoon baking soda
1 teaspoon pure vanilla extract
1½ cups all-purpose flour
1 cup granulated sugar
½ cup cocoa powder
1½ teaspoons baking powder
½ teaspoon salt
½ cup unsalted butter, cold and cut into ½-inch cubes
1 large egg, room temperature
1 cup semi-sweet chocolate chunks

Josie was working as the morning baker at our farmers' market location one day when she had a sudden craving for chocolate while deciding on the daily menu. Instead of the walnut coffee cake she had planned, she envisioned layers of shortbread in place of crumble and dark chocolate cake studded with semi-sweet chocolate chunks. The name is a reference to the classic Black and White Cookie, a New York staple. This coffee cake definitely satisfied those early-morning cravings and became a bakery favourite. This cake is fairly tall, so if you want to cut it into bite-size pieces, try baking it in a 9-inch square pan instead of the 8-inch square pan and reduce the cooking time by 10 minutes. To make this a true coffee cake, replace half the buttermilk with strongly brewed room-temperature coffee.

1. Preheat the oven to 350°F (180°C). Grease an 8-inch square cake pan with canola oil cooking spray and line with parchment paper.

2. Make the shortbread crumble: In the bowl of a stand mixer fitted with the paddle attachment, combine the flour, butter, and icing sugar. Mix on medium-low speed until the mixture is mealy, there is very little dry flour, and it is just starting to come together as a dough, 2 to 3 minutes. Transfer the crumble to a small bowl and set aside. There's no need to wash the bowl before mixing the cake batter.

3. Make the chocolate cake batter: In a small bowl, whisk together the buttermilk, baking soda, and vanilla. Set aside.

4. In the bowl of a stand mixer fitted with the paddle attachment, combine the flour, granulated sugar, cocoa, baking powder, and salt. Mix on medium-low speed for 1 to 2 minutes until the ingredients are well combined. Add the butter and mix on medium-low speed until the mixture is mealy, 2 to 3 minutes.

5. Whisk the egg into the buttermilk mixture and add the wet ingredients and chocolate chunks to the dry ingredients in the bowl of the stand mixer. Mix on low speed, increasing to medium speed until almost fully incorporated, less than 1 minute. Scrape down the sides and bottom of the bowl. Mix on medium-high speed for 30 seconds until the batter is well combined.

6. Assemble and bake: Scoop half the cake batter into the prepared pan and, using a small offset palette knife, smooth out the top. Sprinkle half the shortbread crumble evenly over the surface of the batter. Repeat with the remaining batter and crumble. Bake for 45 to 60 minutes, or until a toothpick inserted into the centre of the cake comes out clean.

7. Cut the cake into 2½-inch squares using a bread knife. Wipe the knife clean with a warm cloth between each cut to get nice clean cuts.

Quiche Two Ways

Ham and Cheddar Quiche Filling
⅓ pound (150 g/¾ cup) Black Forest ham, cubed
4 ounces (115 g/1 cup) shredded old cheddar cheese

Roasted Vegetable and Goat Cheese Quiche Filling
½ cup ½-inch-thick portobello mushroom slices
½ cup ½-inch-thick red onion slices
½ cup ½-inch-thick red bell pepper slices
½ cup ¼-inch-thick zucchini slices
½ cup ¼-inch-thick eggplant slices
2 tablespoons olive oil
½ teaspoon salt
½ teaspoon freshly ground black pepper
4 ounces (115 g/½ cup) soft goat cheese, cut into ½-inch chunks

Butter Pastry
1½ batches Butter Pastry (page 296)

Egg Mixture
4 large eggs
½ cup whole milk
½ cup whipping (35%) cream
½ teaspoon salt
¼ teaspoon freshly ground black pepper

These two quiche flavours are our best-selling quiches: Ham and Cheddar and Roasted Vegetable and Goat Cheese. What we love about quiche, though, is that it is so easy to swap out the fillings for what you have on hand. Any cooked vegetables will work, as well as any leftover cooked meats or cheeses. One of our favourite summer quiches is roasted tomato and basil fresh from the garden with mozzarella. Get creative with your fridge leftovers and discover your favourite quiche combination. If you have it on hand, you can swap half-and-half cream for the milk and whipping cream; it will work just as well. But avoid replacing the whipping cream with milk, as the cream adds body to your quiche and using just milk won't give you the rich custard this quiche deserves.

1. Preheat the oven to 400°F (200°C). Generously grease a 12-cup muffin pan with canola oil cooking spray and line a baking sheet with parchment paper or a silicone baking mat.

2. Prep the ham and cheddar quiche filling: Organize and set aside the cubed ham and shredded cheese.

3. Make the roasted vegetable quiche filling: Toss together the mushrooms, red onion, bell pepper, zucchini, eggplant, olive oil, salt, and pepper on the prepared baking sheet until the vegetables are fully coated in oil. Spread the vegetables into an even layer on the baking sheet and roast until they are cooked all the way through and slightly blackened around the edges, 15 to 20 minutes. Allow the vegetables to cool to room temperature on the baking sheet before filling the tart shells in step 8. Keep the oven at 400°F (200°C) to blind-bake the tart shells (step 5).

4. Roll out the butter pastry dough for the tart shells: On a lightly floured work surface, roll out the butter pastry dough into a rough rectangle, about ⅛-inch thickness. Cut out twelve 5-inch circles of dough, rerolling scraps if necessary. Gently press the dough circles into the muffin cups, making sure not to stretch the dough. Place the muffin pan, uncovered, in the refrigerator for 15 to 20 minutes to allow the pastry to relax and firm up a bit. (CONTINUES)

DO AHEAD

You can make these quiches ahead and store them in an airtight container in the refrigerator for up to 3 days. To serve, warm them in a 325°F (160°C) oven for 15 to 20 minutes. The butter pastry can be made ahead, wrapped tightly in plastic wrap, and stored in the refrigerator for up to 1 week or in the freezer for up to 6 months. If frozen, thaw in the refrigerator overnight before using. The tart shells can be baked, cooled thoroughly and left in the pan, wrapped in beeswax or plastic wrap, and stored at room temperature for up to 3 days. The egg mixture can be made ahead and stored in an airtight container in the refrigerator for up to 3 days. Whisk the mixture well before using.

5. Blind-bake the tart shells: Line each shell with a parchment paper square and fill with ½ cup dried beans or pie weights. Bake for 20 to 25 minutes, or until the edges of the shells are golden brown. Lift the parchment squares and beans or weights out of the tart shells. Reduce the oven temperature to 325°F (160°C).

6. Make the egg filling: In a medium bowl, whisk together the eggs, milk, cream, salt, and pepper until thoroughly combined.

7. Assemble the ham and cheddar quiches: Divide the ham and shredded cheese evenly among 6 of the tart shells, filling them to the top of the pastry.

8. Assemble the roasted vegetable quiches: Evenly divide the roasted vegetable mixture among the remaining 6 tart shells and top with the goat cheese.

9. Pour the egg mixture evenly over the filling up to ¼ inch from the top of the pastry. Bake for 20 to 25 minutes, or until the egg filling is puffed and light golden brown in places and no wetness is visible. These quiches are best enjoyed hot on the day of baking, but they can also be served chilled or at room temperature.

Mini-Cinny Buns

Enriched Dough
1 batch Enriched Dough (page 304)
½ cup unsalted butter, melted and cooled to room temperature, for brushing the dough

Filling
¾ cup packed dark brown sugar
2 tablespoons granulated sugar
2 tablespoons cinnamon
½ teaspoon salt

Dreamy Cream Cheese Icing
⅓ batch Dreamy Cream Cheese Icing (page 295)

Our cinnamon bun recipe was developed by Josie in her home kitchen when we didn't yet have a bricks-and-mortar bakery and were still just doing farmers' markets and a Community Supported Bakery (CSB) program. This is a pretty classic cinnamon bun. Warm spices caramelized within layers of soft buttery dough, finished with a sweet cream cheese icing. These are the half-size version we often make at the bakery that are perfect for parties. They are also a pretty great mini bump before the tail end of a workday when paired with that final dose of caffeine. They are baked in a muffin pan and need to be turned out of the pan as soon as they emerge from the oven, to prevent them from sticking as the sugar cools. This is a versatile base dough, and you'll see it in a couple of recipes throughout this book. We love to double the dough recipe and freeze half so that the next time you want cinnamon buns you can just defrost the dough in the fridge overnight and use the dough in the morning.

1. Generously grease a 12-cup muffin pan with canola oil cooking spray.

2. Roll out the enriched dough: On a lightly floured work surface, roll out the dough into a 24- × 12-inch rectangle that is ¼ inch thick. Move the dough around and check underneath it a couple of times to make sure it is not sticking to the work surface, dusting lightly with more flour as needed. Brush any flour off the top of the dough with a dry pastry brush. Let the dough rest on the counter for 5 minutes.

3. With a long side facing you, using a pastry brush, brush the melted butter evenly over the whole surface of the rectangle.

4. Make the filling: In a small bowl, mix together the brown sugar, granulated sugar, cinnamon, and salt until thoroughly combined. Sprinkle the cinnamon sugar evenly over the dough, leaving a 1-inch border of exposed dough along the edge of the long side farthest from you.

5. Roll and cut the dough and let rise: Starting at the long side closest to you, roll the dough away from you into a tight roll, sealing it closed with the 1 inch of exposed buttered dough.   (CONTINUES)

DO AHEAD

The dough can be made ahead and stored, covered with beeswax or plastic wrap, in the refrigerator for up to 36 hours or frozen for up to 1 month. If frozen, thaw in the refrigerator overnight. Allow refrigerated or previously frozen dough to sit at room temperature for 45 to 60 minutes before rolling it out. These buns are best served immediately, but they can be stored, covered, at room temperature for up to 12 hours or in an airtight container in the refrigerator for up to 1 day, then warmed in a 325°F (160°C) oven for 5 minutes.

TEA PARTY

113

6. Using a serrated knife, cut the roll crosswise into twelve 2-inch slices. Carefully lift the slices so that they don't unroll and place them, cinnamon sugar spiral side up, in the wells of the greased muffin pan. Allow the buns to rise, uncovered, in a warm, humid area for 45 to 60 minutes, or until they double in size. If the surface of the buns seems to be drying out, lightly spray them with warm water every 10 to 15 minutes using a spray bottle.

7. Meanwhile, preheat the oven to 325°F (160°C).

8. Bake the buns: Slide the buns into the oven and bake for 18 to 25 minutes, or until they are puffed and golden brown. Remove from the oven and immediately invert the pan over a serving plate or clean baking sheet. Using metal tongs or 2 forks so that the sugar doesn't burn you, reposition the buns top side up. Allow the buns to cool for 15 minutes, then flip them back over.

9. Ice the buns: Spread 3 tablespoons of dreamy cream cheese icing over each warm bun and serve immediately.

For the dad(s) that raised you and the dad(s) that raised you up, Father's Day is the day to celebrate all the father figures in your life. The dads in our lives have a distinct preference for bacon, pretzels, and chocolate, but if that's not your dad(s), feel free to pull recipes from other chapters. We know that no matter what, your dad(s) will appreciate anything homemade. After all, the secret ingredient when you are baking for family, or chosen family, really is love. For a small family dinner, we suggest picking just two or three recipes to focus on. Maybe Soft Pretzels (page 129) with a selection of mustards, followed by Cheesy Shepherd's Pie (page 133) and a green salad, topped off with decadent PB Chocolate Cream Pie (page 123) for dessert. Finish off your gathering with a round of games or a movie marathon with a Bacon Butter Tart (page 119) late-night snack. For a large Father's Day party, bake the whole spread and serve it buffet style. Cut the Salted Caramel Pretzel Bars (page 121) and Banana Chocolate Chip Slab Cake (page 127) into bite-size pieces, make mini muffin cup versions of the Bacon Butter Tarts (page 119) and half-size pretzels, and allow people to help themselves to servings of Cheesy Shepherd's Pie (page 133) and PB Chocolate Cream Pie (page 123). Balance out all that butter with a green salad or veggie platter and an alternative main for any dietary restrictions. Set up a few card game stations or outdoor games so that folks can mingle and play between nibbles.

Father's Day

Bacon Butter Tarts 119

Salted Caramel Pretzel Bars 121

PB Chocolate Cream Pie 123

**Banana Chocolate Chip
Slab Cake 127**

Ⓥ Soft Pretzels 129

Cheesy Shepherd's Pie 133

Bacon Butter Tarts

Butter Pastry

1½ batches Butter Pastry (page 296)

Filling

1 cup packed dark brown sugar

2 teaspoons cornstarch

¼ cup unsalted butter, melted
    and room temperature

3 large eggs, room temperature

½ cup pure maple syrup

½ cup golden corn syrup

1 teaspoon pure vanilla extract

1 teaspoon salt

1 cup cooked 1-inch pieces bacon
    (14 ounces/400 g uncooked)

These smoky, salty, and sweet tarts will please any meat lover. If possible, purchase unsliced bacon so that you can cut it into ½-inch cubes. If unsliced bacon is not available, seek out extra-thick-cut bacon to create those chunky bits. These tarts are hearty treats, so if you are serving them in a buffet or as appetizers, try making them in a mini muffin pan instead. For minis, cut your pastry rounds out with a 2½- to 3-inch round cookie cutter and use just two pieces of bacon per tart. Fill the tarts, leaving ¼-inch headspace, and bake for 20 to 25 minutes.

1. Preheat the oven to 400°F (200°C). Generously grease a 12-cup muffin pan with canola oil cooking spray.

2. Prepare the tart shells: Roll out the butter pastry dough to about ⅛-inch thickness. Cut out twelve 5-inch circles of dough. Gently press the dough circles into the muffin cups, making sure not to stretch the dough and forming walls that extend about ½ inch above the rims of the muffin cups. Place the muffin pan in the refrigerator for 15 to 20 minutes while you make the filling to allow the pastry to relax and firm up a bit.

3. Make the filling: In a medium bowl, whisk together the brown sugar and cornstarch. Whisk in the melted butter. Add the eggs and continue whisking until the mixture is smooth and no oily film remains around the edges.

4. Whisk in the maple syrup, corn syrup, vanilla, and salt until fully incorporated.

5. Fill and bake the tarts: Remove the muffin pan from the refrigerator and add ½ tablespoon of bacon pieces to each tart shell. Pour the filling over the bacon, filling each tart shell level with the pan, leaving about ½-inch headspace of pastry for the filling to bubble up as it cooks. Bake for 35 to 40 minutes, or until the filling has puffed up above the tart and the pastry is deep golden brown. The filling will settle as it cools. Using a small offset palette knife, remove the tarts from the pan immediately so that they do not stick to the pan as they cool.

DO AHEAD

The butter pastry can be made ahead, wrapped tightly in plastic wrap, and stored in the refrigerator for up to 1 week or in the freezer for up to 6 months. If frozen, thaw in the refrigerator overnight before using.

The pastry circles can be rolled, cut, and stored in the refrigerator, covered with beeswax or plastic wrap, for up to 2 days. The filling can be made ahead and stored in an airtight container in the refrigerator for up to 1 week. Serve

the tarts warm, reheated in the oven at 350°F (180°C) for 5 to 10 minutes. Store, covered, at room temperature for 1 day or in the refrigerator for up to 6 days.

FATHER'S DAY

MAKES one 8-inch square pan, nine 2½-inch square bars • **PREP:** 25 minutes, plus cooling and chilling time • **COOK:** 45 minutes

Salted Caramel Pretzel Bars

Brownie
½ cup all-purpose flour
½ cup cocoa powder
½ teaspoon salt
¾ cup granulated sugar
2 large eggs
7 ounces (200 g/1 cup) milk
  chocolate callets or good-quality
  chopped chocolate
½ cup unsalted butter
½ cup buttermilk
1 tablespoon pure vanilla extract
¼ cup Caramel (page 317)

Ganache
7 ounces (200 g/1 cup) milk
  chocolate callets or good-quality
  chopped milk chocolate
½ cup whipping (35%) cream

To finish
¼ cup Caramel (page 317)
1 cup hard pretzel pieces
¼ to 1 teaspoon flaky sea salt
  (we use Maldon)

When developing this recipe, Josie asked each of her family members to describe their perfect caramel pretzel brownie. She baked eight versions and we had a tasting party. This extra ooey-gooey, lick-your-fingers, soft milk chocolate, sweet and salty version won out. But a close second was her son Finn's version. He loves this recipe but replaces the caramel with the same amount of smooth, sweetened peanut butter. So, if you don't have a caramel fan on your hands, try Finn's version! We love it extra salty but feel free to amp up or decrease the salt to your liking. If you are worried about sticky fingers at your gathering, you might want to serve these in muffin cups to keep the caramel contained or skip the caramel on top. To keep the pretzels extra crunchy for your guests, hold back the pretzels and stick a whole pretzel into the top of each brownie after slicing and right before serving.

1. Preheat the oven to 350°F (180°C). Grease an 8-inch square cake pan with canola oil cooking spray and line it with parchment paper.

2. Make the brownie: Sift the flour, cocoa, and salt into a small bowl and stir together. Set aside.

3. In the bowl of a stand mixer fitted with the whisk attachment, add the sugar and eggs and whisk on high speed until the mixture is thick, light, and airy, about 10 minutes.

4. Meanwhile, in a medium heat-resistant bowl, melt the milk chocolate and butter in the microwave in 30-second intervals, stirring vigorously after each interval, until melted and smooth.

5. Reduce the mixer speed to low and, with the mixer running, slowly add the chocolate butter mixture, then increase the speed to medium-high and whisk until a pudding consistency is achieved, 2 to 3 minutes. Scrape down the sides and bottom of the bowl.

6. Add the buttermilk, vanilla, and dry ingredients and whisk on medium speed just until combined, about 1 minute. Scrape down the sides and bottom of the bowl. Mix again on medium-high speed for 30 seconds.   (CONTINUES)

DO AHEAD

These brownies can be baked and stored un-iced, covered, in the refrigerator for up to 3 days. The caramel can be made ahead and stored in an airtight container at room temperature for up to 1 month. Finished brownies with pretzels can be stored in an airtight container at room temperature for up to 1 day. Finished brownies without pretzels can be stored in an airtight container in the refrigerator for up to 3 days.

7. Scoop two-thirds of the brownie batter into the prepared pan and spread it out in an even layer. Drizzle the ¼ cup caramel evenly over the surface of the batter. Do not try to spread out the caramel. Top with the remaining brownie batter and, using a small offset palette knife, smooth the batter flat. Bake for 35 to 45 minutes, or until the brownie jiggles just slightly when the pan is shaken and the top is puffed up. Allow the brownies to cool completely in the pan for 1 to 2 hours before icing them.

8. Ice the brownies: In a medium heat-resistant bowl, heat the milk chocolate and cream in the microwave in 30-second intervals, stirring vigorously after each interval, until smooth and the chocolate is melted, 1 to 1½ minutes total. Stir the ganache until silky smooth, then pour it over the cooled brownie, evenly spreading it out with an offset palette knife.

9. Finish the brownies: Drizzle the caramel over the ganache, allowing it to sink into the ganache. Sprinkle the pretzels over the ganache while it is still wet. Sprinkle the flaky salt, to taste, on top. Allow to set, uncovered, in the refrigerator for 1 hour.

10. Cut the brownies using a warm chef's knife by dipping it into hot water and drying it on a clean kitchen towel. Wipe the knife between each cut to get nice clean cuts.

PB Chocolate Cream Pie

Chocolate Graham Crumb Crust
1 batch Chocolate Graham Crumb
   Crust (page 299)

Peanut Butter Crumble
1½ cups icing sugar
¾ cup smooth peanut butter
   (sweetened, not natural)

Chocolate Filling
1 cup whipping (35%) cream
½ cup whole milk
10 ounces (285 g/1½ cups)
   semi-sweet chocolate callets or
   good-quality chopped chocolate
2 large eggs, room temperature
2 tablespoons granulated sugar
¼ teaspoon salt

Peanut Butter Whipped Cream
2 cups whipping (35%) cream, cold
¼ cup icing sugar
3 tablespoons smooth peanut butter
   (sweetened, not natural)

To finish
½ batch Dark Chocolate Ganache
   (page 307)
1 tablespoon dark chocolate crisp
   pearls

If your dad(s) like Reese's Peanut Butter Cups, they will love this pie. It's the more sophisticated version of your favourite corner store treat, and we love sprinkling a few Reese's mini peanut butter cups on top of this pie to drive home that familiarity. Just lightly chop the mini peanut butter cups and sprinkle them over the whipped cream in lieu of the crisp pearls and ganache drizzle. The chocolate graham crumb crust is a touch salty by design, but you will find that it really balances out the dark chocolate, and salt is a natural partner for peanut butter. Serve this pie at room temperature to keep the chocolate pudding silky smooth and to get the full flavour profile.

1. Preheat the oven to 375°F (190°C).

2. Prepare the chocolate graham crumb crust: Firmly and evenly press the graham crust mixture into the bottom and all the way up the sides of a 9-inch pie plate to form a pie crust. Bake for 10 minutes, or until the crust has puffed up slightly and appears dry. Allow the crust to cool completely before adding the fillings.

3. Make the peanut butter crumble: In a medium bowl, mix together the icing sugar and peanut butter until it forms a crumble. Reserve ½ cup of the crumble to finish the pie in step 8. Sprinkle the remaining crumble over the baked pie crust and gently pat it down to form an even layer on top of the graham crust.

4. Make the chocolate filling: In a medium saucepan over medium heat, bring the cream and milk to a simmer, stirring frequently. When you see steam dancing across the top of the mixture, remove the pot from the heat and stir in the chocolate until melted.

5. Whisk in the eggs, sugar, and salt until the mixture is smooth. Return the saucepan to the stovetop over low heat and cook, stirring constantly, for 7 to 8 minutes, or until the filling has thickened slightly to a thin pudding texture. Do not let it come to a boil. (CONTINUES)

DO AHEAD

The graham crust and ganache can be made ahead. Let the crust cool completely in the pie plate, then wrap the pie plate in beeswax or plastic wrap and store at room temperature for up to 1 week. The ganache can be stored in an airtight container in the refrigerator for up to 2 weeks. This pie is best enjoyed on the day it is assembled and served at room temperature. Store, covered, at room temperature for 1 day or in the refrigerator for up to 3 days. If refrigerated, allow the pie to come to room temperature, uncovered, for 1 to 2 hours before serving.

6. Fill the pie crust and chill: Pour the filling over the peanut butter crumble in the pie crust. Place in the refrigerator for 2 to 3 hours until completely cool. Any filling that doesn't fit in your pie plate makes a delicious pudding.

7. Make the peanut butter whipped cream: In the bowl of a stand mixer fitted with the whisk attachment, combine the cream, icing sugar, and peanut butter and whip on medium speed until the mixture starts to get frothy and begins to thicken, 2 to 3 minutes. Increase the speed to high and whip for another 30 to 60 seconds, or until the cream looks fluffy and the whisk leaves deep markings in the whipped cream.

8. Finish the pie: Spoon the peanut butter whipped cream over the top of the pie for a rustic finish or fill a 16-inch piping bag fitted with a No. 825 star tip and finish the pie by piping lines of star drops across the pie to cover the whole surface (see Buttercream and Whipped Cream Piping Styles, page 286, C). Drizzle the dark chocolate ganache over the whipped cream. Sprinkle with the reserved peanut butter crumble and crisp pearls.

Banana Chocolate Chip Slab Cake

Banana Chocolate Chip Cake

2 cups all-purpose flour

1½ teaspoons baking powder

1 teaspoon baking soda

½ teaspoon salt

2 ripe bananas

½ cup full-fat sour cream

1 teaspoon pure vanilla extract

½ cup unsalted butter,
    room temperature

1 cup sugar

2 large eggs, room temperature

7 ounces (200 g/1 cup) semi-sweet
    chocolate callets or good-quality
    chopped chocolate

Dreamy Cream Cheese Icing

1 batch Dreamy Cream Cheese Icing
    (page 295)

For assembly

¼ batch Caramel (page 317)

1 to 1½ cups dried banana chips

You can guarantee that a pan of fresh-baked cake will be ready to greet you when visiting Nickey's mother's home. Banana cake is frequently on rotation, and our version pays deep respect to her traditional take with a few additions. In our version we add sour cream for extra moisture and flavour and chocolate chips because, why not? And we add our dreamy cream cheese icing and finish it with a caramel drizzle. Dried banana chips are a great decorative touch and take this cake from kitchen staple to dinner party ready.

1. Preheat the oven to 350°F (180°C). Grease a 9- × 13-inch pan with canola oil cooking spray. Line the pan with parchment paper, allowing excess paper to hang over each side for easy removal.

2. Make the cake: Sift the flour, baking powder, baking soda, and salt into a small bowl and stir together.

3. In a medium bowl, using a fork, mash the bananas completely. Stir in the sour cream and vanilla.

4. In the bowl of a stand mixer fitted with the paddle attachment, cream the butter and sugar on medium-high speed until pale and fluffy, about 4 to 5 minutes. Scrape down the sides and bottom of the bowl.

5. Add the eggs, one at a time, and beat well on medium-high speed. Scrape down the sides and bottom of the bowl after each addition. Add the mashed banana mixture and beat on medium speed for 1 to 2 minutes until combined. Scrape down the sides and bottom of the bowl.

6. Add the flour mixture and chocolate and mix on low speed until just combined.

7. Scoop the batter into the prepared pan. Level the top of the batter with a small offset palette knife or spoon. Bake for 35 to 45 minutes, or until a toothpick inserted into the centre of the cake comes out clean. Remove from the oven and let sit for at least 30 minutes before removing the cake from the pan. Allow the cake to cool to room temperature for 1 to 2 hours. (CONTINUES)

DO AHEAD

This cake can be baked and stored un-iced, wrapped in beeswax or plastic wrap, at room temperature for up to 3 days. You can make the cream cheese icing and caramel ahead. Store the cream cheese icing in an airtight container in the refrigerator and the caramel in an airtight container at room temperature for up to 1 month. The iced cake is best enjoyed at room temperature on the day of baking. Store (without the banana chips), covered, in the refrigerator for up to 5 days and add the banana chips just before serving to keep them crisp.

8. Ice and finish cake: In the bowl of a stand mixer fitted with the paddle attachment, beat the dreamy cream cheese icing on medium-high speed for 3 to 4 minutes. Spread the icing over the top of the cake with an offset palette knife, leaving it rustic looking with swirls and lines.

9. In a small heat-resistant bowl, heat the caramel in the microwave for 10 seconds to achieve a drizzling consistency. Use a spoon to drizzle the caramel over the top of the cake. Slice the cake and finish each piece with a sprinkle of banana chips.

Soft Pretzels Ⓥ

Pretzel Dough

4¾ cups all-purpose flour
2 tablespoons packed dark
    brown sugar
1 tablespoon instant dry yeast
1½ teaspoons salt
1½ cups warm water
6 tablespoons canola oil,
    more for greasing the bowl

Water Bath

7½ cups water
3 tablespoons baking soda

To finish

2 tablespoons flaky sea salt or
    pretzel salt (we use Maldon)

This is one vegan crowd-pleaser everyone loves. Eat these warm from the oven and they are pillowy soft and airy; as they cool (if you can wait!), they get that classic pretzel chew. We know dads love knowing how stuff works, so impress your dad(s) with this tidbit: whenever you are enjoying a food that browns and changes flavour while cooking, from a perfectly grilled steak to a chocolate chip cookie, you are enjoying a Maillard reaction. The beautiful deep golden brown of this pretzel is a result of this chemical reaction, in which amino acids and sugars break down and rearrange themselves to create a variety of aromas and flavours. It occurs at 310°F (154°C) and works best in alkaline conditions; that's why we bake these pretzels in a hot oven, and a quick boil in the baking soda bath is essential. If you make a couple of ⅛-inch-deep cuts in the pretzels between their bath and the oven, right before you sprinkle the salt on, you will see the Maillard reaction clearly, the dough's surface will bake up deep brown and shiny, and the cuts will open up to reveal a creamy white interior. These are big-as-your-face snacking pretzels, but you can make half-size ones—just bake them for 10 to 14 minutes.

1. Make the pretzel dough: In the bowl of a stand mixer fitted with the dough hook attachment, add the flour, brown sugar, instant yeast, and salt and stir on low speed for 1 minute to evenly distribute the yeast.

2. Add the warm water and canola oil and mix on medium speed until no wet flour remains and you are left with a sticky dough that sticks to the bottom of the bowl, about 2 minutes. If there is still dry flour in the bowl, scrape down the sides and bottom of the bowl. With the mixer running on medium speed, add more water, 1 tablespoon at a time, up to ¼ cup total depending on the humidity in your kitchen. Mix just until the water is incorporated and you have a sticky dough.

3. Reduce the speed to low and allow the mixer to knead the dough until it comes away from the sides of the bowl and is soft and pillowy, 10 to 15 minutes.

4. Remove the dough from the mixer bowl and form it into a ball. Grease the bowl with canola oil and place the dough ball seam side down in the bowl. Allow the dough to rise in a warm area, covered with beeswax or plastic wrap, until it has doubled in size, about 1 hour. (CONTINUES)

DO AHEAD —————

These pretzels are best enjoyed warm or within 4 hours of baking, but they can be stored in an airtight container for up to 2 days, then warmed in a 325°F (160°C) oven for 5 minutes.

5. Shape the pretzels: Divide the dough into 8 equal pieces. Shape the pieces of dough into short logs, about 10 to 12 inches long. Once you have rolled out all 8 pieces, return to the first log you rolled and continue to roll it out into a longer rope shape, about 30 inches long.

6. Place the rope on the work surface in front of you, parallel to your body. With both hands, lift the rope from either end so that the middle of the rope is still touching the work surface and both ends are about 12 inches in the air. Twist the two ends together twice to make a double twist about 2 inches below the ends of the rope. Drape the ends back down onto the work surface toward you through the centre of the U-shape to form a circle, then gently press the ends of the rope onto the dough, leaving as much overhang as you like in your pretzels. Push firmly to seal and form a pretzel shape. Transfer the pretzel to a baking sheet greased with canola oil. Repeat to shape the remaining pieces of dough.

7. Preheat the oven to 400°F (200°C) and line 2 baking sheets with parchment paper or silicone baking mats.

8. Prepare the water bath for the pretzels, then bake them: Fill a large shallow pot with the water and bring to a boil over high heat. Once the water is boiling, reduce the heat to low and stir in the baking soda. You want to maintain a very gentle boil, so adjust the heat as needed from low to medium. Using your hands, carefully lower the pretzels into the water and baking soda solution, 2 or 3 at a time. Simmer the pretzels until they puff up, 90 seconds per side.

9. Remove the pretzels from the liquid with a slotted spatula, drain well, and transfer to the prepared baking sheets, evenly spaced. Sprinkle with flaky sea salt. Bake until golden brown and cooked through, about 15 to 18 minutes.

Cheesy Shepherd's Pie

Meat Filling

1 tablespoon olive oil
1 pound (450 g) lean ground pork
1 pound (450 g) lean ground beef
1 cup diced peeled carrot
1 cup diced celery
1 cup diced white onions
2 cloves garlic, finely chopped
1 can (5.5 ounces/156 mL)
   tomato paste
⅓ cup Worcestershire sauce
½ cup dark ale
1 tablespoon Sriracha sauce
⅔ cup fresh or frozen corn kernels
Salt and freshly ground black pepper

Mashed Potato Topping

1 batch Mashed Potato Topping
   (page 300)

For assembly

3 cups grated old cheddar cheese,
   divided

Cheesy and meaty, with a touch of ale and spice from the Sriracha sauce, this is our spin on a classic invented by Stephanie, a former cook at the bakery. She was an amazing co-worker, always full of enthusiasm as a superfan turned employee, and a great chef. We recommend baking this casserole on a baking sheet lined with parchment paper because it may bubble up over the sides and burn as the liquid hits the pan. Like all Shepherd's pies, this dish tastes even better the next day, so don't be afraid to make it in advance and add the cheddar on top when you reheat it for serving.

1. Make the meat filling: In a large skillet, heat the olive oil over medium-high heat. Add the ground pork and beef and brown the meat, stirring occasionally, about 5 to 7 minutes. Strain any excess fat from the meat using a fine metal mesh sieve. Return the meat to the pan. Reduce the heat to medium and add the carrots, celery, onions, and garlic. Cook, uncovered, stirring occasionally, until the onions are soft and transparent, about 10 minutes.

2. Add the tomato paste, Worcestershire sauce, dark ale, and Sriracha and continue cooking, stirring occasionally, until the liquid has mostly evaporated, 5 to 7 minutes.

3. Add the corn and season to taste with salt and pepper. Remove from the heat and set aside at room temperature while you prepare the mashed potato topping.

4. Preheat the oven to 400°F (200°C).

5. Assemble and bake the pie: Scoop the meat filling into the base of an 11- × 7-inch (2 L) casserole dish. Sprinkle 2 cups of the grated cheese evenly over the filling. Spoon the mashed potatoes over the top of the pie for a rustic finish, or fill a 16-inch piping bag fitted with a No. 825 star tip and finish the pie by piping lines of star swirl border across the pie to cover the whole surface (see Buttercream and Whipped Cream Piping Styles, page 286, C).

6. Place the casserole dish on a baking sheet and bake until the potatoes have golden brown edges, 35 to 45 minutes. Remove the pie from the oven and sprinkle the remaining 1 cup grated cheese over top. Return the pie to the oven and bake until the cheese is bubbly, about 10 minutes. Serve hot.

DO AHEAD

This dish can be made ahead through step 5 and stored, covered, in the refrigerator for up to 3 days or in the freezer for up to 2 months. Allow the pie to defrost in the refrigerator overnight before reheating at 325°F (160°C) for 1 hour. Remove the pie from the oven and sprinkle the remaining 1 cup cheese over top. Return the pie to the oven and bake until the cheese is bubbly, about 15 minutes. The meat filling can be made ahead and stored in an airtight container in the refrigerator for up to 3 days. Store leftovers, covered, in the refrigerator for up to 6 days.

FATHER'S DAY

Backyard barbecue, picnic in the park, or poolside bash, summertime calls for gatherings, and we embrace any excuse to make Chocolate Mint Ice Cream Sandwich Bars (page 139). Any one of these recipes would be a welcome addition to a potluck celebration, which is our favourite low-effort approach to summer gatherings. Call up your friends and assign them a course to bring. For your foodie friends, challenge them to make something fun by sending them recipe suggestions from our cookbook or letting their imaginations soar. S'mores Bars (page 137), Peach Custard Pie (page 145), and Summer Berry Trifle (page 147) are all travel friendly and will be welcome at any gathering. Mile-High Pulled Pork Mac and Cheese Pie (page 149) makes an impressive centrepiece for a formal sit-down dinner or as a buffet feature. The Cheddar Onion Beer Buns (page 153) are delicious as a snack on their own, but they really shine when paired with a juicy hamburger or veggie burger. Celebrate summer's natural bounty by making the Fresh Fruit Passion Puffs (page 141) with a variety of fresh fruit fillings. Those who don't cook can always bring chips and dips, fresh fruits and veggies, or even crackers and cheese. As host, provide all the serving and eating essentials like cutlery, plates, and napkins. Set up defined food areas so that guests can just drop their dishes and party or provide clear kitchen space for those who need to finish dishes. Make sure you have enough ice water and cups but request BYOB (Bring Your Own Beverage) so that guests can indulge in whatever meets their needs.

Summer Eats

S'mores Bars

¾ cup unsalted butter, melted
  and warm
½ cup packed dark brown sugar
1½ teaspoons pure vanilla extract
½ teaspoon salt
1 cup graham cracker crumbs
1 cup all-purpose flour
1¼ cups Nutella, divided
8 ounces (225 g/2½ cups)
  Marshmallows (page 314),
  cut into ½-inch pieces

When a campfire isn't readily available, these bars will fulfill that summer craving for s'mores and then some. A layer of buttery graham base topped with milk chocolate hazelnut spread and homemade marshmallow make for the perfect s'mores experience. The crowning layer of creamy Nutella drizzle on top of these bars completes the experience, complementing the dense, fudge-like, baked Nutella inside the bar. These are most scrumptious when slightly warm and you can still get that pull-apart marshmallow gooeyness, but they will firm up nicely for bite-size party treats when refrigerated.

1. Preheat the oven to 350°F (180°C). Grease an 8-inch square pan with canola oil cooking spray and line with parchment paper.

2. In a medium bowl, whisk together the melted butter, brown sugar, vanilla, and salt until smooth and the sugar has dissolved.

3. Add the graham crumbs and flour and stir until well combined and no dry flour remains.

4. Press the graham mixture evenly into the bottom of the prepared pan. Using an offset palette knife, spread 1 cup of the Nutella evenly over the base.

5. Evenly distribute the marshmallow pieces over the Nutella layer. Bake for 35 to 40 minutes, or until the top of the marshmallow is a deep toasty brown and the Nutella has bubbled up a little around the edges. Allow to cool at room temperature for at least 30 minutes.

6. In a small heat-resistant bowl, heat the remaining ¼ cup Nutella in the microwave for 30 to 45 seconds to make it easier to drizzle. Using a spoon, generously drizzle the Nutella over the bars in diagonal lines across the top.

7. Cut the bars using a warm chef's knife by dipping it into hot water and drying it on a clean kitchen towel. Wipe the knife between each cut to get nice clean cuts.

DO AHEAD

These bars can be baked and stored, uncut, without the final Nutella drizzle, wrapped in beeswax or plastic wrap, at room temperature for up to 3 days. The marshmallows can be made ahead and stored in an airtight container at room temperature for up to 2 months. Store the finished bars in an airtight container at room temperature for up to 5 days.

Chocolate Mint Ice Cream Sandwich Bars

Chocolate Mint
No-Churn Ice Cream

1 can (15 ounces/350 mL)
  sweetened condensed milk
½ teaspoon pure vanilla extract
½ teaspoon vanilla bean paste
½ teaspoon mint extract
1 drop leaf green gel food coloring
2 cups whipping (35%) cream
¾ cup mini semi-sweet
  chocolate chips

Brownie Sandwich Cookies

1 cup all-purpose flour
¾ cup cocoa
¾ teaspoon baking powder
¾ teaspoon salt
1½ cups unsalted butter,
  room temperature
1 cup granulated sugar
2 eggs, room temperature
2 teaspoons pure vanilla extract

In the early years, we catered to every possible customer craving, and we even created ice cream for a short period. Our small, previously loved ice cream machine churned out some interesting varieties, but believe it or not we never consistently made ice cream sandwiches, even though we fantasized about them constantly. Nickey felt that this cookbook needed an ice cream sandwich to fill that void, and we hope this easy recipe entices you to create a number of your own signature no-churn ice cream flavours with our complementary soft and chewy brownie sandwich cookie as its base. You will need to plan ahead for this recipe; it's best to give yourself two days. The ice cream needs to be made one day in advance of assembling the bar, and the bar needs at least 2 hours or overnight to set up before you can cut and serve.

1. Make the chocolate mint no-churn ice cream: Line a 9- × 13-inch cake pan in plastic wrap, with enough overhang to cover the surface area of the ice cream once in the pan. Ensure that the stand mixer bowl and whisk attachment are clean and place them in the freezer until ready to use.

2. In a small bowl, whisk together the sweetened condensed milk, vanilla extract and bean paste, mint extract, and food colouring until well combined. Set aside.

3. In the chilled bowl of a stand mixer fitted with the chilled whisk attachment, add the cream and whip on high speed until stiff peaks form, 3 to 5 minutes.

4. Remove the bowl from the mixer and, using a silicone spatula, fold in the condensed milk mixture until just combined. Fold in the chocolate chips. Pour the ice cream into the prepared cake pan, spreading it out evenly using an offset palette knife.

5. Carefully cover the ice cream with the overhanging plastic wrap, using light pressure to adhere the wrap directly to the surface. Ensure that the entire surface is covered and sealed, then place the cake pan on a flat surface in the freezer overnight. (CONTINUES)

DO AHEAD

Wrap the bars individually in pieces of parchment paper and store in an airtight container in the freezer for up to 2 weeks. The ice cream can be made ahead, wrapped as instructed in the recipe, and frozen for up to 1 week. The brownie sandwich cookies can be baked, cut in half with parchment intact and stored in an airtight container in the freezer for up to 2 weeks.

6. Meanwhile, make the brownie sandwich cookies: Preheat the oven to 350°F (180°C). Grease a 13- × 18-inch baking sheet with canola oil cooking spray and line with parchment paper, allowing excess paper to hang over each side for easy removal. The cooking spray under the parchment helps to keep the sheet in place while spreading the thick batter.

7. Sift the flour, cocoa, baking powder, and salt into a medium bowl. Set aside.

8. In the bowl of a stand mixer fitted with the paddle attachment, beat the butter and sugar on medium-high speed until light and fluffy, about 3 to 5 minutes. Add the eggs, one at a time, scraping down the sides and bottom of the bowl after each addition. Add the vanilla and beat until smooth, 1 to 2 minutes.

9. Add the flour mixture and beat on medium speed until smooth. Using a silicone spatula, scoop the thick batter onto the prepared baking sheet.

10. Using an offset palette knife, spread the batter out evenly over the entire baking sheet, meeting all sides. Bake for 10 to 12 minutes until a toothpick inserted into the centre of the brownie comes out clean. Allow the brownie to cool to room temperature and then wrap the whole pan with beeswax or plastic wrap and store at room temperature for up to 2 days.

11. Assemble the ice cream bars: Unwrap the brownie and run a paring knife around the edges to loosen it from the pan without cutting the parchment paper. Lift the brownie from the baking sheet using the parchment paper handles and place it on a cutting board. With a chef's knife, cut the brownie sheet in half to create two 9- × 13-inch pieces. Peel the parchment paper from the brownies and set aside one brownie sheet.

12. Remove the ice cream pan from the freezer, discard the plastic wrap, and place the ice cream on the brownie sheet that is still on the cutting board. Place the other brownie sheet upside down on top of the ice cream to form a sandwich.

13. Wrap the top and sides of the assembled ice cream sandwich in plastic wrap and place it in the freezer for up to 2 hours before cutting.

14. Cut the bars using a warm chef's knife, wiping between each cut. Trim any overhanging ice cream to make a cleanly cut rectangle. Cut the ice cream bar into twelve 4¼ × 2¼-inch rectangles (4 × 3 grid).

Fresh Fruit Passion Puffs

Puff Pastry Dough
1 batch Blitz Puff Pastry (page 298)

Egg Wash
1 large egg
1 tablespoon water,
    room temperature
1 tablespoon granulated sugar

Pastry Cream
½ batch Pastry Cream (page 315)

Fresh Fruit
1¼ cups fresh berries

Whipped Cream
1 batch Whipped Cream (page 300)

This recipe entails some planning and prep, but then it comes together quickly and with very little skill required. It's a great dish to get a guest to finish during the party to help them feel involved or to give yourself an uplifting sense of accomplishment mid-party. We guarantee at least a few squeals over how adorable these little puffs are! They are a childhood favourite revisited for many but elevated with juicy fresh fruit, rich pastry cream, and fresh whipped cream. Upon first bite, you'll know you can never go back to those processed pockets. Don't let puff pastry scare you. This recipe has been engineered for its simplicity, and once you have mastered it, you'll find many reasons to make more puffs.

1. Preheat the oven to 400°F (200°C). Line a baking sheet with parchment paper or a silicone baking mat.

2. Roll out the puff pastry dough: On a lightly floured surface, roll out the puff pastry dough into a 9½-inch square, about ½ inch thick. Lift the dough to make sure it isn't sticking to the counter and let it rest for 5 minutes.

3. Cut and chill the puff pastry: Trim the edges of the pastry with a very sharp chef's knife to make a 9-inch square with 4 cleanly cut edges. Cut the square into nine 3-inch square pieces (3 × 3 grid). Place the pastry squares evenly on the prepared baking sheet. Cover the baking sheet lightly with plastic wrap or parchment paper and refrigerate for 20 minutes to allow the pastry to relax and firm up before baking.

4. Egg wash, sprinkle with sugar, and bake the puff pastry: In a small bowl, thoroughly whisk together the egg and water until combined. Remove the baking sheet from the refrigerator and discard the plastic wrap or parchment paper. Brush the tops of the pastry squares with egg wash and sprinkle with a thin layer of sugar. Bake for 20 to 25 minutes until the pastry has at least tripled in height and is a dark golden brown all over. Do not open the oven while baking. Steam is important to achieve the desired height. Allow the puff pastry to cool completely on the baking sheet before filling. (CONTINUES)

DO AHEAD

These puffs are best enjoyed within 4 hours of being assembled, as they do get soggy. The puff pastry can be made ahead, wrapped tightly in plastic wrap, and stored in the refrigerator for up to 3 days or in the freezer for up to 6 months. If frozen, thaw in the refrigerator overnight before using. Unfilled, baked puffs can be stored at room temperature in an airtight container for up to 24 hours. The pastry cream can be made ahead and stored in an airtight container in the refrigerator for up to 2 weeks.

thin layer
of baked
on sugar

piped
whipped
cream

pastry
cream

fresh fruit

puff pastry

5. Fill the puffs and top with berries: When you are ready to serve, split each puff pastry in half horizontally using your hands or a serrated knife. In the bowl of a stand mixer fitted with the paddle attachment, beat the pastry cream on medium speed to return it to a smooth consistency, about 2 minutes (or whisk it thoroughly by hand in a medium bowl for about 3 minutes). Fill each bottom half of the pastry with 2 tablespoons of pastry cream, spreading it to just meet the edges of the puff pastry using the back of a spoon or small palette knife. Top the pastry cream with 2 tablespoons of berries, evenly arranged in a single layer.

6. Pipe the whipped cream and finish: Using a piping bag fitted with a No. 824 star tip, pipe 2 rows of star swirl border whipped cream (see Buttercream and Whipped Cream Piping Styles, page 286, C) to cover the berries. Place the top halves of the pastry puff on top of the whipped cream and press down gently to attach it to the cream layer. Serve immediately.

Peach Custard Pie

DO AHEAD: You can blind-bake the crust ahead and store it, tightly wrapped in beeswax or plastic wrap, at room temperature for up to 3 days. Serve the pie warm to highlight the smooth custard and juicy fruit or refrigerate for at least 2 hours and serve chilled to cut beautiful clean slices perfect for plating. Store the finished pie, covered, at room temperature for 1 day or in the refrigerator for up to 3 days.

Sugar Cookie Dough
½ batch Sugar Cookie Dough (page 301)

Custard Filling
1¼ cups granulated sugar
6 tablespoons all-purpose flour
1 teaspoon cinnamon
½ teaspoon salt
1 cup whipping (35%) cream
3 large eggs
2 teaspoons pure vanilla extract

Fruit Filling
1⅓ pounds (600 g) peaches, peeled, pitted, and cut into ¼- to ½-inch slices (5 large peaches)

Nothing can compare to freshly picked ripe peaches, and our city has a whole festival just to celebrate this sunset-coloured fruit. We hope you can take advantage of local markets and farms in your community to get your hands on baskets of these sunny globes when they're in season. This pie originated as a pear pie recipe from Nickey's sister-in-law, Barb. At first, we made a pear custard bar that we sold in the shop, and then it evolved into this peach custard pie we're sharing with you. Fresh peaches hovering in a not-too-sweet, lightly spiced cinnamon custard filling atop a sweet cookie pie shell perfectly balances this peachy pastry.

1. Preheat the oven to 350°F (180°C).

2. Roll out the sugar cookie dough: On a lightly floured work surface, roll out the sugar cookie dough into an 11- to 12-inch circle, about ¼ inch thick. Fold the dough in half to lift it without stretching and gently unfold it into a 9-inch pie plate. Gently press the dough into the sides and bottom of the plate, pushing any cracks back together to seal the dough. Trim the dough as needed and crimp the edges of the pastry or use the tines of a fork to press ridges along the edges. Place the pie plate in the refrigerator to allow the dough to relax and firm up a bit, at least 15 minutes.

3. Blind-bake the crust: Using the tines of a fork, poke holes in the bottom and sides of the pastry shell. Line the shell with a piece of foil large enough to tuck around the edges of the pastry and fill it with about 2 cups of dried beans or pie weights. Wrap the foil around the edges of the pan lightly. Do not press into the dough. Bake for 25 to 35 minutes, or until the crust appears dry and is a very light brown. Remove the beans and foil. Allow the pie shell to cool completely on a wire rack.

4. Make the custard filling: In a medium bowl, whisk together the sugar, flour, cinnamon, and salt until combined. Whisk in the cream until smooth. Whisk in the eggs and vanilla and mix until smooth.

5. Assemble and bake the pie: Arrange the peach slices in the baked pie crust in concentric circles starting from the outside to the centre, piling the peaches to meet the top of the pie crust.

6. Place the pie on a baking sheet and pour the custard filling over the peaches, leaving about ¼-inch headspace of crust so that the filling can bubble up as it cooks. It's okay if the peaches are floating. Bake for 50 to 60 minutes until the custard is firm and lightly browned.

7. Serve the pie hot or allow it to cool completely for beautiful slices.

Summer Berry Trifle

Vanilla Cake
1 batch Vanilla Cake Batter (page 282) or 12 cups packed vanilla cake trimmings

Pastry Cream
2 batches Pastry Cream (page 315)

Strawberry Compote
½ batch Strawberry Compote (page 309; reserve ¼ cup for the Strawberry Simple Syrup, recipe below)

Strawberry Simple Syrup
1 batch Simple Syrup (page 316)
¼ cup Strawberry Compote (reserved; recipe above)

Mixed Berry Compote
½ batch Mixed Berry Compote (page 309)

Whipped Cream
1 batch Whipped Cream (page 300)

For assembly
1 cup fresh raspberries
1 cup fresh blueberries
1 cup fresh blackberries

One of our best-selling summer products are our trifle cups—fresh cake trimmings layered with seasonal compotes or chocolate ganache, vanilla pastry cream, or fruit curds, and a whipped cream crown with various toppings. For some, trifle will always bring them back to their family's dinner table; for others, it will be the first time they are enjoying the combination of different textures and flavours that make trifle a classic. Summer is bursting with seasonal goodness, and this trifle is not shy in taking advantage of all the bright, sweet and sour, flavourful, juicy summer fruits. Feel free to use any variety of our compotes (pages 309 to 310), to swap Lemon Curd (page 316) for pastry cream, or to top this with toasted Meringue (page 301) instead of whipped cream.

1. Preheat the oven to 350°F (180°C). Grease a 9- × 13-inch cake pan with canola oil cooking spray. Line the bottom with a parchment paper rectangle. If using cake trimmings (instead of vanilla cake batter), skip step 3.

2. Bake the cake: Pour the vanilla cake batter into the prepared pan and, using a small offset palette knife, smooth out the top. Bake for 30 to 45 minutes, or until a toothpick inserted into the centre of the cake comes out clean. Allow the cake to cool in the pan on a wire rack for 20 minutes. Remove the cake from the pan, leaving the parchment paper on the bottom, and cool completely on the wire rack.

3. Tear the cooled vanilla cake with your hands or, using a serrated knife, cut the cake into 1-inch square pieces. Transfer to a medium bowl and set aside.

4. Refresh the pastry cream: In the bowl of a stand mixer fitted with the paddle attachment, beat the pastry cream on medium speed to return it to a smooth consistency, about 2 minutes. Set aside.

5. Make the strawberry simple syrup: In a small bowl, mix the reserved ¼ cup strawberry compote into the simple syrup. Set aside

6. Assemble the trifle: Layer half of the cake pieces in the bottom of a large glass bowl or trifle dish and build them about halfway up the bowl. You want to cover the bottom completely. Using your hands, lightly push down on the cake to create a packed layer, limiting any air pockets or empty spaces. Using a spoon or pastry brush, cover the entire surface of the cake pieces with ½ cup of the strawberry simple syrup, making sure they are well moistened. (CONTINUES)

DO AHEAD

The cake can be baked and stored, wrapped in beeswax or plastic wrap, at room temperature for up to 3 days. You can make the pastry cream, compotes, and simple syrup ahead. The pastry cream can be stored in an airtight container in the refrigerator for up to 2 weeks. Store the compotes in separate airtight containers in the refrigerator for up to 1 month or in the freezer for up to 6 months. If frozen, thaw in the refrigerator overnight before using. The simple syrup can be stored in an airtight container in the refrigerator for up to 3 weeks. The trifle can be made up to step 8 and stored, covered, in the refrigerator for up to 3 days. Add the whipped cream and fresh berries right before serving. Leftovers can be stored, covered, in the refrigerator for up to 3 days.

whipped cream

fresh berries

pastry cream

mixed berry
compote

strawberry
compote

all cake moistened
with strawberry
simple syrup

vanilla cake

trifle bowl

7. Spoon half of the pastry cream over the moistened cake pieces, creating an even layer, then spoon heaping tablespoons of strawberry compote and mixed berry compote over the pastry cream, creating pockets of each colour. Check to see how the colours look through the sides of the bowl while assembling to ensure that you're happy with the look.

8. Place the remaining cake pieces on top of the compotes. Using your hands, gently pack the cake down slightly. Drizzle or brush the cake with the remaining strawberry simple syrup, followed by the remaining pastry cream.

9. To finish, spoon enough freshly whipped cream to cover the trifle completely. Using an offset palette knife and with even pressure, gently press down and smooth the whipped cream flat and even with the rim around the dish. This seals the trifle and allows all the flavours to mingle undisturbed. Clean the outside of the rim and bowl with a clean kitchen towel. Dollop the remaining whipped cream on top or pipe decorative rosettes as a border around the outside edge of the trifle, using a 12-inch piping bag fitted with a No. 824 star tip (see Buttercream and Whipped Cream Piping Styles, page 286, C). Arrange the raspberries, blueberries, and blackberries on top of the whipped cream.

Mile-High Pulled Pork Mac and Cheese Pie

Pulled Pork

3 pounds (1.35 kg) boneless, skinless pork shoulder

¼ cup Barbecue Spice Mix (page 313)

1 tablespoon salt

2 large onions, trimmed and peeled (keep whole)

2 cans (12 ounces/355 mL each) root beer

1 cup water, if needed

Apple Cider Honey Barbecue Sauce

1½ cups ketchup

1 cup apple cider vinegar

½ cup packed brown sugar

½ cup honey

⅓ cup Worcestershire sauce

3 tablespoons Dijon mustard

2 tablespoons canola oil

4 cloves garlic, crushed

4 teaspoons soy sauce

1 tablespoon Barbecue Spice Mix (page 313)

Butter Pastry

1½ batches Butter Pastry (page 296)

(INGREDIENTS CONTINUE)

This towering beauty will have everyone licking their lips. It retains heat well, so it makes for a stunning centrepiece on the table while guests mingle. Mac and cheese and barbecued pulled pork go hand in hand, and it felt only natural to make it into a pie, topped with caramelized onions, crispy bread crumbs, and from-scratch barbecue sauce. The results are a mind-blowing savoury summer pie. Big flavour, big texture, and big presence. If you're wondering how to tell if the interior is perfectly heated due to the immense height of this pie, poke a sharp knife halfway into the centre of the pie, remove the knife, and feel the blade for heat. If it is still room temperature to the touch, place the pie in the oven for another 15 to 20 minutes.

1. Make the pulled pork: Rub the pork shoulder with ¼ cup of the barbecue spice mix and the salt until the pork is entirely encrusted in the spices and salt. Place the pork and whole onions in a slow cooker. Add the root beer, then up to 1 cup of water so that the liquid covers at least half the pork. Cover and cook over high heat until the meat is tender and shreds easily with a fork, about 6 hours. Remove the pork and onions from the liquid and allow them to cool to room temperature in a large bowl or 9- × 13-inch baking pan. Discard the cooking liquid.

2. Meanwhile, make the apple cider honey barbecue sauce: Combine the ingredients in a medium saucepan and bring to a boil over high heat, stirring frequently with a silicone spatula. Reduce to a low boil over low to medium-low heat and cook, stirring occasionally, for 60 to 90 minutes until the sauce thickens and is the texture of ketchup. Allow the sauce to cool to room temperature before using.

3. Roll out the dough for the pie crust: Preheat the oven to 400°F (200°C). Generously grease an 8-inch springform pan with canola oil cooking spray. On a lightly floured work surface, roll out the butter pastry dough into a 14- to 15-inch circle, about ³⁄₁₆-inch thick. Fold the dough in half to lift it without stretching and gently unfold it into the pan. Gently press the dough into the sides and bottom of the pan, making sure not to stretch the dough. Tuck the edges up and over the top of the springform pan. Trim the dough as needed and crimp the edges of the pastry. Place the springform pan in the refrigerator to allow the dough to relax and firm up a bit, at least 15 minutes. (CONTINUES)

DO AHEAD

All the components of this pie can be made ahead to simplify the recipe. The butter pastry can be made ahead, wrapped tightly in plastic wrap, and stored in the refrigerator for up to 1 week or in the freezer for up to 6 months. If frozen, thaw in the refrigerator overnight before using. The pie shell can be blind-baked and stored, covered, at room temperature for up to 24 hours. The pulled pork can be stored, covered, in the refrigerator for up to 2 days. The barbecue sauce can be stored in an airtight container in the refrigerator for up to 3 months. The mac and cheese mixture can sit, covered, at room temperature for up to 1 hour before you assemble the pie. Leftovers can be stored, covered, in the refrigerator for up to 4 days.

Mac and Cheese

1 pound (450 g) dried macaroni
¼ cup unsalted butter
¼ cup all-purpose flour
2 cups whole milk, divided
1 pound (450 g/4 cups) shredded
    old cheddar cheese
1 teaspoon salt
½ teaspoon freshly ground
    black pepper
½ cup panko bread crumbs, divided

4. Blind-bake the crust: Line the pie shell with parchment paper and fill it with about 5 to 6 cups of dried beans, rice, or pie weights. Bake for 25 to 30 minutes, or until the crust is a deep golden brown. Remove the parchment paper and beans, rice, or pie weights carefully and set aside. Allow the pie shell to cool completely in the pan on a wire rack.

5. Make the mac and cheese—cook the pasta: Bring a large pot of salted water to a boil over high heat. Once the water is boiling, add the macaroni. Stir to separate the noodles so that they don't clump together as the water comes back to a boil and cook, according to the package directions, until al dente. Drain the pasta.

6. Meanwhile, make the cheese sauce: Melt the butter in a medium pot over medium heat to start the roux. Once the butter has melted, mix in the flour with a wooden spoon or silicone spatula until smooth and cook, stirring constantly, while the mixture bubbles for 1 minute.

7. While the mixture is still bubbling, add ⅓ cup of the milk and stir until the mixture has thickened to a stiff paste. Add another ⅓ cup of the milk and continue to stir until the paste is smooth again. Increase the heat to medium-high and continue to add about ⅓ cup of the milk at a time until all the milk has been added and the mixture has thickened and is smooth. Allow to boil for 3 minutes, stirring frequently, to cook out the starch.

8. Reduce the heat to low and stir in the shredded cheese, salt, and pepper. Stir continuously until the cheese has melted and the sauce is smooth.

9. Stir the drained macaroni into the cheese sauce and mix together.

10. Assemble and bake the pie: Preheat the oven to 350°F (180°C).

11. Remove the root end of the cooked onions and slice the onions into strips using a chef's knife. Shred the pork and remove any fat or gristle. In a large bowl, mix together the shredded pork with ½ cup of the apple cider honey barbecue sauce and ½ cup of the sliced onions. Reserve the remaining 1 cup of sliced onions for step 14.

12. Sprinkle the bottom of the empty baked pie shell with ¼ cup of the panko. Evenly spread the pork mixture over the panko. Pour ¼ cup of the apple cider honey barbecue sauce over the pork mixture, spreading it out evenly with the back of a spoon.

13. Spoon the prepared mac and cheese over the pork layer, filling the pie shell to the top and mounding the mac and cheese slightly in the centre to create a dome shape. Sprinkle the remaining ¼ cup panko evenly over the surface of the mac and cheese.

14. Arrange the reserved 1 cup sliced onions around the top outer edge of the pie to create a 2-inch border. Bake the pie until the top starts to brown, 45 to 50 minutes. Remove the pie from the oven. Using a spoon or a 12-inch piping bag fitted with a No. 4 round tip, drizzle ¼ cup of the apple cider honey barbecue sauce over the pie in a crosshatch pattern. Bake the pie for another 15 to 20 minutes or until the panko is golden brown and the onions are caramelized. Serve immediately or allow to sit at room temperature for up to 1 hour.

Cheddar Onion Beer Buns

DO AHEAD: The dough can be made ahead; allow it to rise for just 30 minutes at room temperature in step 4 and then store it, covered, in the refrigerator for up to 24 hours. Allow refrigerated dough to sit at room temperature for 45 to 60 minutes before shaping. Store the baked buns in an airtight container at room temperature for up to 2 days.

1 pound (450 g/4 cups) bread flour
2 ounces (50 g/½ cup) whole wheat flour
2 tablespoons granulated sugar
1 tablespoon instant dry yeast
1½ teaspoons salt
1 cup 2% milk, room temperature
1 cup dark ale, room temperature
¼ cup unsalted butter, room temperature
4 large green onions (green and white parts), sliced into ¼-inch pieces (about ¾ cup)
3 cups grated old cheddar cheese

Our cheddar onion beer bread was created specifically for the Ottawa Street Farmers' Market. It features garden-fresh green onions, old cheddar hand-selected from a local cheesemonger, a full-bodied ale, and a buttery milk bread base. Occasionally we even layer cooked bacon into these loaves. This dough makes an excellent sandwich loaf as well; just form a loaf, bake it in a 9- × 5-inch loaf pan, and increase the baking time to 50 minutes. These buns are heavenly when toasted and used as hamburger buns, eaten fresh from the oven with salted butter, or used to make delicious deli meat sandwiches. At the bakery we love them as the base of a classic ham and cheese sandwich with a touch of Dijon mustard and mayonnaise.

1. Make the dough and let it rise: In the bowl of a stand mixer fitted with the dough hook attachment, add the bread flour, whole wheat flour, sugar, instant yeast, and salt, then stir together on low speed for 1 minute to evenly distribute the yeast.

2. Add the milk, ale, and butter and mix on medium speed until no dry flour remains, about 1 minute. If there is still dry flour in the bowl, scrape down the sides and bottom of the bowl, add 1 to 2 tablespoons of water, and mix on medium speed for another minute until no dry flour remains. Continue mixing on medium-low speed for 8 to 12 minutes, or until the dough has pulled away from the sides and bottom of the bowl.

3. Allow the dough to rest in the mixer bowl, covered loosely with a kitchen towel, for 10 minutes.

4. Add the green onions and grated cheddar and mix on medium-low speed for 2 minutes until the onions and cheese are evenly distributed in the dough. Lightly grease a large bowl with olive oil. Shape the dough into a ball and place it in the oiled bowl. Cover the bowl with beeswax or plastic wrap and allow the dough to rise at room temperature until doubled in size, about 1 hour.

5. Shape the dough and let the buns rise: Turn the dough out onto a lightly floured surface. Divide the dough into 15 equal pieces. Working with one piece of dough at a time and keeping the other pieces covered with beeswax or plastic wrap, shape each piece into a smooth bun. Place the 15 buns on a baking sheet lined with parchment paper, spacing them evenly (3 × 5 grid).

6. Let the buns rise in a humid and warm area until doubled in size, about 1 hour. If you don't have a humid area, you can mist the buns with warm water in a spray bottle every 15 minutes. After 30 to 45 minutes of rising, preheat the oven to 375°F (190°C).

7. Bake the fully risen buns: Bake for 18 to 25 minutes, or until the tops are golden brown all over. Allow the buns to cool for 1 hour before serving.

Birthday parties should really be all about the birthday person, so make sure first and foremost that you've established their needs and centred their wants in your planning. The perfect birthday party can be big and grand and full of colourful foods and exciting entertainment, or it can be three or four people gathered around a backyard fire with an acoustic guitar and some finger foods. Show your birthday love by considering the perfect event for your individual birthday star. When we celebrate our bakery's anniversary each year, it's always a big, colourful shindig full of sprinkles and loud laughter. To highlight the best of this menu, we suggest an afternoon party starting around noon so that folks expect to come hungry. Prepare a food spread including lots of fresh fruit and vegetables and a charcuterie platter that stays set up for the whole party so that folks can graze as they please. The Raspberry Pop Tart Banner (page 163), Cheesy Fish Crackers (page 170), and Sprinkle Surprise Cupcakes (page 169) make natural single-serving snacks. Cut the Goat Cheese Brownies (page 157) into bite-size pieces and consider mini White Chocolate Marshmallow Surprise Sandwich Cookies (page 159). Serve the Rainbow Pie (page 165) as your birthday "cake" or a big platter of full-size White Chocolate Marshmallow Surprise Sandwich Cookies (page 159) for impact. Since blowing out candles on a communal cake has become passé, we love using fondant to create a decorative mini cake just for holding candles or preparing a single serving of the pie or a cake ready for the birthday person to blow out the candles. You can buy white or coloured fondant at most bulk food stores, and it's just like playing with playdough.

Birthdays

Goat Cheese Brownies

Brownie Batter

½ cup cocoa powder, sifted
1 cup granulated sugar
½ teaspoon salt
½ cup unsalted butter, melted
1 large egg
1½ teaspoons pure vanilla extract
¼ cup buttermilk
½ cup all-purpose flour, sifted

Goat Cheesecake Filling

9 ounces (250 g) soft goat cheese
½ cup granulated sugar
1 egg yolk

These brownies may have you scratching your head, but trust us, they are worth every single crumb. The goat cheese brownie is an employee favourite, and for longtime customers it's something like "if you know, you know." It was a staple in our pastry case for a few years during our early days. The tart and slightly sour goat cheese plays well with the decadent chocolate and makes for a fudge-like brownie experience. We hope you enjoy this flavour journey, and we hope these brownies become a regular in your household. Several employees demanded that we make an extra tray for snacking when we made them for this book, so they must be good! We love these for birthday parties because they are easy to make (no fussy icings) and they fulfill everyone's cravings for chocolate while being just different enough to encourage curiosity.

1. Preheat the oven to 350°F (180°C). Line an 8-inch square cake pan with parchment paper.

2. Make the brownie batter: In a medium bowl, whisk together the cocoa, sugar, salt, and melted butter until the mixture is smooth and no oily film remains around the edges.

3. Whisk in the egg and vanilla, adding a little air, until the mixture is smooth and has lightened slightly in colour. Whisk in the buttermilk until the mixture is smooth. Using a silicone spatula, stir in the flour and mix until no dry flour remains and the batter is smooth. Set aside.

4. Make the cheesecake filling and bake the brownies: In the bowl of a stand mixer fitted with the paddle attachment, beat the goat cheese, sugar, and egg yolk on medium-high speed for 1 to 2 minutes until smooth. Scrape down the sides and bottom of the bowl. Mix again on medium-high speed for 30 seconds. Do not overmix or the mixture will become too liquid.

5. Scoop the brownie batter into the prepared pan, alternating with smaller scoops of the cheesecake filling. Using a butter knife, swirl the two batters together a little. You want to leave distinct areas of cheesecake and brownie batter. Tap the pan lightly on the counter to level out the batters. Bake for 35 to 45 minutes, or until a toothpick inserted into the centre of the brownie comes out clean. Allow the brownie to cool at room temperature for 1 to 2 hours and, once cooled, cover the pan and refrigerate overnight before cutting.

6. Cut the brownies using a warm chef's knife by dipping it into hot water and drying it on a clean kitchen towel. Wipe the knife between each cut to get nice clean cuts.

DO AHEAD

These brownies can be made ahead and stored in an airtight container in the refrigerator for up to 5 days.

Remove them from the refrigerator at least 1 hour before serving and serve them at room temperature.

BIRTHDAYS

White Chocolate Marshmallow Surprise Sandwich Cookies

White Chocolate Rainbow Cookies

1½ cups all-purpose flour

¾ teaspoon baking soda

½ cup unsalted butter, melted

½ cup granulated sugar

½ cup packed dark brown sugar

½ teaspoon salt

1 large egg

1 teaspoon pure vanilla extract

7 ounces (200 g/1 cup) good-quality white chocolate chunks or chopped chocolate

4 tablespoons rainbow sprinkles, divided

Vanilla Bean Buttercream

¼ batch Vanilla Bean Buttercream (page 293)

Blue Marshmallow Filling

¼ batch (8 ounces/225 g) Marshmallows (page 314)

2 drops sky blue gel food colouring

Our sandwich cookies are just like little cakes: two delectable cookies layered and filled with ganache and buttercream and often encrusted in sprinkles or nuts. We have made dozens of variations over the years; if you love sandwich cookies, we have a whole chapter devoted to them in our first cookbook, *Cake & Loaf*. This is our most celebratory sandwich cookie, made with colourful white chocolate rainbow cookies sandwiching our classic vanilla bean buttercream but with a centre of surprising, festive, bright blue marshmallow. You can tint the marshmallow whatever colour fits your theme best or even make a couple of different coloured fillings. For an extra punch, add sprinkles to the outside of the buttercream for even more festive fun. To make irresistible mini sandwich cookies, scoop 1-tablespoon portions of dough and bake for 10 minutes.

1. Preheat the oven to 350°F (180°C). Line 2 baking sheets with parchment paper or silicone baking mats.

2. Make the cookies: Sift the flour and baking soda into a medium bowl.

3. In a large bowl, whisk together the melted butter, granulated sugar, brown sugar, and salt until the mixture is smooth and no oily film remains around the edges. Whisk in the egg and vanilla until the mixture is smooth and light in colour.

4. Using a spatula, stir in the flour mixture and white chocolate and mix until almost no dry flour remains. Add 3 tablespoons of the rainbow sprinkles and continue to mix until no dry flour remains and the sprinkles are evenly distributed. The dough may look a little wet, but it will firm up as the butter cools.

5. Scoop six 3-tablespoon portions of the cookie dough onto each baking sheet, leaving ample space between them. Gently press down on the cookies to flatten them to about ¾-inch thickness. Sprinkle the remaining 1 tablespoon of sprinkles over the tops of 6 of the cookies. These will be the tops of the sandwich cookies. Bake, one sheet at a time, for 15 to 18 minutes, or until the cookies are puffed up and light brown all over. Allow the cookies to cool on the baking sheets. (CONTINUES)

DO AHEAD

It is best to assemble the sandwich cookies on the day the white chocolate rainbow cookies are baked, but you can store un-iced cookies in an airtight container at room temperature for up to 2 days. The buttercream can be made ahead and stored in an airtight container in the refrigerator for up to 2 months (allow it to come up to room temperature for 4 hours before using). The marshmallows can be made ahead and stored in an airtight container at room temperature for up to 2 months. Store assembled sandwich cookies in an airtight container in the refrigerator for up to 4 days.

BIRTHDAYS

159

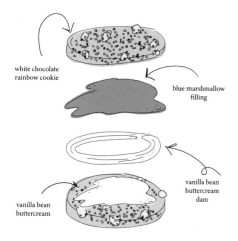

white chocolate
rainbow cookie

blue marshmallow
filling

vanilla bean
buttercream
dam

vanilla bean
buttercream

6. Assemble the sandwich cookies: In the bowl of a stand mixer fitted with the paddle attachment, beat the vanilla bean buttercream on medium-high speed for 7 to 10 minutes, until light and fluffy. Place the cookies without sprinkles, upside down, on a baking sheet. Spread about 1 tablespoon of the buttercream on each cookie, leaving a ½-inch border of exposed cookie around the edge (see page 286, photo A).

7. Fill a piping bag fitted with a No. 824 star tip with the remaining buttercream. Pipe a thick circle of buttercream around the border of each iced cookie to create a well for the marshmallow filling, leaving a ¼-inch border of exposed cookie around the edge (see page 286, photo B).

8. In a heat-resistant medium bowl, heat the marshmallows in the microwave for 1 minute, or until melted. Stir in the food colouring and stir vigorously for 1 to 2 minutes until the colour is evenly distributed.

9. Fill the well of each cookie with 2 tablespoons of the marshmallow. Generously grease your spoons with canola oil cooking spray to make the marshmallow easier to handle and scoop (see page 286, photo C).

10. Place the remaining cookies, sprinkles side up, on top of the filled cookies to form sandwiches. Using even pressure, gently push down on the tops to form a bond with the filling (see page 286, photo D).

A

B

C

D

Raspberry Pop Tart Banner

Butter Pastry
1 batch Butter Pastry (page 296)

Raspberry Jam
¼ batch Raspberry Jam (page 310)
    or ½ cup store-bought

Egg Wash
1 large egg
1 tablespoon water,
    room temperature

To finish
⅓ cup granulated sugar,
    for sprinkling

Pop tarts are one of Josie's go-to breakfast offerings for family and friends. They're easy to throw together if you make the pastry the day before or have some pastry dough in the freezer, and it's a great way to show off preserves. Josie loves making jams and jellies and has an extensive collection. Raspberry is a popular classic, but some of her favourite pop tart fillings are gooseberry jam, apple butter, marmalade, and Nutella. The nostalgic commercial pop tarts were usually short crust and very sweet, but ours focus on a crisp, flaky butter crust so that the filling can shine. You can even add in chopped-up marshmallows, chocolate chips, or nuts. Just be sure not to overstuff the pop tarts. You should be able to tightly seal the edges without much fuss, which is important so that they don't burst during baking. We've made these pop tarts even more fun by miniaturizing them and adding letters so that you can spell out messages for your party as a fun alternative centrepiece. Double the recipe if your message is longer than fifteen letters.

1. Preheat the oven to 400°F (200°C). Line 2 baking sheets with parchment paper or silicone baking mats.

2. Roll out the butter pastry: On a lightly floured surface, roll out the butter pastry to about ⅛-inch thickness. Allow the pastry to rest for 10 minutes so that it doesn't shrink after cutting. Using a metal ruler and pizza cutter, cut the pastry into thirty 2-inch squares. Reroll the scraps into a rough ball to roll out in step 3. Lay the squares flat on a baking sheet, with parchment paper between layers. Place the baking sheet in the refrigerator, covered with beeswax or plastic wrap, for at least 20 minutes to firm up.

3. Cut out the letters: Meanwhile, roll out the reserved ball of scrap pastry to ⅛-inch thickness. Using ¾-inch- to 1-inch-tall letter-shaped cookie cutters, cut out your message. Place the letters on a flat plate and chill them in the refrigerator, covered, for at least 10 minutes before applying them to your tarts in step 5. (CONTINUES)

DO AHEAD

These tarts are best enjoyed on the day they are baked, but the components can be prepared ahead. The butter pastry can be made ahead, wrapped tightly in plastic wrap, and stored in the refrigerator for up to 1 week or in the freezer for up to 6 months. If frozen, thaw in the refrigerator overnight before using. The pastry squares can be rolled, cut, covered with beeswax or plastic wrap, and stored in the refrigerator for up to 2 days. Store the jam in an airtight container in the refrigerator for up to 1 month or in the freezer for up to 4 months. If frozen, thaw in the refrigerator overnight before using. Store finished tarts in an airtight container at room temperature for up to 2 days. If desired, warm the pop tarts in a 325°F (160°C) oven for 4 to 5 minutes.

BIRTHDAYS

163

4. Make the egg wash and assemble the pop tarts: In a small bowl, thoroughly whisk together the egg and water until combined. Working with 6 chilled pastry squares at a time and keeping the other squares covered and in the refrigerator, using a pastry brush, lightly brush egg wash over the entire surface of 3 pastry squares, all the way to the edges. Scoop 1 teaspoon of raspberry jam into the centre of each egg washed square. Working with one square at a time, place a plain pastry square directly on top of the jam and, with your fingers, gently press around the outside border of the square, lining up the edges and pushing out any air, to attach the squares like a ravioli. Using a fork, go around the edge of the square, pressing the fork ⅛ inch into the outside edge of the pastry to create a crimped border all the way around the pop tart to seal in the jam. Repeat with the remaining pastry squares to assemble all the pop tarts. Place the pop tarts on the prepared baking sheets, leaving 1 inch of space between them.

5. Lightly brush the egg wash over the entire surface of the pop tarts. Arrange the pastry letters in the centre of the squares and gently press down to adhere to the egg wash. Egg wash the whole surface lightly one more time. Sprinkle 1 teaspoon of sugar over each pop tart to create a sparkly crust as they bake.

6. Bake the pop tarts: Bake for 12 to 18 minutes, or until the pastry is a deep golden brown. Using a large offset palette knife, transfer the pop tarts to a wire rack to cool for 10 to 15 minutes and then serve warm or at room temperature. Be careful, as the jam can be very hot right out of the oven.

Rainbow Pie

Butter Pastry

1 batch Butter Pastry (page 296)

Lemon Layer

½ cup granulated sugar

⅓ cup + 2 tablespoons water

1 tablespoon unsalted butter

Zest of 1 lemon

6 tablespoons fresh lemon juice

2 tablespoons cornstarch

2 egg yolks

1 drop golden yellow gel food
    colouring (optional)

Lime Layer

½ cup granulated sugar

⅓ cup + 2 tablespoons water

1 tablespoon unsalted butter

Zest of 1 lime

6 tablespoons fresh lime juice

2 tablespoons cornstarch

2 egg yolks

2 drops leaf green gel food colouring
    (optional)

Raspberry Layer

13 ounces (370 g) frozen raspberries,
    thawed

½ cup granulated sugar

1 tablespoon butter

2 tablespoons cornstarch

2 egg yolks

1 tablespoon fresh lemon juice

(INGREDIENTS CONTINUE)

This pie was originally developed for our biggest Pride celebration a few years ago, just after the success of our viral cake, the Gayke. We had been hearing stories about queer couples being refused wedding cakes and we were outraged. Planning your wedding cake should be a joyful and delicious experience, definitely free of discrimination and hate. A longtime collaborator and business buddy of ours reached out about creating "the gayest possible cake" to celebrate the anniversary of his engagement. Chris and his fiancé, Jared, had also been disturbed by these stories of rejection. Chris posted the cake to his social media with the message: "In Canada, when you ask for a gay cake, you get a gay cake!" It went viral, with the image of the cake being shared millions of times. Chris turned the cake into a graphic and then a shirt, and we used the shirts to fundraise for local LGBTQ2+ initiatives, paying forward the love.

1. Preheat the oven to 400°F (200°C).

2. Roll out the butter pastry: On a lightly floured work surface, roll out the butter pastry dough into an 11- to 12-inch circle, about ⅛ inch thick. Fold the dough in half to lift it without stretching and gently unfold it into a 9-inch pie plate. Gently press the dough into the sides and bottom of the plate, making sure not to stretch the dough. Trim the dough as needed and crimp the edges of the pastry. Place the pie plate in the refrigerator to allow the pastry to relax and firm up a bit, at least 15 minutes.

3. Blind-bake the crust: Line the shell with parchment paper and fill it with 2 to 3 cups of dried beans or rice or with pie weights. Bake for 20 to 25 minutes, or until the crust is a deep golden brown. Remove the parchment paper and beans, rice, or pie weights. Allow the pie shell to cool completely in the pan on a wire rack.

4. Make the lemon layer: In a small saucepan, combine the sugar, water, butter, and lemon zest and bring to a boil, stirring occasionally, over high heat. Boil for 1 minute and then remove from the heat. (CONTINUES)

DO AHEAD

You can make the pie (minus the whipped cream) and store it, covered, in the refrigerator for up to 3 days. Just add the whipped cream when you are ready to serve the pie. The butter pastry can be made ahead, wrapped tightly in plastic wrap, and stored in the refrigerator for up to 1 week or in the freezer for up to 6 months. If frozen, thaw in the refrigerator overnight before using. The pie shell can be blind-baked, covered, and stored at room temperature for up to 24 hours. Store the finished pie, covered, in the refrigerator for up to 2 days.

Blueberry Layer

14 ounces (400 g) frozen blueberries, thawed

½ cup granulated sugar

1 tablespoon butter

2 tablespoons cornstarch

2 egg yolks

1 tablespoon fresh lemon juice

1 drop royal blue gel food colouring (optional)

Whipped Cream

1 batch Whipped Cream (page 300)

5. In a medium bowl, combine the lemon juice, cornstarch, and egg yolks and whisk until the cornstarch is fully dissolved. Temper the egg mixture by slowly adding the hot sugar mixture, 2 tablespoons at a time, stirring constantly. Pour the mixture back into the saucepan and return it to a boil, whisking constantly, over medium-high heat. Reduce the heat to medium to maintain a low boil and continue to cook, stirring constantly, for 1 to 2 minutes, or until the mixture has thickened. Stir in the food colouring, if using. Scoop the filling into the baked pie crust and, using a small offset palette knife, smooth it out into an even layer. Place the pie in the refrigerator, uncovered, while you prepare the lime layer.

6. Make the lime layer: Repeat steps 4 and 5 using the ingredients for the lime layer.

7. Make the raspberry layer: Place the thawed raspberries, with their juices, in a large fine-mesh strainer set over a large bowl. Using a silicone spatula or wooden spoon, press the fruit and juices through the strainer. Some small seeds may get through, but that is okay. This is your raspberry purée. You should have ¾ cup.

8. In a small saucepan, combine the sugar, ½ cup of the raspberry purée, and butter and bring to a boil, stirring occasionally, over high heat. Boil for 1 minute and then remove from the heat.

9. In a medium bowl, combine the remaining ¼ cup raspberry purée, cornstarch, egg yolks, and lemon juice and whisk until the cornstarch is fully dissolved. Temper the egg mixture by slowly adding the hot mixture, 2 tablespoons at a time, stirring constantly. Pour the mixture back into the saucepan and bring to a boil, whisking constantly, over medium-high heat. Reduce the heat to medium to maintain a low boil and cook, stirring constantly, for 1 to 2 minutes, or until the mixture has thickened. Scoop the filling into the baked pie crust over the lime layer and, using a small offset palette knife, smooth it out into an even layer. Return the pie to the refrigerator, uncovered, while you prepare the blueberry layer.

10. Make the blueberry layer: Repeat steps 7 to 9 using the ingredients for the blueberry layer, stirring in the food colouring (if using) before you scoop the filling into the pie shell. Cover the top of the pie with plastic wrap to prevent a skin from forming and allow the pie to cool completely in the refrigerator for 1 to 2 hours.

11. Finish the pie: Spoon the whipped cream over the top of the pie for a rustic finish, or fill a 16-inch piping bag fitted with a No. 825 star tip and finish the pie by piping lines of star swirl border across it to cover the whole surface (see Buttercream and Whipped Cream Piping Styles, page 286, C).

Sprinkle Surprise Cupcakes

Vanilla Cupcakes
½ batch Vanilla Cake Batter
 (page 282)

Vanilla Bean Buttercream
½ batch Vanilla Bean Buttercream
 (page 293)
2 or 3 different colours of gel
 food colouring

Simple Syrup
1 batch Simple Syrup (page 316)

For assembly
1¼ cups sprinkles of choice

Sprinkles bring joy and a sense of playfulness to everything they adorn. When you bite into these light and fluffy vanilla cupcakes, you will be surprised by a colourful assortment of sprinkles in the centre. Get creative and choose different sizes, colours, and shapes of sprinkles that complement your celebration theme. If you do not have an apple corer, you can use the opposite end of a large piping tip or a one-inch round cookie cutter to cut holes in the top of the cupcakes to fill with sprinkles. A paring knife will also work to carve out holes. For a fun birthday party activity, prepare these cupcakes plain with no sprinkles on top and provide bowls of chopped-up chocolate bars, candy, and sprinkles. Let your guests go wild building the most extreme cupcakes they can imagine.

1. Preheat the oven to 350°F (180°C). Line a muffin pan with 12 paper liners or generously grease with canola oil cooking spray.

2. Make the cupcakes: Fill the muffin cups three-quarters full with the vanilla cake batter. Bake for 16 to 20 minutes, or until a toothpick inserted into the centre of a cupcake comes out clean. Cool the cupcakes in the pan or wait 5 to 10 minutes, then turn them out onto a wire rack to cool completely.

3. Prepare the buttercream: In the bowl of a stand mixer fitted with the paddle attachment, beat the vanilla bean buttercream for 5 minutes on medium-high speed until light and fluffy. Divide the buttercream into 2 or 3 small bowls and whisk your choice of food colouring into each bowl. Fill separate piping bags fitted with a No. 827 star tip with each coloured buttercream. Set aside.

4. Fill the cupcakes: Using an apple corer or a paring knife, create holes in the centres of the cupcakes. Moisten the top of each cupcake with up to 2 tablespoons of simple syrup. Fill each hole with 1½ to 2 tablespoons of sprinkles, filling the entire cavity.

5. Decorate the cupcakes: Pipe rosettes (see Buttercream and Whipped Cream Piping Styles, page 286, D) on the tops of all the cupcakes and finish with ¼ teaspoon of sprinkles per cupcake.

DO AHEAD

The iced cupcakes are best enjoyed at room temperature on the day they are assembled, but they can be stored, covered, in the refrigerator for up to 2 days. Remove the cupcakes from the refrigerator and let sit at room temperature for 2 to 4 hours before serving. Un-iced cupcakes can be stored in an airtight container at room temperature for up to 2 days. The simple syrup can be stored in an airtight container in the refrigerator for up to 3 weeks. The buttercream can be stored in an airtight container in the refrigerator for up to 2 months or in the freezer for up to 6 months. If refrigerated, let soften at room temperature for 4 hours. If frozen, thaw in the refrigerator overnight.

BIRTHDAYS

Cheesy Fish Crackers

12 ounces (340 g/3 cups) shredded old cheddar cheese

½ cup unsalted butter, cold and cut into ½-inch cubes

1 cup all-purpose flour, more for dusting

½ cup whole wheat flour

½ teaspoon onion powder

½ teaspoon sweet paprika

½ teaspoon salt

½ teaspoon freshly ground black pepper

Josie originally developed this recipe when her child, Lily, was a toddler and she was looking for homemade alternatives to grocery-store favourites. The dough comes together easily, and you get to play with shapes and designs. What could be more satisfying than playing with your food? Make a double batch of dough and bake half the crackers in advance of your party. Store the extra dough, wrapped tightly in beeswax or plastic wrap, in the refrigerator until an hour before you want to roll it out. During the party, provide a variety of cookie cutters and get the kids, or guests who are kids at heart, to help create their own unique designs and bake them mid-party for snacking or take-home goodies. At a past event, we had a lot of fun creating a fish-themed birthday party with these crackers—they made waves with our guests, and we hope they will with yours, too.

1. Preheat the oven to 400°F (200°C). Line 2 baking sheets with parchment paper or silicone baking mats.

2. In a food processor, combine all the ingredients and pulse until the cheddar and butter are fully incorporated and a dough forms.

3. On a lightly floured work surface, roll out the dough to about ⅛-inch thickness. Move the dough around and check underneath it frequently to make sure it is not sticking to your work surface, dusting lightly with more flour as needed.

4. Using a fish-shaped cookie cutter, cut out the crackers and place them on the prepared baking sheets, leaving ample space between them. (Instead of using a cookie cutter, you can use a paring knife to create original shapes for your crackers. If you wish to create a design on your crackers, use a little bit of water between pieces of cracker dough to stick them together. Ensure that the crackers on each baking tray are about the same size for even baking.)

5. If there is any flour on top of the crackers, brush it off with a pastry brush before baking. Bake the crackers, one sheet at a time, for 14 to 16 minutes, or until they are puffed up and appear dry. Allow the crackers to cool completely on the baking sheets.

DO AHEAD

These crackers are best enjoyed on the day they are baked, but they can be stored in an airtight container at room temperature for up to 1 week. The dough can be made ahead, wrapped tightly in beeswax or plastic wrap, and stored at room temperature for up to 12 hours or in the refrigerator for up to 3 days. Warm chilled dough to room temperature for 1 to 2 hours before rolling it out.

S ometimes we find ourselves rushing through life from goal to goal, and we forget to celebrate our and our loved ones' accomplishments and milestones. We are personally guilty of skipping the celebration part of events and over-focusing on just making it to the finish line. But the magic of life happens in between, in the moments we take to breathe, look around, and give ourselves a well-earned high-five. Make it a habit to recognize the positives and celebrate special moments big and small with your family and friends. Milestone gatherings could be anything from celebrating the acceptance of a new job or a small wedding to a sixtieth wedding anniversary or hundredth birthday. This menu works best for a cocktail party with passed appetizers. If it's within your budget, splurge for some staff to serve the food and drinks and tidy up afterward. That way, you'll actually get to enjoy the party as a guest! If you are working with a caterer for any of the food or renting a venue, they can usually connect you with serving staff for hire. For a more intimate milestone celebration, invite folks for after-dinner drinks and serve the Lemon Poppy Seed Penthouse Bars (page 175) cut into bite-size pieces, the Sugar Dot Cookies (page 177), Nut-Free Mini Linzer Tarts (page 181), and Jalapeño Cheddar Stuffed Pretzel Balls (page 185) along with a selection of alcoholic cocktails, THC-infused beverages, and mocktails. Allow the Strawberries and Cream Celebration Cake (page 183) to act as your centrepiece until near the end of the night, then serve it as a midnight snack.

Milestone Party

Lemon Poppy Seed Penthouse Bars

Lemon Poppy Seed Cake Base

1½ cups all-purpose flour

½ teaspoon baking powder

¼ teaspoon baking soda

4 ounces (115 g/½ cup) cream
    cheese, room temperature

½ cup unsalted butter,
    room temperature

¾ cup granulated sugar

1 large egg, room temperature

1 teaspoon pure vanilla extract

2 teaspoons poppy seeds

Zest of 1 lemon

Lemon American Buttercream

1 batch Vanilla Bean American
    Buttercream (page 294)

Zest of 1 lemon

2 tablespoons fresh lemon juice

Lemon Simple Syrup

¼ cup Simple Syrup (page 316;
    ¼ batch)

2 tablespoons fresh lemon juice

Sugared Lemon Zest

Zest of ½ lemon

2 tablespoons granulated sugar

To finish

1 tablespoon white chocolate
    crisp pearls

A quick online search will bring up an abundance of recipes featuring lemon and poppy seed, and we aren't surprised. It is a delightful combination, with the bright sour lemon contrasting with nutty and underlying fruitiness that blends beautifully with buttery vanilla bases. Our OG Penthouse bar was an attempt to capture the nostalgia of the grocery-store staple Lofthouse cookies (impossibly soft vanilla cookies topped with garishly bright icing and sprinkles). This is just one of our variations on that classic. One of our favourite things is taking commercially produced grocery-store favourites and making them our own with much better ingredients but flavours that are as recognizable as the classic. Cut these lemony fresh bars in bite-size pieces to feed a crowd.

1. Preheat the oven to 350°F (180°C). Grease an 8-inch square cake pan with canola oil cooking spray and line with parchment paper.

2. Make the lemon poppy seed cake base: Sift the flour, baking powder, and baking soda into a medium bowl and stir together.

3. In the bowl of a stand mixer fitted with the paddle attachment, beat the cream cheese on medium-high speed until smooth. Scrape down the sides and bottom of the bowl. Add the butter and beat until smooth. Scrape down the sides and bottom of the bowl.

4. Add the sugar and beat on medium-high speed for 3 to 5 minutes until the batter is pale and fluffy. Scrape down the sides and bottom of the bowl.

5. Add the egg and vanilla and continue to beat on medium-high speed for 3 to 5 more minutes until the batter is smooth and fluffy. Scrape down the sides and bottom of the bowl.

6. Add the poppy seeds and lemon zest and continue to beat on medium-high speed for 1 more minute to evenly distribute them in the batter. Scrape down the sides and bottom of the bowl.

7. Reduce the speed to low and add the flour mixture. Gradually increase the speed to medium and mix until the batter is smooth, 1 to 2 minutes. The batter will be quite thick. (CONTINUES)

DO AHEAD

These bars are best enjoyed at room temperature on the day they are made but can be stored in an airtight container at room temperature for up to 4 days. All the components of the finished bar can be made ahead to simplify assembly. Once the cake base is baked, cool it thoroughly, wrap it tightly in beeswax or plastic wrap, and store at room temperature for up to 3 days. Store the American buttercream in an airtight container in the refrigerator for up to 1 month or in the freezer for up to 6 months. Allow chilled icing to come up to room temperature for 4 hours before using. If frozen, thaw in the refrigerator overnight before using. The simple syrup can be stored in an airtight container in the refrigerator for up to 3 weeks.

8. Scoop the batter into the prepared pan, level it with an offset palette knife, and bake for 20 to 25 minutes, or until a toothpick inserted into the centre of the cake comes out clean. Cool at room temperature for 2 hours before icing.

9. Meanwhile, make the lemon American buttercream: In the bowl of a stand mixer fitted with the paddle attachment, beat the vanilla bean American buttercream on medium-high speed for 2 to 3 minutes until fluffy. Add the lemon zest and juice and continue to beat on medium-high for 2 to 3 minutes until the juice is fully incorporated and the icing is fluffy.

10. Make the lemon simple syrup: In a small bowl, stir together the simple syrup and lemon juice.

11. Finish the bars: Using a pastry brush, brush the simple syrup over the top of the cake until all the syrup is absorbed. Spread the buttercream evenly over the syrup-soaked bar.

12. Make the sugared lemon zest: In a small bowl, rub together the lemon zest and sugar. Sprinkle the sugared lemon zest evenly over the top of the bar. Finish by sprinkling white chocolate crisp pearls evenly over the bar. Refrigerate for 20 to 30 minutes to allow the icing to set.

13. Cut the bars using a warm chef's knife by dipping it into hot water and drying it on a clean kitchen towel. Wipe the knife between each cut to get nice clean cuts.

Sugar Dot Cookies

Sugar Cookie Dough
1 batch Sugar Cookie Dough
  (page 301)

Royal Icing
2 batches Royal Icing (page 295)
1 to 2 drops rose gel food colouring
1 to 2 drops lemon yellow gel food
  colouring
1 to 2 drops purple gel food colouring

To finish
2 to 3 tablespoons edible gold flake

One of our favourite sights at the bakery is stacks of these rainbow-hued mini cookies piled high on baking racks waiting to be packaged. They look like you could just dive in and surround yourself in cookies. Mini everything has a great appeal for adults and kids alike, and we decided one day that our cookie lineup needed something perfect for dipping in milk that would also have a long shelf life. Our vanilla bean sugar dot cookies and their siblings, iced gingerbread dots, have been a staple item ever since. Being that they are tiny and need one dollop of royal icing, they dry quickly and require minimal fuss. Get fancy with different coloured sprinkles, edible gold flakes, different piping tips, and lustre or sparkle dusts. Customize the colours to tie in with your celebration theme for a complementary look. These can also be bagged up by the dozen for fun edible favours to hand out to your guests as a "thank you."

1. Preheat the oven to 350°F (180°C). Line 3 baking sheets with parchment paper or silicone baking mats.

2. Make the cookies: The dough must be rolled immediately after mixing. On a lightly floured work surface, roll out the sugar cookie dough to about ¼-inch thickness. Move the dough around and check underneath it frequently to make sure it is not sticking, dusting lightly with flour as needed. Use a floured metal ruler to run under the dough to release any stuck areas.

3. Using a 1½-inch round cookie cutter, cut out at least 144 rounds, rerolling the dough up to twice if necessary. Place the cookies on the prepared baking sheets, evenly spaced (6 × 8 grid per baking sheet). Bake, one sheet at a time, for 10 to 14 minutes, or until the cookies have puffed up and are slightly golden on top and slightly browned on the bottom. Allow the cookies to cool completely on the baking sheet. While the cookies are cooling, prepare the royal icing.

4. Decorate the cookies: Evenly divide the royal icing into 3 small bowls, one for each colour used. Add the food colouring one drop at a time, stirring vigorously with a silicone spatula between each addition, until the desired colour is reached. The royal icing should be a stiff texture (see Royal Icing Piping Styles, page 288, Stiff Texture). (CONTINUES)

DO AHEAD

Make these cookies and ice them with royal icing at least 1 day ahead of serving or packaging. You can store the finished cookies in an airtight container at room temperature for up to 1 month. Individually packaged and sealed iced cookies can be stored at room temperature for up to 2 months. Un-iced cookies can be stored in an airtight container at room temperature for 1 month or in the freezer for up to 3 months. Place frozen cookies, uncovered, on a baking sheet in a single layer to thaw at room temperature for 30 minutes before icing them. The royal icing can be made ahead and stored in an airtight container in the refrigerator for up to 1 month. When ready to use, in the bowl of a stand mixer fitted with the paddle attachment, beat on high speed for 5 to 7 minutes to refresh the icing.

MILESTONE PARTY

5. Pipe kisses or rosettes: Fill three 12-inch piping bags fitted with No. 824 star tips using plastic couplers with 1½ cups of a different colour of royal icing in each bag. Pipe a kiss or rosette with the star tips or a dot on each cookie using the round tip in step 6. Once you have piped about 6 cookies, sprinkle with gold flake to ensure that it adheres while the icing is freshly piped and wet. Continue to pipe and sprinkle the cookies with gold flake until you have iced about two thirds of the cookies. Return any unused icing to the bowls to pipe dots on the remaining third.

For kisses (see Royal Icing Piping Styles, page 288, Stiff Texture J): Using even pressure, attach the royal icing to the cookie, pull up and away from the cookie slightly to build a wide bottom, and continue pulling up, releasing pressure completely to create a point.

For rosettes (see Royal Icing Piping Styles, page 288, Stiff Texture J): Using even pressure, attach the royal icing to the cookie and begin to move the tip counter-clockwise in a tight circle. End the rosette once you have closed the circle, then begin to release pressure and with a flick of the wrist, end pressure completely to create a point ending on the starting point laying down. Once you have piped about 6 cookies, sprinkle with gold flake to ensure that it adheres while the icing is freshly piped and wet. Continue to pipe and sprinkle the cookies with gold flake until you have iced about two-thirds of the cookies. Return any unused icing to the bowls to pipe dots.

6. Pipe dots: To each bowl of the remaining royal icing, add 1 to 2 teaspoons of water, a teaspoon at a time, stirring thoroughly after each addition, until the icing has reached a "stable flooding consistency" (See Royal Icing Piping Styles, page 288, Stable Flooding Texture). The icing is fluid yct when piped has a limited amount of spread but is able to settle while holding its shape. Once you have piped about 6 cookies, sprinkle them with gold flake. Continue to pipe and sprinkle the cookies with gold flake until all the cookies are iced.

7. For dots (see Royal Icing Piping Styles, page 288, Stable Flooding Texture K): Fill three 12-inch piping bags fitted with No. 4 small round tips using plastic couplers with the remaining royal icing. Pipe dots, starting in the centre and leaving ¼ inch of exposed cookie around the edge to allow the icing to settle. Once you have piped about 6 cookies, sprinkle with gold flake to ensure that it adheres while the icing is freshly piped and wet. Continue to pipe and sprinkle the cookies with gold flake until all the cookies are iced.

8. Allow the piped cookies to dry, undisturbed and uncovered, at room temperature, for 12 to 24 hours to ensure that they dry completely. Decorated cookies can be served once dried.

Nut-Free Mini Linzer Tarts

DO AHEAD: These tarts are best enjoyed on the day they are baked but can be made ahead and stored in an airtight container at room temperature for up to 6 days. The raspberry jam can be made ahead and stored in an airtight container in the refrigerator for up to 1 month or in the freezer for up to 4 months. If frozen, thaw in the refrigerator overnight before using.

Sugar Cookie Dough
1 batch Sugar Cookie Dough (page 301)

Filling
1 cup speculoos cookie butter
¾ cup Raspberry Jam (page 310) or store-bought
1 tablespoon lemon juice

To finish
¼ cup turbinado sugar

The original Linzer torte is a recipe from the 1600s and, according to some, is the oldest recorded cake recipe. It is traditionally a squat, crumbly, nut-based short-crust pastry flavoured with lemon and cinnamon, generally filled with raspberry or red currant jam and topped with a lattice design of thin pastry. It's a classic we all made in culinary school, and it has lasted this long for a reason—it is a delicious traditional combination. We have reimagined this torte as a nut-free handheld version. It has all the deliciousness of a peanut butter and jelly sandwich cookie without the nuts. The buttery sugar cookie isn't too sweet, so it lets the cookie butter and jam shine. These tarts are downright addictive!

1. Preheat the oven to 350°F (180°C). Generously grease 2 muffin pans with canola oil cooking spray. Line a baking sheet with parchment paper.

2. **Roll out the sugar cookie dough:** The dough must be rolled immediately after mixing. On a lightly floured work surface, roll out the sugar cookie dough to about ⅛-inch thickness. Move the dough around and check underneath it frequently to make sure it is not sticking, dusting lightly with flour as needed. Cut out forty-eight 2½-inch circles of dough. Place 24 dough circles on the prepared baking sheet, evenly spaced. Cover with beeswax or plastic wrap and set aside until step 5—these will be the pastry tops. Gently press the remaining 24 dough circles into the muffin cups, forming walls that extend about three-quarters up the cups.

3. **Fill the tart shells:** Add 2-teaspoon portions of speculoos cookie butter to each tart shell and spread it out with the back of a small spoon, flattening the cookie butter evenly into each base. Be sure to completely cover the bottom.

4. In a small bowl, stir together the raspberry jam and lemon juice. Add 1½ teaspoons of jam to each tart shell and spread it out with the back of a small spoon, evenly covering the cookie butter.

5. **Add the pastry tops and bake:** Using a small pastry brush, lightly brush the rims of the 24 tart shells with water. (This will help attach the tops to the tarts.) Using a ½-inch cookie cutter (circle or other small shape), punch out the centres of the pastry tops. Cover the tarts with the tops and, using your fingertips, gently press the edges together around the tart, then crimp the edges with the tines of a fork.

6. Brush the tops of the tarts lightly with water and sprinkle ½ teaspoon of the turbinado sugar over each tart.

7. Bake for 25 to 30 minutes, or until the jam is bubbling up a little and the pastry is golden brown. The filling will settle as it cools. Using a small offset palette knife, remove the tarts from the pan immediately, so that they do not stick to the pan as they cool.

Strawberries and Cream Celebration Cake

Vanilla Cake Batter
1½ batches Vanilla Cake Batter
  (page 282)

Strawberry Compote
½ batch Strawberry Compote
  (page 309; reserve ¼ cup for
  the Strawberry Simple Syrup,
  recipe below)

Strawberry Simple Syrup
1 batch Simple Syrup (page 316)
¼ cup Strawberry Compote
  (reserved; recipe above)

Vanilla Bean Buttercream
1 batch Vanilla Bean Buttercream
  (page 293)

Pastry Cream
1 batch Pastry Cream (page 315)

For assembly (optional)
Prepared floral decoration

It can't be a party without cake! And what better way to celebrate than with a vanilla bean cake featuring fresh strawberry compote, silky-smooth pastry cream, and vanilla bean buttercream. Fresh florals and a rustic finish give this cake a versatile appearance that can shine at any milestone celebration. Decorate the cake simply with some edible flowers or consult your local flower shop about appropriate flowers to dress up your cake. You can usually order pre-made floral cake toppers that you can add to your cake, or the florist will suggest flowers that are food-safe you can add yourself.

1. Preheat the oven to 350°F (180°C). Grease two 8-inch round cake pans with canola oil cooking spray and line the bottoms with parchment paper circles.

2. Make the cake layers: Divide the vanilla cake batter evenly between the prepared pans and, using a small offset palette knife, smooth out the tops. Bake for 60 to 75 minutes, or until a toothpick inserted into the centres of the cakes comes out clean. Allow the cakes to cool in the pans on a wire rack for 20 minutes. Remove the cakes from the pans, leaving the parchment paper circles on the bottoms, and cool completely on the wire rack. Once the cakes are cool, wrap them tightly in plastic wrap and store at room temperature for up to 3 days.

3. Assemble and decorate the cake—prepare the cake layers: Trim the domes off the tops of the baked vanilla cake layers and cut the cakes in half horizontally. Use the cake assembly and decorating instructions (follow instructions on page 283, step 1, photo A).

4. Make the strawberry simple syrup: In a small bowl, mix the reserved ¼ cup strawberry compote into the simple syrup.   (CONTINUES)

DO AHEAD

It is best to make the components of this cake ahead, then assemble the layered cake on the day you wish to serve it. The cake layers can be baked and stored, wrapped in beeswax or plastic wrap, at room temperature for up to 3 days. The pastry cream can be stored in an airtight container in the refrigerator for up to 2 weeks. The compote can be stored in an airtight container in the refrigerator for up to 1 month or in the freezer for up to 6 months. If frozen, thaw the compote in the refrigerator overnight before using. The simple syrup can be stored in an airtight container in the refrigerator for up to 3 weeks. The assembled cake can be stored, covered, in the refrigerator up to 4 days.

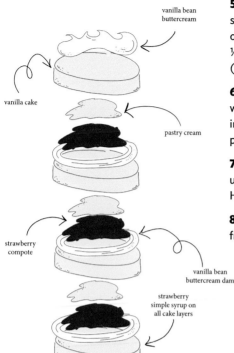

vanilla bean
buttercream

vanilla cake

pastry cream

strawberry
compote

vanilla bean
buttercream dam

strawberry
simple syrup on
all cake layers

5. Stack the cake: Moisten each layer with ¼ cup of the strawberry simple syrup. Stack the cake with vanilla bean buttercream on a 10-inch cake board or serving plate, adding ¼ cup of the strawberry compote topped with about ½ cup of the pastry cream to each cake layer with a dam of vanilla buttercream (follow instructions on page 283, step 2, photos B to E).

6. Crumb coat the cake: Crumb coat the top and sides of the stacked cake with a thin layer of vanilla bean buttercream and place the cake, uncovered, in the refrigerator for 15 minutes (follow instructions on page 284, step 3, photos F to G).

7. Mask the cake: Mask the chilled cake with the vanilla bean buttercream using a rustic finish (follow instructions on page 284, step 4 to 5, photos H to J).

8. Finish the cake (optional): Decorate the cake by preparing and placing fresh florals on the top and sides of the cake.

Jalapeño Cheddar Stuffed Pretzel Balls

Cheese Whiz
½ cup condensed milk

4 ounces (115 g/1 cup) shredded old cheddar cheese

3 to 4 tablespoons chopped pickled or fresh jalapeño peppers

Pretzel Dough
½ batch Pretzel Dough (page 129)

Water Bath
7½ cups water

3 tablespoons baking soda

For assembly
1 tablespoon flaky sea salt (we use Maldon) or pretzel salt

There was a time we regularly made stuffed pretzels at the bakery. Our bakers made so many amazing stuffed pretzels from dill cream cheese to Reuben (corned beef and sauerkraut). Our bread baker at the time, Kyle, was frustrated with our stuffed cheddar pretzels because he wanted more cheese flavour. So, his brilliant experiment to create homemade Cheez Whiz began. We think he nailed it, and you are going to find all sorts of items to dip into or stuff with this luscious, intensely cheesy, creamy spread. If you don't like spice, you can skip the jalapeños and just stuff the balls with our cheese whiz. Either way, serve these golden orbs warm, if possible. They will still be delicious at room temperature but not as satisfyingly soft and cheesy.

1. Make the cheese whiz: In a small heat-resistant bowl, combine the condensed milk and shredded cheese and heat in the microwave for 1 minute. Vigorously stir until the cheese is melted and the mixture is glossy and smooth. If you see any lumps, heat in the microwave in 15-second intervals, stirring after each interval, until smooth. Store in an airtight container in the refrigerator for at least 4 hours or overnight to firm up.

2. Remove the cheese whiz from the refrigerator and stir it with a spoon to create a smooth texture. Stir in 3 tablespoons of the jalapeños and taste for spice level. Add up to 1 tablespoon remaining jalapeños to taste.

3. Preheat the oven to 400°F (200°C). Line 2 baking sheets with parchment paper or silicone baking mats.

4. Make the pretzels: Prepare the pretzel dough as instructed on page 129, steps 1 to 4. Divide the dough into 12 equal pieces and form into small balls. Working with one ball of dough at a time and keeping the other balls covered with beeswax or plastic wrap, use your hands to flatten the ball into a 3-inch disc, thinner around the edges than in the middle. Place 1 tablespoon of the cheese whiz filling in the centre of the disc and, using the back of a spoon, gently press the filling into the dough. Bring the edges of the dough up around the filling and pinch the bun closed, ensuring that it's tightly sealed. Roll it gently in your hands to round off the bun. Once the filling is covered and no bits are peeking through the dough, place it sealed side down on one of the prepared baking sheets. Repeat until all the discs are stuffed and evenly spaced on the baking sheets. (CONTINUES)

DO AHEAD

Make the cheese whiz at least 1 day ahead and store it in an airtight container in the refrigerator for up to 1 week. These pretzel balls are best served warm immediately but will keep, uncovered, at room temperature for up to 18 hours. The pretzel balls can be reheated in the oven at 300°F (150°C) for 5 minutes.

MILESTONE PARTY

5. Prepare the water bath and boil the pretzel balls: In a large shallow pot, bring the water to a boil over high heat. Once the water is boiling, reduce the heat to low and stir in the baking soda. You want to maintain a very gentle boil, so adjust the heat to medium if needed. Using a spider strainer to transfer the pretzel balls in and out of the water bath, cook the balls 2 or 3 at a time until puffed, 90 seconds per side. Drain well and transfer the pretzel balls to the prepared baking sheets, evenly space, and make one cut down the centre of each ball with a very sharp knife. Do not cut deep enough to pierce the cheese whiz.

6. Top the pretzel balls and bake: Sprinkle the pretzel balls with flaky sea salt and bake until golden brown and cooked through, about 15 minutes.

Fresh Vegetable Pizza

Puff Pastry Dough

1 batch Blitz Puff Pastry (page 298)

Buttermilk Ranch Cream Cheese

8 ounces (225 g/1 cup) cream
  cheese, room temperature
¼ cup buttermilk
1 tablespoon Ranch Spice Mix
  (page 312)
¼ teaspoon salt
¼ teaspoon freshly ground
  black pepper

Toppings

2 tablespoons finely chopped
  red onion
½ cup chopped English cucumber
1 red bell pepper, chopped
¾ cup small broccoli florets
¾ cup cauliflower florets
1 carrot, peeled and grated
¼ cup fresh dill leaves
Edible flowers (optional)

This recipe originated with a trip to a friend's cottage in high school. Josie's best friend, Neil, had invited her to the family cottage and Neil's mom, Barb, prepared an appetizer based on Pillsbury Crescent Rolls, topped with cream cheese mixed with salad dressing and whatever fresh veggies were in the fridge. It didn't seem like much at first, but Josie couldn't stop eating it. Then she couldn't stop making it. Eventually this version emerged with homemade puff pastry, our own buttermilk ranch cream cheese, a rainbow of vegetables, and an elegant garnish. The result is an accessible dish, popular at parties, and a great weekday family meal.

1. Preheat the oven to 400°F (200°C). Grease a 13- × 18-inch baking sheet generously with canola oil cooking spray.

2. Roll out the puff pastry dough: On a lightly floured work surface, roll out the puff pastry dough into a 13- × 18-inch rectangle, about ⅛ inch thick. Fold the dough in half to lift it without stretching and gently unfold it into the baking sheet. Gently press the dough into the sides and bottom of the sheet, making sure not to stretch the dough. Place the baking sheet in the refrigerator to allow the dough to relax and firm up a bit, at least 15 minutes.

3. Brush any flour off the surface of the dough using a dry pastry brush and prick all over with the tines of a fork. (Pricking holes, or docking, allows the dough to rise evenly.) Bake for 20 to 25 minutes, or until the pastry has puffed up and is a deep golden brown colour. Allow the puff pastry to cool completely on the baking sheet.

4. Make the buttermilk ranch cream cheese: In the bowl of a stand mixer fitted with the paddle attachment, beat the cream cheese on medium-high speed until smooth, 2 to 3 minutes. Scrape down the sides and bottom of the bowl.

5. Add the buttermilk, ranch spice mix, salt, and pepper. Mix on medium speed until the mixture is homogenous and the spices are evenly distributed.

6. Using a small offset palette knife, evenly spread the cream cheese mixture over the puff pastry base, leaving a ½-inch border of exposed pastry around the edges.

7. Finish the pizza with toppings: Evenly sprinkle the onions, cucumber, bell pepper, broccoli, cauliflower, and carrot over the cream cheese mixture.

8. Cut the pizza into 20 squares (4 × 5 grid) and garnish with fresh dill and edible flowers, if using. Serve immediately.

DO AHEAD

This pizza is best enjoyed within 4 hours of being assembled. The puff pastry can be made ahead, wrapped tightly in plastic wrap, and stored in the refrigerator for up to 3 days or in the freezer for up to 6 months.

If frozen, thaw in the refrigerator overnight before using. The puff pastry base can be baked and stored, tightly wrapped in beeswax or plastic wrap, at room temperature for up to 24 hours. The buttermilk ranch cream cheese

can be made ahead and stored in an airtight container in the refrigerator for up to 1 week. Store leftovers in an airtight container in the refrigerator for up to 2 days.

We believe that outdoor fall gatherings hold a special magic, just like the fall harvest fairs of our childhood. Pile your seating high with comfy blankets and request that guests dress warmly. Set up outdoor games like ring toss to keep people moving, and provide warm apple cider or coffee to keep everyone toasty. The colour theme for these baked goods is burnt orange, with all their pumpkin and pecan accents, so run with that theme and decorate with sunflowers, mini pumpkins, or fall grasses. For a special treat, you can hire a coffee food truck or mobile coffee shop to come right to your party with a full latte bar so that guests can indulge in a pumpkin spice latte along with your baked goods. Set up a little bakery of your own with platters of Pumpkin Spice Latte Bars (page 193), Sea Salt Brown Butter Pecan Cookies (page 199), Cheesecake Stuffed Pumpkin Snickerdoodles (page 195), and Nutty Pumpkin Squares (page 200). If you are aiming for more of a sit-down meal, the Turkey and Wild Rice Pie with Mashed Potato Topping (page 207) has everything you need in one delicious dish, side salad optional. Serve the Pumpkin Cheesecake Pie with Pecan Praline (page 203) or Apple Cinnamon Bundt Cake (page 204) for dessert and you are set!

Fall Feelings

Pumpkin Spice Latte Bars

Coffee Blondie Layer

2 teaspoons hot water

1 teaspoon instant coffee granules

¼ cup unsalted butter

4 ounces (115 g/⅔ cup) white chocolate callets or good-quality chopped chocolate

¼ cup granulated sugar

1 teaspoon pure vanilla extract

1 egg

½ cup all-purpose flour

¼ teaspoon salt

Pumpkin Cake Layer

½ cup all-purpose flour

1½ teaspoons Pumpkin Spice Mix (page 312)

½ teaspoon baking powder

¼ teaspoon baking soda

½ teaspoon salt

½ cup + 1 tablespoon pure pumpkin purée

6 tablespoons granulated sugar

¼ cup canola oil

1 large egg

Espresso Ganache

12 ounces (340 g/1¾ cups) white chocolate callets or good-quality chopped chocolate

6 tablespoons hot espresso

Meringue

1 batch Meringue (page 301)

We know that some of you count down the days to PSL (Pumpkin Spice Latte) season. Get it any time with these caffeine-infused blondies. While brainstorming for fall bar ideas one year, Nickey challenged the bakers to create a flavour profile that was reminiscent of all those warm and snuggly feelings associated with the popular PSL. The bakers set to work with different approaches involving freshly brewed coffee, shots of espresso, and instant coffee granules. In the end, we had two winners that gave the most pronounced coffee flavour in two different layers—instant coffee granules in the blondie base and fresh espresso in the top layer. We were presented with stunning layers, rich coffee flavour from the espresso ganache and coffee blondies, a spicy pumpkin centre, and a toasted pillowy meringue flourish on top that is a nod to a barista-worthy latte finish.

1. Preheat the oven to 350°F (180°C). Grease an 8-inch cake pan with canola oil cooking spray and line with parchment paper.

2. **Make the coffee blondie layer:** In a small bowl, stir together the hot water and instant coffee until the coffee granules are dissolved. Set aside.

3. In a large heat-resistant bowl, melt the butter and white chocolate in the microwave for 1 minute. Stir until all the chocolate is melted and then add the sugar and vanilla. Mix vigorously until the sugar is dissolved. Add the egg and mix well until smooth. Add the instant coffee mixture and mix until smooth.

4. Sift the flour and salt into the wet ingredients and stir until no dry flour remains and the batter is smooth. Scoop the batter into the prepared cake pan and bake for 18 to 20 minutes, or until a toothpick inserted into the centre of the cake comes out clean.

5. **Make the pumpkin cake layer:** Sift the flour, pumpkin spice mix, baking powder, baking soda, and salt into a large bowl and stir together.

6. In a medium bowl, mix the pumpkin purée, sugar, canola oil, and egg until the sugar is dissolved and no oily film remains around the edges. (CONTINUES)

DO AHEAD

These bars are best enjoyed at room temperature on the day they are made, but cut bars can be stored in an airtight container in the refrigerator for up to 2 days. The bars can be made ahead (without meringue) and stored, covered, in the refrigerator for up to 2 days before you cut and top them with meringue.

7. Add the wet ingredients to the dry ingredients and stir just until the ingredients are fully incorporated and no dry flour remains. Scoop the batter evenly over the baked blondie layer and, using a small offset palette knife, smooth out the top. Bake for 20 to 25 minutes, or until a toothpick inserted into the centre of the cake comes out clean. Allow to cool at room temperature for 2 to 3 hours.

8. Make the espresso ganache: In a medium heat-resistant bowl, heat the white chocolate and espresso in the microwave for 1 minute. Vigorously stir until the ingredients are incorporated and the mixture is glossy and smooth. If you see any lumps, heat in the microwave in 15-second intervals, stirring after each interval, until smooth. Pour the ganache over the cooled pumpkin cake layer, allowing the ganache to settle level. Store, uncovered, in the refrigerator for 1 hour to allow the ganache to firm up.

9. Top with meringue: Insert a hot knife between the parchment paper and the ganache to create clean edges as you remove the paper. Cut the bars using a warm chef's knife by dipping it into hot water and drying it on a clean kitchen towel. Wipe the knife between each cut to get nice clean cuts.

10. Fill a large piping bag fitted with a No. 126 petal icing tip with the meringue and pipe a latte swirl design on top of each bar. Turn the bar to face you diagonally so that it looks like a diamond. Hold the piping bag so that the thinner opening of the tip is at the top and the wider opening of the tip connects with the bar. Start by attaching the meringue to the top corner of the bar surface and begin building out a ridged diamond shape with horizontal lines. Weaving back and forth to meet the sides of the bar with even pressure, leave a ¼-inch border of exposed ganache around the edges. End this diamond-shaped swirl design with a point at the other end by releasing pressure on the piping bag and flicking your wrist down and away.

11. Toast the top of each meringue swirl with a handheld kitchen torch, being careful to avoid the ganache. Serve immediately, as these bars are best eaten on the day they are topped with meringue.

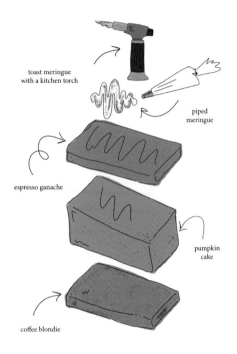

toast meringue with a kitchen torch

piped meringue

espresso ganache

pumpkin cake

coffee blondie

Cheesecake Stuffed Pumpkin Snickerdoodles

Cheesecake Filling

8 ounces (225 g/1 cup) cream cheese, room temperature
¼ cup packed dark brown sugar
1 tablespoon pure vanilla extract
¼ teaspoon salt

Pumpkin Snickerdoodle Cookies

3¼ cups all-purpose flour
2 teaspoons Pumpkin Spice Mix (page 312)
1½ teaspoons baking powder
½ teaspoon salt
1 cup unsalted butter
1 cup granulated sugar
½ cup packed dark brown sugar
¾ cup pure pumpkin purée
1 large egg
2 teaspoons pure vanilla extract

Coating

2 cups granulated sugar
2 tablespoons cinnamon

Have your favourite hot drink at the ready with these festive beauties. These soft pumpkin snickerdoodle cookies with a sweet vanilla centre and a crisp cinnamon sugar crust will transport you to a slower time. Give into that feeling and drift away on the fall harvest like a fluttering autumnal leaf in a crisp wind. The cheesecake filling and cookie dough can be made in advance, the filling left in the freezer, and the cookie dough in the refrigerator so that you can also bake a few cookies each day if you desire! We suggest eating these pumpkin cookies within the first day or two after baking, because they do get soggy over time.

1. Line 2 baking sheets that will fit in your refrigerator and freezer with parchment paper or silicone baking mats.

2. Make the cheesecake filling: In the bowl of a stand mixer fitted with the paddle attachment, beat the cream cheese on medium-high speed until smooth, 2 to 3 minutes. Scrape down the sides and bottom of the bowl. Add the brown sugar, vanilla, and salt. Cream the mixture on medium-high speed until smooth, 1 to 2 minutes.

3. Scoop 1-tablespoon portions of the filling onto one of the prepared baking sheets, leaving ample space between them so that they do not touch. Place the baking sheet in the freezer for at least 4 hours or overnight, until the cheesecake portions are frozen solid and easy to remove from the parchment paper or silicone mat.

4. Make the cookie dough: Sift the flour, pumpkin spice mix, baking powder, and salt into a small bowl and stir together.

5. In the bowl of a stand mixer fitted with the paddle attachment, cream the butter, granulated sugar, and brown sugar on medium-high speed until the mixture is pale and fluffy. Scrape down the sides and bottom of the bowl.

6. Add the pumpkin purée, egg, and vanilla and continue to cream on medium-high speed for 2 to 3 minutes until the mixture is smooth and has lightened in colour. Scrape down the sides and bottom of the bowl. (CONTINUES)

DO AHEAD

These cookies are best enjoyed on the day of baking. Store baked cookies in an airtight container at room temperature for up to 2 days.

You can make both components of the cookie ahead for easy assembly. Once the cheesecake filling portions are frozen solid, they can be transferred to

an airtight container and stored in the freezer for up to 1 month. The cookie dough portions can be stored, covered, in the refrigerator for up to 1 week.

7. Mix in the flour mixture on medium-low speed until fully incorporated. Scrape down the sides and bottom of the bowl. Mix the dough one last time on medium-high speed for 30 seconds to make sure it's evenly mixed. Scoop eighteen 3-tablespoon portions of cookie dough onto the second prepared baking sheet, leaving ample space between them so that they do not touch. Place the baking sheet, covered, in the refrigerator for at least 4 hours or overnight, until the dough is firm, not sticky, and easy to remove from the parchment paper or silicone mat.

8. Make the coating and finish the cookies: Preheat the oven to 350°F (180°F). Line 3 baking sheets with parchment paper or silicone baking mats.

9. In a medium bowl, mix together the sugar and cinnamon for the coating.

10. Remove the cookie dough from the refrigerator and the filling from the freezer. Using your hands, flatten the cold cookie dough balls, one portion at a time, into discs. Place a portion of frozen cheesecake filling in the centre of each disc and fold the edges of the dough around it. Once the cheesecake is covered and no bits are peeking through the dough, flatten the cookie slightly into a thick disc. Immediately, completely coat the dough in the cinnamon sugar.

11. Place 6 portions of coated dough, evenly spaced, on one of the prepared baking sheets and bake immediately. If you let the sugar-covered cookies sit for too long at room temperature, the sugar will start to melt and you'll get a glaze effect instead of sparkly cinnamon sugar. Bake for 16 to 20 minutes, or until the cookies are puffed and appear dry. Allow the cookies to cool on the baking sheet. Continue to assemble, coat, and bake the remaining cookies.

Sea Salt Brown Butter Pecan Cookies

1¼ cups all-purpose flour
1 tablespoon cornstarch
½ teaspoon baking soda
½ teaspoon cinnamon
½ cup + 2 tablespoons unsalted butter
½ cup granulated sugar
½ cup packed dark brown sugar
1 teaspoon sea salt
1 large egg
2 teaspoons pure vanilla extract
¾ cup chopped toasted pecans
24 whole pecan halves

Never underestimate the power of salt in a recipe; it helps improve overall flavour and encourages browning. And with this recipe, we were looking for all that wonderful browning and caramel flavour, so that's where the addition of brown butter comes in. Brown butter is butter that has been slowly heated until the milk solids in the butter separate from the fat and they cook until caramelized. The caramelized milk solids impart a nutty flavour and aroma to the butter. To achieve the perfect brown butter, remember that the butter will go from brown to burnt quickly, so stay close to the pan when you make it. These cookies are a combination of salty and sweet with a rich butter flavour that is heightened by scrumptious pecans. To keep these cookies at their peak brown-buttery goodness, put them in a sealed container shortly after cooling to keep them soft.

1. Preheat the oven to 350°F (180°C). Line 2 baking sheets with parchment paper or silicone baking mats.

2. Sift together the flour, cornstarch, baking soda, and cinnamon into a medium bowl and set aside.

3. In a small saucepan, melt the butter over medium heat, then bring to a boil, stirring frequently, until the milk solids in the butter have turned a deep brown and the butter has a pleasant nutty smell. Immediately pour the browned butter into a large bowl to stop the cooking process.

4. Whisk the granulated sugar, brown sugar, and salt into the warm browned butter until the mixture becomes smoother, the sugars start to dissolve, and no oily film remains around the edges. Whisk in the egg and vanilla, adding a little air, until the mixture is smooth and has lightened in colour.

5. Stir in the flour mixture and chopped pecans and mix until no dry flour remains. Do not overmix. The dough may look a little wet, but it will firm up as the butter cools.

6. Scoop twelve 1½-tablespoon portions of cookie dough onto each prepared baking sheet, leaving ample space between them. Top each cookie with 1 pecan half, gently pressing it into the dough to adhere. Bake, one sheet at a time, for 12 to 15 minutes, or until lightly browned all over. For chewier, gooey cookies, bake until the centre is risen but a little shiny and wet looking. Allow the cookies to cool completely on the baking sheet.

DO AHEAD

These cookies are best enjoyed on the day of baking but can be stored in an airtight container at room temperature for up to 5 days. You can scoop the cookie dough and store unbaked cookies in an airtight container in the refrigerator for up to 3 days before baking them. Place the chilled cookies, uncovered, on a prepared baking sheet with ample space between them. Let them come to room temperature for 30 minutes before baking.

Nutty Pumpkin Squares

Nutty Pumpkin Cake
1½ cups all-purpose flour
1½ teaspoons baking powder
¾ teaspoon baking soda
1½ teaspoons cinnamon
½ teaspoon salt
¼ teaspoon ground cloves
12 ounces (340 g/1¼ cups) pure
    pumpkin purée
1 cup + 2 tablespoons granulated
    sugar
¾ cup canola oil
3 large eggs
¾ cup roughly chopped toasted
    pecans
¼ cup Caramel (page 317)

Glaze
½ cup icing sugar
1 to 1½ tablespoons warm water

As the seasons change, these tender pumpkin cake squares with caramel pecans baked right in to create gooey pockets of pumpkin caramel are one of the first signs of fall at the bakery. When we start loading up our pantry with extra cases of pumpkin purée, cinnamon, cloves, nutmeg, cardamom, ginger, and allspice, all bakers recognize that pumpkin spice season has arrived. The neighbourhood surrounding the bakery is enveloped by the sweet, spicy pumpkin scent and we all settle into those "fall feelings." To us, these bars feel just like your favourite fall sweaters, cozy scarves, and walks in the leaves with a hot beverage. Peaceful, familiar, and full of potential for cuddles.

1. Preheat the oven to 350°F (180°C). Grease an 8-inch cake pan with canola oil cooking spray and line with parchment paper.

2. Make the cake: Sift the flour, baking powder, baking soda, cinnamon, salt, and cloves into a large bowl and stir together.

3. In a medium bowl, mix together the pumpkin purée, sugar, canola oil, and eggs until the sugar is dissolved and no oily film remains around the edges.

4. Add the wet ingredients to the dry ingredients and stir just until the ingredients are fully incorporated and no dry flour remains. Scoop the batter into the prepared cake pan and, using a small offset palette knife, smooth out the top.

5. In a small bowl, stir together the chopped pecans and caramel. Drop teaspoonfuls of caramel pecan mixture evenly over the batter to cover as much surface area as possible. Do not mix it in. Bake for 40 to 50 minutes, or until a toothpick inserted into the centre of the cake comes out clean. Allow the cake to cool at room temperature for 1 to 2 hours.

6. Make the glaze: In a small bowl, whisk together the icing sugar and water until smooth. Drizzle the glaze diagonally over the cooled cake in a zig-zag pattern.

7. Cut the squares using a serrated knife. Wipe the knife clean with a warm cloth between each cut to get nice clean cuts.

DO AHEAD

The cake can be baked ahead and stored, un-glazed and wrapped in beeswax or plastic wrap, at room temperature for up to 2 days.

You can make the caramel ahead and store it in an airtight container at room temperature for up to 1 month. The glazed squares are best enjoyed

at room temperature on the day of baking but can be stored in an airtight container at room temperature for up to 2 days.

Pumpkin Cheesecake Pie with Pecan Praline

DO AHEAD: Make the pecan praline at least 1 day ahead and store it in an airtight container at room temperature for up to 2 months. The graham crust can be baked ahead. Let the crust cook in the pie plate, then wrap the pie plate in beeswax or plastic wrap and store at room temperature for up to 1 week. The cheesecake filling (unbaked) can be made ahead and stored in an airtight container in the refrigerator for up to 2 weeks. Once assembled, store the finished pie, covered, in the refrigerator for up to 3 days.

Graham Crumb Crust
1 batch Graham Crumb Crust (page 299)

Cheesecake Filling
1 pound (450 g/2 cups) cream cheese, room temperature
½ cup packed dark brown sugar
1 tablespoon Pumpkin Spice Mix (page 312)
½ teaspoon salt
1 tablespoon bourbon
2 teaspoons pure vanilla extract
1 cup pure pumpkin purée
2 large eggs

For assembly
2 ounces (55 g/¼ cup) white chocolate callets or good-quality chopped chocolate
¼ batch Pecan Praline (page 318)

This bestselling pie has been a constant on our fall menu for more than a decade. On occasion, during our pie-making marathon that is Thanksgiving weekend, this pumpkin cheesecake pie has been even more popular than the classic pumpkin pie. It may have something to do with the silky-smooth cheesecake packed with warm spices and pumpkin flavour, the crunchy buttery praline, and the subtle sweet touch of white chocolate drizzle on top. You can make the cheesecake base up to one week in advance and store it, covered, in the refrigerator until you are ready to serve. Top the cheesecake with the white chocolate and pralines right before you serve the pie.

1. Make the graham crumb crust: Preheat the oven to 350°F (180°C). Firmly and evenly press the graham crumb crust mixture into the bottom and all the way up the sides of a 9-inch pie plate to form a pie shell. Bake for 10 to 15 minutes, or until light golden brown. Reduce the oven temperature to 300°F (150°C).

2. Make the cheesecake filling: In the bowl of a stand mixer fitted with the paddle attachment, beat the cream cheese on high speed until smooth and no lumps remain. Scrape down the sides and bottom of the bowl.

3. Add the brown sugar, pumpkin spice mix, salt, bourbon, and vanilla and beat on medium-high speed just until smooth and fully combined. Scrape down the sides and bottom of the bowl.

4. Add the pumpkin purée and beat on medium-high speed just until smooth and combined. Do not overbeat. It is important to keep air bubbles to a minimum. Scrape down the sides and bottom of the bowl.

5. Add the eggs and beat on medium-high speed just until fully incorporated and the batter is smooth. Pour the batter over the graham crumb crust. Bake for 30 to 40 minutes. Do not open the oven door during the baking time. The cheesecake is done when it looks nearly set and only a small circle in the centre appears when the pan is jiggled slightly. Turn off the heat and leave the cheesecake in the oven for 10 minutes. Allow the pie to cool to room temperature and then chill in the refrigerator for 1 hour; the centre will firm up as the pie cools.

6. Finish the pie: In a small heat-resistant bowl, melt the white chocolate in the microwave in 30-second intervals, stirring after each interval, 1 minute total. Fill a 12-inch piping bag fitted with a No. 3 round tip with the white chocolate. Pipe a crosshatch design by drizzling the chocolate in opposing diagonal zig-zag patterns.

7. Sprinkle the pecan praline over the wet chocolate, forming a 2-inch border of praline around the edge of the pie.

Apple Cinnamon Bundt Cake

Apple Cinnamon Bundt Cake

4 small or 3 medium Granny Smith
   apples (about 1 pound/450 g),
   peeled, cored, and cut into
   ¼-inch chunks (3 cups)
1 tablespoon lemon juice
½ tablespoon granulated sugar
1 tablespoon + 1 teaspoon cinnamon,
   divided
3 cups all-purpose flour
2 teaspoons baking powder
1 teaspoon baking soda
1 teaspoon salt
2 cups packed brown sugar
1⅓ cups canola oil
3 large eggs
1 teaspoon pure vanilla extract

Cinnamon Sugar Glaze

1 cup icing sugar
1 teaspoon cinnamon
2 tablespoons water, warm

As soon as this tender apple cinnamon Bundt cake starts caramelizing in your oven, the sweet, warm scent will have you waiting anxiously for the cake to cool so you can finish it with the sweet cinnamon sugar drizzle and dig in. We suggest bringing this cake to a fall gathering to share, but don't be surprised if people start requesting it as your signature contribution.

1. Preheat the oven to 350°F (180°C). Thoroughly grease a 10-inch Bundt pan with canola oil cooking spray.

2. Make the cake: In a medium bowl, toss together the chopped apples, lemon juice, granulated sugar, and 1 teaspoon of the cinnamon to coat. Set aside.

3. Sift the flour, remaining 1 tablespoon cinnamon, baking powder, baking soda, and salt into a large bowl and stir together using a whisk.

4. In another medium bowl, whisk together the brown sugar, canola oil, eggs, and vanilla until fully incorporated and pale in colour.

5. Add the wet mixture and apple mixture to the dry ingredients and, using a silicone spatula, mix until combined.

6. Scoop the batter into the prepared pan. Level the top of the batter with a small offset palette knife or spoon. Bake for 50 to 65 minutes, or until a toothpick inserted into the centre of the cake comes out clean. Allow the cake to cool in the pan for at least 15 minutes. Tap the bottom of the pan sharply against the counter to release the cake, invert the pan on a wire rack, and allow the cake to cool completely.

7. Make the cinnamon sugar glaze: In a small bowl, whisk together the icing sugar, cinnamon, and just enough warm water to form a thick yet pourable glaze. Using a spoon, drizzle the glaze over the top of the Bundt cake. Serve at room temperature.

DO AHEAD

This cake is best served within 12 hours after it is glazed. Store leftovers, covered, at room temperature for up to 3 days.

Turkey and Wild Rice Pie with Mashed Potato Topping

Cranberry Sauce

1 batch Cranberry Sauce (page 311)

Turkey Filling

3 pounds (1.35 kg) skin-on, bone-in
   turkey breasts and/or thighs
   (3 cups cubed cooked turkey)
1 tablespoon olive oil
1 teaspoon salt, more for seasoning
1 teaspoon freshly ground black
   pepper, more for seasoning
3 tablespoons unsalted butter
1 cup chopped leeks (white and
   light green parts only)
½ cup chopped celery
½ cup peeled and chopped carrots
¼ cup uncooked wild rice
2 cups Poultry Stock (page 319)
   or store-bought chicken stock
1 cup peeled and cubed sweet
   potatoes
1 cup cubed butternut squash
1 tablespoon chopped fresh thyme
2 tablespoons chopped fresh sage
1 cup whipping (35%) cream
2 tablespoons cornstarch
½ cup frozen kernel corn niblets
2 tablespoons Cranberry Sauce
   (recipe above), more for serving

Butter Pastry Dough

1 batch Butter Pastry (page 296)

Mashed Potato Topping

1 batch Mashed Potato Topping
   (page 300)

We aren't joking when we say that this pie is a whole Thanksgiving dinner rolled into one. It is loaded with roasted turkey, seasonal vegetables, nutty wild rice reminiscent of stuffing, mashed potatoes, and a creamy gravy with a touch of cranberry sauce. Creating this pie is a labour of love, so consider doubling the recipe and making a second pie or some mini pies for your freezer. This makes a wonderful easy weeknight meal when winter is creeping in and you want to return to those fall feelings again.

1. Make the turkey filling: Prepare the filling a day in advance of baking the pie. Preheat the oven to 375°F (190°C). Line a baking sheet with parchment paper.

2. Place the turkey on the prepared baking sheet. Rub the turkey with the olive oil, salt, and pepper to evenly distribute the oil and seasoning over the meat. Roast the turkey until it reaches an internal temperature of at least 170°F (77°C) and the juices run clear, 30 to 45 minutes. Allow the turkey to cool to room temperature. Remove all the meat from the bones and cube the turkey meat, set aside. Discard the skin but reserve the bones to make stock (Poultry Stock, page 319).

3. In a large heavy pot, heat the butter over medium heat. When the butter is melted, add the leeks, celery, and carrots and cook, stirring frequently, until the vegetables are soft and fragrant, 3 to 4 minutes. Add the wild rice and continue to cook, stirring frequently, for 1 minute to toast the rice. Add the stock, increase the heat to high, and bring to a boil, stirring occasionally. Once the stock is boiling, reduce the heat to medium-low to maintain a gentle boil and cook the rice, covered, for 35 minutes or until it is mostly cooked but still firm in the centre.

4. Add the sweet potatoes, squash, thyme, and sage, then increase the heat to high and bring to a boil. Once the mixture is boiling, reduce the heat to medium-low and maintain a gentle boil, covered, for 10 to 15 minutes, or until the sweet potatoes and squash are fork-tender. (CONTINUES)

DO AHEAD

You can make this pie up to 2 days ahead and store it, covered, in the refrigerator. To serve, warm it in a 325°F (160°C) oven for 50 to 60 minutes. The butter pastry can be made ahead, wrapped tightly in plastic wrap, and stored in the refrigerator for up to 1 week or in the freezer for up to 6 months. If frozen, thaw in the refrigerator overnight before using. The pie shell can be blind-baked and stored at room temperature, covered, for up to 24 hours. Store the cranberry sauce in an airtight container in the refrigerator for up to 1 month or in the freezer for up to 6 months. If frozen, thaw in the refrigerator overnight before using. The turkey filling must be made at least 1 day ahead and can be stored in an airtight container in the refrigerator for up to 3 days. Store leftovers, covered, in the refrigerator for up to 6 days.

5. In a small bowl, stir together the cream and cornstarch until the cornstarch is dissolved. Add this slurry to the filling and, stirring constantly, bring the mixture back to a boil over high heat and cook until thickened, 2 to 3 minutes.

6. Remove the pot from the heat and stir in the cubed turkey, corn, and the 2 tablespoons cranberry sauce. Season to taste with salt and pepper. You should slightly overseason the filling, as the pastry tends to absorb the salt in the filling as the pie bakes. Allow the filling to cool to room temperature and store, covered, in the refrigerator overnight to allow the flavours to mingle.

7. Make the pie crust: Preheat the oven to 400°F (200°C). Generously grease a 9-inch pie plate with canola oil cooking spray.

8. On a lightly floured work surface, roll out the butter pastry dough into an 11- to 12-inch circle, about ⅛ inch thick. Fold the dough in half to lift it without stretching and gently unfold it into the pie plate. Gently press the dough up the sides and into the bottom of the pan, making sure not to stretch the dough. Trim the dough as needed and crimp the edges of the pastry. Place the pie plate in the refrigerator to allow the pastry to relax and firm up a bit, at least 15 minutes.

9. Blind-bake the pie shell: Line the shell with parchment paper and fill it with 2 to 3 cups of dried beans or rice or fill it with pie weights. Bake for 20 to 25 minutes, or until the crust is a deep golden brown. Remove the parchment paper and beans, rice, or pie weights. Allow the pie shell to cool completely on a wire rack. The pie shell can sit at room temperature, covered, for up to 24 hours before you assemble the pie.

10. Assemble the pie: Preheat the oven to 400 °F (200°C). Scoop the turkey filling into the baked pie shell. Spoon the mashed potato topping over the filling, smoothing them into an even layer to seal in the filling. (Alternatively, you can fill a 16-inch piping bag fitted with a No. 825 star tip with the mashed potato topping and finish the pie by piping lines of star swirl border across the filling to cover the whole surface of the pie; see Buttercream and Whipped Cream Piping Styles, page 286, C). Place the pie on a baking sheet to catch any juices that bubble over and bake until the potatoes have golden brown edges and the filling is heated all the way through, 50 to 60 minutes.

11. Serve hot with the remaining cranberry sauce on the side.

Dressing up is fun, and often we need a reason not to take ourselves too seriously. Take a break from your everyday routine to throw a costume party and engage in some fantasy. Halloween parties can be kid friendly and lighthearted, a little scary and playfully gory, or the stuff of nightmares. Keep it light and fun with Chocolate Dipped Brownie Mummies (page 213), 3D Jack-O'-Lantern Cookies (page 217), or Monster Krispies (page 219). Or perhaps up the gore factor with Ghost Bread Dippers (page 229) served with a blood red pepper hummus dip. To keep people entertained, consider a pumpkin carving competition or costume contest with some sweet prizes of baked goodies to take home. Have fun with your table spread and carry the theme over to the serving platters and decor: use black tablecloths and top them with old yellowed lacy cloths for interest, set different-shaped clear bowls upside down as platforms with lights inside them, hit up a thrift store for a variety of candelabras, and be sure to grab some fake spider webs to string up and stretch over everything. The Pumpkin Spice Monster Cake (page 225) or PB&J Crunch Pie (page 223) makes an excellent centrepiece for the table. To give decor an old, dirty look, find some old mason jars and dry-brush them with black acrylic paints on the outside—the paint scrapes and peels off after use. Creating the ambiance is easy with a playful approach using light and sound. Keep things dim and mysterious but, depending on your guests, consider using LED candles instead of wax so you won't have to keep them lit all night or worry about safety. String up some light strands in oranges, reds, and purple and maybe even include a strobe light or two facing different corners of a room. Make a playlist with some spooky retro or ambient scary soundtracks to enhance the experience; just be sure it doesn't drown out conversations. Cue up some classic horror flicks on a TV or computer, run them all party long as a visual effect, but keep them on mute so they don't compete with the music or conversation.

Halloween

Chocolate Dipped Brownie Mummies

Royal Icing (for the eyeballs and mummy wrap)

1½ batches (4½ cups) Royal Icing
(page 295)

4 to 5 drops black gel food colouring

Brownie

1 cup cocoa powder, sifted

2 cups granulated sugar

½ teaspoon salt

1 cup unsalted butter, melted and warm

2 large eggs

1 tablespoon pure vanilla extract

½ cup buttermilk, room temperature

1 cup all-purpose flour, sifted

For dipping

3½ pounds (1.5 kg/7½ cups) milk chocolate couverture callets (we use Callebaut)

Halloween is a fun time for all of us at the bakery, especially for the front-of-house staff when they witness the sheer joy of neighbourhood kids getting their first glimpse of our offerings. These mummies are a favourite among the young ones for two reasons: the fudge brownie coated in couverture chocolate is to die for and the decor is approachable for kids of all ages. They tend to peel off the googly eyes first and then devour the entire mummy in one sitting. Not only are these portable and long-lasting for easy gift giving, but they are a fun and spooky way to celebrate with your favourite ghouls. Pair these with some dry hot chocolate mix for a spooky yet sweet party favour. These Halloween treats take three days total to make but don't require much work on each day; they just require some planning. You'll need sixteen ice pop sticks or 4½-inch wooden skewers.

1. Line a baking sheet with parchment paper or a very clean silicone baking mat.

2. Make the mummy eyeballs: Once you have made the royal icing, transfer 1½ cups to a small bowl to make your eyeballs. Reserve the remaining royal icing to create the bandages for your mummies on the next day (step 17); store in an airtight container at room temperature.

3. Thin the royal icing with 1 to 2 teaspoons of water until it is thin enough to settle flat when dropped on a surface but not as thin as a flooding consistency (see Royal Icing Piping Styles, page 288, Stable Flooding Texture K). Fill a piping bag fitted with a No. 4 round tip with 1 cup of the royal icing.

4. Mix the black food colouring into the remaining ½ cup royal icing until you have a deep black icing.

5. Pipe thirty-two ¼- to ¾-inch white circles on the prepared baking sheet in a variety of sizes.

6. Fill a piping bag fitted with a No. 2 round tip with the black royal icing. Pipe a small dot in the centre of each "eyeball" to form a "pupil."

7. Allow the eyeballs to dry completely, uncovered, at room temperature in a dry area overnight. Once hardened, the eyeballs should be easy to lift off the prepared baking sheet.

8. Make the brownie: Preheat the oven to 350°F (180°C). Grease a 9- × 13-inch cake pan with canola oil cooking spray and line with parchment paper. (CONTINUES)

DO AHEAD

Make the eyeballs at least 2 days ahead and, once they harden, store them in an airtight container at room temperature for up to 6 months. You can make the brownies ahead

and store them wrapped tightly in beeswax or plastic wrap for up to 3 days before cutting them. Dip the brownies in chocolate and finish them with the royal icing bandages at

least 1 day ahead so that they can dry. Store the finished brownie mummies individually packaged or in an airtight container at room temperature for up to 1 week.

9. In a large bowl, whisk together the cocoa, granulated sugar, salt, and warm butter until the mixture is smooth and no oily film remains around the edges.

10. Vigorously whisk in the eggs and vanilla, incorporating a little air, until the mixture is smooth and has lightened slightly in colour. Whisk in the buttermilk until the mixture is smooth.

11. Stir in the flour and mix just until no dry flour remains and the batter is smooth. Pour the batter into the prepared pan and smooth out the surface with an offset palette knife. Bake for 30 to 35 minutes, or until a toothpick inserted into the centre of the brownie comes out clean. You need the brownie to be completely cooked and not fudgy in the middle. Allow the bar to cool to room temperature, then wrap the entire pan in beeswax or plastic wrap and let sit at room temperature overnight so it is firm enough to dip the next day.

12. Continue making the mummies: Cut the brownies into sixteen 2¼- × 3¼-inch rectangles. Insert the wooden skewers into the shorter end of the brownies, pushing them halfway into each brownie, making sure they are secure (see photos A to C).

13. Start decorating the mummies: Line 2 baking sheets with parchment paper or very clean silicone baking mats. You will need a deep, tall (4-cup) container. Make sure it is spotless and buff it with a clean kitchen towel to remove any oils. Tempering chocolate is time sensitive, so make sure you have your prepared brownies on sticks, lined baking sheets, eyeballs, and deep, tall container ready and within reach before you begin to temper the chocolate (step 14).

14. Prepare the tempered chocolate following the instructions on page 305. Once the chocolate is tempered, it is important to work quickly before the chocolate hardens. Pour the tempered chocolate into the deep, tall container, leaving a 1-inch headspace. The container won't hold all the chocolate, so you will need to refill the container as you coat the brownies.

15. Holding the stick firmly, insert a brownie all the way into the chocolate until it's completely covered. Slowly pull the brownie back out of the chocolate, tilting it as you go to gently scrape the excess chocolate off the bottom of the brownie (see photo D). Place the brownie top side up on one of the prepared baking sheets and add the eyeballs while the chocolate is still wet (see photo E). Repeat to coat the remaining brownies and attach the eyeballs, evenly spacing the brownies on the baking sheets. If your chocolate is setting up too quickly and you don't feel you have time to add the eyeballs, you can attach them later with royal icing.

16. Allow the chocolate to firm up fully for 1 to 2 hours before adding the royal icing wrappings.

17. Finish decorating the mummies: Fill a piping bag fitted with No. 46 basket weave tip with the reserved white royal icing. Position a baking sheet of chocolate brownies in front of you and pipe "mummy wrappings," criss-crossing horizontally on angles across the brownie and around the eyeballs (see photo F). Add some diagonal lines too, being sure to avoid covering the eyeballs (see Royal Icing Piping Styles, page 288, Stiff Texture I). Enjoy immediately with soft icing or allow the mummies to dry overnight, uncovered, at room temperature until the icing has hardened.

A

B

C

D

E

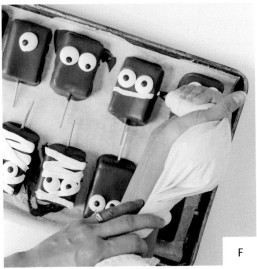

F

3D Jack-O'-Lantern Cookies Ⓥ

Vanilla Dough

1 cup soft vegan margarine, cold
  (we use Crystal)
½ cup granulated sugar
2 teaspoons pure vanilla extract
2½ cups all-purpose flour
½ teaspoon salt
12 to 20 drops orange gel food
  colouring (optional)

Chocolate Dough

½ cup soft vegan margarine, cold
  (we use Crystal)
¼ cup granulated sugar
1 teaspoon pure vanilla extract
1 cup all-purpose flour
¼ cup cocoa powder, sifted
¼ teaspoon salt

These striking orange and black cookies are so fun to make! They make an excellent party activity for any guests since they don't involve flour or water to form them. Just make sure everyone washes their hands first. You can create any shapes you like with the dough—let your imagination soar. It should be similar in texture to playdough and will stick easily to itself. Do not use flour to roll it out but feel free to use a variety of cookie cutters and layering techniques to create your own 3D edible art. Shapes can be ½- to ¾-inch tall maximum and will flatten slightly as they bake. Make sure that, whatever shapes you are making, the cookies are all relatively the same size and height for even baking. Leave 1 to 2 inches between the cookies on the trays so that they can expand while baking.

1. Make the vanilla dough: In the bowl of a stand mixer fitted with the paddle attachment, cream the margarine, sugar, and vanilla on medium-high speed for 3 to 4 minutes until the mixture is light and fluffy and has increased slightly in volume. Scrape down the sides and bottom of the bowl.

2. Add the flour, salt, and food colouring (if using). Mix on low speed, increasing to medium-high, until the flour is fully incorporated and the dough is orange (if using food colouring).

3. Shape the dough into a ball and wrap it in beeswax or plastic wrap. Refrigerate for at least 1 hour.

4. Make the chocolate dough: In the bowl of a stand mixer fitted with the paddle attachment, cream the margarine, sugar, and vanilla on medium-high speed for 3 to 4 minutes until the mixture is light and fluffy and has increased slightly in volume. Scrape down the sides and bottom of the bowl.

5. Add the flour, cocoa, and salt. Mix on low speed, increasing to medium-high, until the flour is fully incorporated and the dough is brown.

6. Shape the dough into a ball and wrap in beeswax or plastic wrap. Refrigerate for at least 1 hour.

7. Make the cookies: Preheat the oven to 350°F (180°C). Line 2 to 3 baking sheets with parchment paper or silicone baking mats.

8. Divide the vanilla dough into 20 equal balls. Each ball will form a cookie.

9. Roll the balls into 12-inch logs. Cut the logs into 6 equal pieces and roll each piece into 2½- to 3-inch logs with tapered, pinched ends. They should look like elongated footballs or batards. (CONTINUES)

DO AHEAD

You can make the cookie doughs ahead and store them separately, tightly wrapped in beeswax or plastic wrap, for up to 3 days. Store the baked cookies in an airtight container at room temperature for up to 2 weeks.

HALLOWEEN

217

10. For each cookie, assembling one at a time, line up the 6 pieces of dough alongside each other, pinch the ends together, then tuck them into the top and bottom of the pumpkin, forming a rippled classic pumpkin shape. You will end up with a rough sphere. Using a bench scraper, transfer the cookie to one of the prepared baking sheets. Form the top and bottom of the pumpkin by pinching it slightly. The cookies don't change shape much as they bake, so make sure you are happy with the shape of your pumpkin. Repeat to form the remaining cookie bases, evenly spaced on the baking sheets.

11. Using your fingers, pinch off a small amount (about 1 teaspoon) of chocolate dough and form it into a triangle shape to make the stem for a pumpkin cookie. Press the stem into the top of a pumpkin. Repeat until all the pumpkins have a stem.

12. Using a paring knife or your fingers, form faces on your jack-o'-lantern with the chocolate dough. Any leftover dough can be shaped into bats, moons, or stars, just like playdough. The cookies must be about the same size on each baking sheet for even baking.

13. Bake, one sheet at a time, for 18 to 22 minutes, or until the cookies are dry and puffy. Allow the cookies to cool completely on the baking sheets before moving them. They are very delicate when first out of the oven. These cookies are best enjoyed on the day of baking.

Monster Krispies

Royal Icing
(for the eyeballs and faces)

1 batch (3 cups) Royal Icing
(page 295)

4 to 5 drops black or purple gel
food colouring

½ cup Halloween sprinkles

Monster Krispies Base

¼ cup unsalted butter,
room temperature

9 ounces (250 g) Marshmallows
(¼ batch; page 314) or
store-bought

1 teaspoon pure vanilla extract
(only if using store-bought
marshmallows)

8 to 12 drops gel food colouring
in preferred colour

6 cups Rice Krispies cereal

For dipping

1 pound, 9 ounces (700 g/3½ cups)
milk chocolate couverture callets
(we use Callebaut)

Once you have dipped these monster heads in the tempered chocolate and added the hair, these are a great build-your-own activity for any age, with yummy, ooey-gooey edible take-home results. Make separate trays of different-coloured rice krispy treats a day in advance and create your royal icing ahead of the gathering as well. Get your guests involved and creative by piping and decorating personalities on their monster krispies. Folks will love applying their own jagged smiles and gnarly eyebrows to the krispies. Devour at your own delicious risk!

1. Line a baking sheet with parchment paper or a very clean silicone baking mat.

2. Make the eyeballs: Once you have made the royal icing, transfer 1½ cups to a small bowl to make your eyeballs. Reserve the remaining royal icing to create the faces for your monsters on the next day (step 16); store in an airtight container at room temperature.

3. Thin the royal icing with 1 to 2 teaspoons of water until it is thin enough to settle flat when piped on a surface but not as thin as a flooding consistency (see Royal Icing Piping Styles, page 288, Stable Flooding Texture K). Fill a piping bag fitted with a No. 4 round tip with 1 cup of the royal icing.

4. Mix the black or purple food colouring into the remaining ½ cup royal icing until you have a deep coloured icing.

5. Pipe 24 to 30 ¼- to ¾-inch white circles on the prepared baking sheet in a variety of sizes.

6. Fill a piping bag fitted with a No. 2 round tip with the coloured royal icing. Pipe a small dot in the middle of each "eyeball" to form a "pupil" (see Royal Icing Piping Styles, page 288, Stable Flooding Texture K).

7. Allow the eyeballs to dry completely, uncovered, at room temperature in a dry area overnight. Once hardened, the eyeballs should be easy to lift off the prepared baking sheet.

8. Make the monster krispies: Grease a 9- × 13-inch baking dish with canola oil cooking spray and line with parchment paper. (CONTINUES)

DO AHEAD

Make the eyeballs at least 2 days ahead and, once they harden, store them in an airtight container at room temperature for up to 6 months. You can make the krispie base ahead and store it wrapped tightly in beeswax or plastic wrap for up to 2 days before cutting. Dip the krispies in chocolate and finish them with the royal icing details at least 1 day ahead so that they can dry fully. Store the finished monster krispies individually packaged or in an airtight container at room temperature for up to 4 days.

9. In a medium heat-resistant bowl, melt the butter and marshmallows in the microwave for 2 to 3 minutes, stirring after 2 minutes and continuing to heat only if the mixture is not fully melted. (Alternatively, you can heat in a medium pot on the stovetop over low heat, stirring frequently, until melted.) Once melted, stir in the vanilla (if using) and food colouring until the mixture is an even colour.

10. Place the Rice Krispies in a large bowl. Pour the marshmallow mixture over the cereal and fold gently with a silicone spatula, trying not to crush the cereal. Gently press the mixture evenly into the prepared dish. Wet your hands slightly or spray them lightly with canola oil cooking spray and press the mixture down to flatten the surface as evenly as possible. (Alternatively, you can cover the mixture with parchment paper and use the bottom of a pan to press the mixture down.)

11. Allow the krispies to cool in the pan to room temperature. Wrap the entire pan in beeswax or plastic wrap and allow the krispies to firm up at room temperature overnight. The next day, cut the krispies into nine 3- × 4-inch rectangles.

12. Start decorating the monster krispies: Line 2 baking sheets with parchment paper or very clean silicone baking mats. You will need a deep, tall (4-cup) container. Make sure it is spotless and buff it with a clean towel to remove any oils. Tempering chocolate is time sensitive, so make sure you have your cut krispies, lined baking sheets, eyeballs, and a deep, tall container ready and within reach before you begin to temper the chocolate (step 13).

13. Prepare the tempered chocolate following the instructions on page 305. Once the chocolate is tempered, it is important to work quickly before the chocolate hardens. Pour the tempered chocolate into the deep, tall container, leaving a 1-inch headspace. The container won't hold all the chocolate, so you will need to refill the container as you coat the krispies.

14. Holding a krispie firmly at one end, insert the head of the monster into the chocolate until it's about one-third covered. Slowly pull the krispie back out of the chocolate, tilting it as you go to gently scrape the excess chocolate off the bottom of the krispie. Place the monster top side up on one of the prepared baking sheets and add the eyeballs and sprinkles while the chocolate is still wet. Repeat to coat the remaining krispies and attach the eyeballs and sprinkles, evenly spacing the krispies on the baking sheets. If your chocolate is setting up too quickly and you don't feel you have time to add the eyeballs, you can attach them later with royal icing.

15. Allow the chocolate to firm up fully for 1 to 2 hours before adding the royal icing details.

16. Finish decorating the monster krispies: Colour the reserved royal icing in the colour(s) of your choosing. Fill a piping bag fitted with a No. 4 round tip with the icing. (If you are using multiple colours, you'll need a piping bag for each.) Position a baking sheet of monsters in front of you and pipe mouths, eyebrows, and scars on the krispies (see Royal Icing Piping Styles, page 288, Stiff Texture H). Enjoy immediately with soft icing or allow the monsters to dry overnight, uncovered, at room temperature until the icing has hardened.

PB&J Crunch Pie Ⓥ

Fondant Spider
1 Fondant Spider (page 292)

Pie Base
1 cup smooth peanut butter
   (sweetened, not natural)
⅓ cup white corn syrup
½ cup granulated sugar
2 teaspoons pure vanilla extract
3 cups Rice Krispies cereal
⅓ cup Raspberry Jam (page 310)
   or store-bought

PB Mousse
6 tablespoons coconut oil
¾ cup smooth peanut butter
   (sweetened, not natural)
1½ cups icing sugar

Topping
9 ounces (260 g/1½ cups)
   vegan semi-sweet chocolate
   callets or good-quality chopped
   chocolate
⅓ cup unsweetened almond milk
¼ cup peanut butter
   (sweetened, not natural)

This no-bake pie is packed with a peanut butter and raspberry jam punch surrounded by a Rice Krispie peanut butter pie shell, surprisingly vegan and worth disturbing a spider to snag a slice. It seemed only fitting to invite our eight-legged friend to the party, and you'll be surprised by how easily a peanut butter and chocolate ganache web design can be achieved by swirling and pulling a toothpick through the topping, creating a home for our spider. Below that web design sits a thick and juicy layer of raspberry jam atop peanut butter mousse that will spill out in epic Halloween effect when cutting each slice. While slicing, be careful not to upset the spider, but if she gives you too much trouble, you can eat that sugary arachnid.

1. Make the pie base: In a large heat-resistant bowl, heat the peanut butter, corn syrup, and sugar in the microwave in 1-minute intervals, stirring after each interval, until the sugar is fully incorporated and the peanut butter is melted. Stir in the vanilla; this addition should smooth out the mixture significantly and make it more pourable.

2. In a large bowl, combine the peanut butter mixture and Rice Krispies and stir together until all the cereal is evenly coated. Using wet hands to prevent the mixture from sticking, press the mixture gently into the bottom and all the way up the sides of a 9-inch pie plate to form a pie shell.

3. Spread a thick layer of raspberry jam over the bottom of the crust but not up the sides.

4. Make the PB mousse layer: In a large heat-resistant bowl, heat the coconut oil and peanut butter in the microwave for 1 minute until melted. Vigorously stir until the ingredients are incorporated and the mixture is glossy and smooth. If you see any lumps, heat in the microwave in 15-second intervals, stirring after each interval, until smooth.

5. Vigorously whisk the icing sugar into the melted coconut oil and peanut butter mixture until no lumps remain and the sugar has dissolved, 2 to 3 minutes. Pour the mixture evenly over the jam layer in the pie shell and refrigerate, uncovered, for 30 minutes, or until the mousse layer is firm. (CONTINUES)

DO AHEAD

Make the fondant spider at least 2 days ahead and allow it to dry, uncovered, at room temperature in a dry area for 2 to 3 days. Once completely dry, you can store the spider in an airtight container at room temperature for up to 6 months. The raspberry jam can be made ahead and stored in an airtight container in the refrigerator for up to 1 month or in the freezer for up to 4 months. If frozen, thaw in the refrigerator overnight before using. Store the finished pie in an airtight container at room temperature for up to 7 days.

6. Finish the pie: In a medium heat-resistant bowl, heat the semi-sweet chocolate and almond milk in the microwave for 1 minute, until the chocolate is melted. Vigorously stir until the ingredients are incorporated and the mixture is glossy and smooth. If you see any lumps, heat in the microwave in 15-second intervals, stirring after each interval, until smooth.

7. In a small heat-resistant bowl, heat the peanut butter in the microwave for 30 seconds or until melted. Fill a 12-inch piping bag fitted with a No. 2 round tip with the melted peanut butter.

8. Pour the melted chocolate mixture evenly over the PB mousse layer and, using the back of a spoon or a small offset palette knife, spread it out level. Pipe even lines of melted peanut butter over the chocolate in a tight swirl pattern, starting from the outer edge. Using a sharp knife or a toothpick, drag the pointed end from the centre of the pie through the rows of the swirl pattern to create a spider web pattern.

9. Refrigerate for 60 minutes to allow the chocolate layer to set up. When firm, place the fondant spider on top and serve.

Pumpkin Spice Monster Cake

Fondant Eyes and Horns
1 batch Fondant Eyes and Horns
   (page 291)

Pumpkin Spice Cake
2 cups all-purpose flour
2 teaspoons baking powder
1 teaspoon baking soda
½ teaspoon salt
1 tablespoon cinnamon
1 tablespoon Pumpkin Spice Mix
   (page 312)
¼ teaspoon ground cloves
15 ounces (425 g/2 cups) pure
   pumpkin purée
1½ cups packed brown sugar
1 cup canola oil
4 large eggs, room temperature

Simple Syrup
1 batch Simple Syrup (page 316)

Vanilla Bean Buttercream
1 batch Vanilla Bean Buttercream
   (page 293)

Maple Cream Cheese Icing
½ batch Dreamy Cream Cheese
   Icing (page 295)
2 tablespoons pure maple syrup
½ teaspoon maple extract

For assembly
2 to 4 drops gel food colouring of
   your choice (at least 2 colours)

Cute and furry or dangerously scary monster?! Take your imagination in all directions with this monster cake by positioning the decorative details in different places, using different colours, and incorporating your own creative icing details to make different hair textures or even a gaping mouth. Whether you choose cute or scary, the pumpkin spice cake interior is really what we are here for. Four soft, spicy pumpkin cake layers with vanilla bean buttercream for stability and three layers of our maple cream cheese icing are truly the main event. This cake is a seasonal favourite and will be as good as gone and banished from your home by the end of your party; not a single slice of pumpkin cake will be left.

1. Preheat the oven to 350°F (180°C). Grease two 6-inch round cake pans with canola oil cooking spray and line the bottoms with parchment paper circles.

2. Make the pumpkin spice cake: Into the bowl of a stand mixer, sift the flour, baking powder, baking soda, salt, cinnamon, pumpkin spice mix, and cloves, then whisk together to fully combine.

3. In a medium bowl, whisk together the pumpkin purée, brown sugar, canola oil, and eggs until the sugar is dissolved, up to 5 minutes. Rub a bit of the mixture between 2 fingertips. It should feel smooth, not gritty.

4. Add the wet ingredients to the dry ingredients in the bowl of the stand mixer. Using the paddle attachment, beat on low speed until almost combined. Scrape down the sides and bottom of the bowl. Beat on medium-low speed until the batter is combined and the dry ingredients are fully incorporated, 1 to 2 minutes. Do not overmix.

5. Divide the batter evenly among the prepared pans and, using a small offset palette knife, smooth out the tops. Bake the cakes at the same time, spacing the pans on the middle rack for even baking, for 50 to 60 minutes, or until a toothpick inserted into the centres of the cakes comes out clean. Allow the cakes to cool in the pans on a wire rack for 30 minutes. Remove the cakes from the pans, leaving the parchment paper circles on the bottoms, and cool completely on the wire rack. (CONTINUES)

DO AHEAD

Make the fondant pieces at least 3 days ahead and allow them to dry, uncovered, at room temperature in a dry area for 3 days. Once completely dry, you can store them in an airtight container at room temperature for up to 6 months. It is best to make the components of this cake ahead and then assemble the layered cake on the day you wish to serve it.

The cake can be baked and stored, wrapped in beeswax or plastic wrap, at room temperature for up to 3 days. The simple syrup can be stored in an airtight container in the refrigerator for up to 3 weeks. You can make the buttercream and cream cheese icing ahead. Store the buttercream in an airtight container in the refrigerator for up to 2 months or in the freezer

for up to 6 months. Store the cream cheese icing in the refrigerator for up to 1 month or in the freezer for up to 2 months. If either is refrigerated, let soften at room temperature before using. If either is frozen, thaw in the refrigerator overnight before using. The assembled cake can be stored, covered, in the refrigerator for up to 4 days.

HALLOWEEN

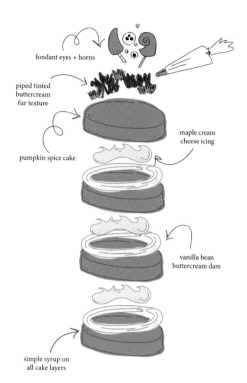

fondant eyes + horns

piped tinted
buttercream
fur texture

pumpkin spice cake

maple cream
cheese icing

vanilla bean
buttercream dam

simple syrup on
all cake layers

6. Make the Maple Cream Cheese Icing: In the bowl of a stand mixer fitted with the paddle attachment, beat the dreamy cream cheese icing on medium-high speed for 1 to 2 minutes. Scrape down the bottom and sides of the bowl. Add the maple syrup and maple extract and beat on medium-high speed for 2 minutes until the icing is smooth.

7. Assemble and decorate the cake—prepare the cake layers: Trim the domes off the tops of the baked cake layers and cut the cakes in half horizontally. Follow the cake assembly and decorating instructions on page 283, step 1, photo A.

8. Stack the cake: Stack the cake on an 8-inch cake board or serving plate following the instructions on page 283, step 2, photos B to E, moistening each layer with 4 tablespoons of simple syrup, using vanilla bean buttercream, and adding ¼ cup of maple cream cheese icing to each layer within a dam of vanilla buttercream.

9. Crumb coat the cake: Empty the piping bag of buttercream into the mixing bowl and divide the remaining buttercream, leaving two-thirds in the mixing bowl for your main colour and placing one-third in a small bowl for your accent colour. Using a whisk, add 2 to 4 drops of food colouring to each bowl and mix until fully combined and fluffy.

10. Crumb coat the top and sides of the stacked cake with a thin layer of the main colour buttercream and place the cake, uncovered, in the refrigerator for 15 minutes (follow instructions on page 284, step 3, photos F and G).

11. Decorate the cake: Fill two 12-inch piping bags fitted with a No. 288 grass tip (one for each buttercream colour). Adhere the eyes to the front side of the cake with a little bit of buttercream applied with a small step pallete knife and place the horns on top of the cake. Begin with the accent colour to create small and large dot variations around the side and top of the cake. Next, fill all the empty spaces with the main colour, starting by outlining the horns and eyes and working your way out from these points. Chill the cake, uncovered, in the refrigerator for 30 minutes before bringing it back to room temperature to serve.

Ghost Bread Dippers ⓥ

Pizza Dough
1 batch Pizza Dough (page 303)

Toppings
Warm water, for brushing
2 tablespoons sesame seeds
2 tablespoons caraway seeds
3 tablespoons flaky sea salt
   (we use Maldon)

For serving
2 cups hummus, tapenade,
   guacamole, or similar dip

When Josie was first learning to bake bread during her apprenticeship, her favourite things to make were the giant leaf-shaped loaves called fougasse. These are similar to focaccia, but the dough is slashed and manipulated by hand to make it look like an ear of wheat. Josie found it so fun to slice and stretch the dough into elaborate shapes and watch it transform as it rose and baked. Capture the same fun here and go wild with ghost shapes—scary or cutesy, it's up to you. We've made these dippers with caraway seeds and sesame seeds, but you can swap them for poppy seeds, flax seeds, or even everything bagel seasoning.

1. Preheat the oven to 400°F (200°C). Line 3 baking sheets with parchment paper or silicone baking mats. If using refrigerated pizza dough, make sure it has come up to room temperature.

2. On a lightly floured work surface, roll out the pizza dough to about ¼-inch thickness. Move the dough around and check underneath it frequently to make sure it is not sticking to the work surface, dusting lightly with more flour as needed. Using a 4-inch, ghost-shaped cookie cutter, cut out 24 ghosts and place 8 on each prepared baking sheet, evenly spaced. To make each ghost unique, use a small paring knife (or No. 825 round tip) to cut eye holes and a mouth and use your hands to stretch the dough as you place it on the baking sheets.

3. If there is any flour on top of your ghosts, brush it off with a dry pastry brush. Use a pastry brush to lightly brush the surface of each ghost with warm water. Sprinkle sesame seeds over 8 ghosts and caraway seeds over 8 ghosts. Sprinkle flaky sea salt over all the ghosts. Bake for 10 to 15 minutes, or until the ghosts are a light golden brown. Allow the ghosts to cool completely on the baking sheets. Serve with the dip of your choice.

DO AHEAD

These dippers are best enjoyed on the day they are baked. The pizza dough can be made ahead and stored, covered with beeswax or plastic wrap, in the refrigerator for up to 36 hours.

Allow chilled dough to come to room temperature, covered, for 45 to 60 minutes before rolling it out. Store baked dippers in an airtight container at room temperature for up to 1 day.

HALLOWEEN

Pierogi Pizza

Bechamel Sauce
3 tablespoons unsalted butter
3 tablespoons all-purpose flour
1⅔ cups whole milk, cold, divided
½ teaspoon dried thyme
½ teaspoon salt
¼ teaspoon freshly ground
    black pepper

Pizza Dough
½ batch Pizza Dough (page 303)

Toppings
1 large Yukon gold potato, peeled
    and very thinly sliced with a
    mandoline
½ large leek (white and light green
    parts only), cleaned, trimmed,
    and thinly sliced on a mandoline
1 cup (4 ounces/115 g) shredded
    mozzarella cheese
½ cup (2 ounces/57 g) shredded
    old cheddar cheese
6 to 8 slices uncooked bacon

To finish
1 cup full-fat sour cream
1 green onion, thinly sliced
½ teaspoon flaky sea salt
    (we use Maldon)
Freshly ground black pepper

Before sealing the deal on their bakery co-ownership, Josie and Nickey got together to create different labour-intensive recipes to test their compatibility as teammates outside of the classroom. Pierogies were their first experiment; from creating a shopping list and gathering ingredients, to cooperating in the same space, organizing the many steps, and handcrafting the pillowy potato and cheddar pockets together, they had a natural ebb and flow. Not to mention that their collaborative efforts made for an exceptional pierogi meal in the end. This Pierogi Pizza pays homage to their earliest milestone in 2007, when they embarked on shared bakery dreams. This is a deconstructed pizza version but a much-requested addition to our pizza bun lineup in the shop.

1. Make the bechamel sauce: In a medium pot, melt the butter over medium heat. Once the butter is melted, mix in the flour with a wooden spoon or silicone spatula until smooth. Continue to cook the mixture, stirring constantly while the mixture bubbles, 1 minute.

2. Add ⅓ cup of the milk and stir hard until the mixture has thickened to a stiff paste. Add another ⅓ cup of the milk and continue to stir until the paste is smooth again. Increase the heat to medium-high and continue to add about ⅓ cup of milk at a time until all the milk is added and the mixture has thickened and is smooth. Allow to boil for 5 minutes, stirring occasionally, to cook out the starch.

3. Stir in the thyme, salt, and pepper. Taste, and adjust seasonings if needed. You want it to be slightly overseasoned to help season the potatoes on the pizza. Allow the sauce to cool, covered, in the refrigerator until it is cold, at least 2 hours.

4. Make the pizza: Preheat the oven to 450°F (230°C). Lightly grease a 13- × 18-inch baking sheet with canola oil or olive oil.

5. If using refrigerated pizza dough, make sure it has come up to room temperature. With oiled hands, patiently stretch the dough into the shape of your baking sheet. You may need to let the dough rest for a few minutes midway so that it can relax.

6. Cover the surface of the dough with the cooled bechamel sauce, leaving a ½-inch border of exposed dough around the edge.

DO AHEAD

The pizza dough can be made ahead and stored, covered with beeswax or plastic wrap, in the refrigerator for up to 36 hours. You can make the bechamel sauce ahead and store it in an airtight container in the refrigerator for up to 1 week. The sauce needs to cool for at least 2 hours before assembling the pizza, but we like to make it a day ahead so that it has time to develop more flavour. The pizza is best served hot from the oven, but it can be stored, covered, at room temperature for up to 12 hours or in an airtight container in the refrigerator for up to 2 days. Reheat in a 350°F (180°C) oven for 5 minutes.

7. Layer the sliced potatoes over the bechamel sauce, overlapping slightly, until the entire surface is covered. Sprinkle the sliced leeks evenly over the potatoes. Sprinkle the shredded mozzarella and cheddar cheeses evenly over the leeks, avoiding the exposed border. Lay the bacon in whole strips over the cheese, covering as much of the surface as possible.

8. Bake the pizza for 20 to 25 minutes, or until the dough is golden brown around the edges and the cheese is golden, melted, and bubbling. Allow the pizza to rest for 5 to 10 minutes.

9. Fill a 12-inch piping bag fitted with a No. 4 round tip with the sour cream. Pipe the sour cream over the pizza in a zig-zag pattern. Sprinkle the green onions over the pizza and finish with the flaky sea salt. Add pepper to taste.

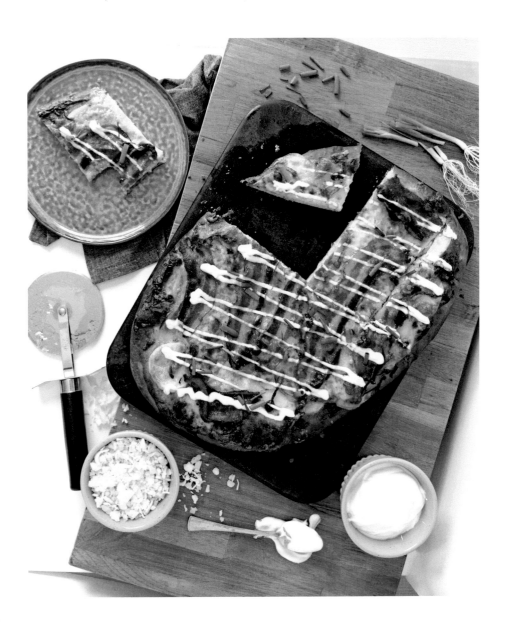

The winter season is by far the most gleeful season at the bakery. We all just love the mass production of cookies—it makes us all feel like little elves in Santa's workshop spreading joy and cheer. There are so many wonderful things to celebrate in December, with more than a dozen cultural and religious holidays filling the month and spilling into January. Everyone is busy producing, packing, and selling thousands of cookies, and it is an impressive logistical feat that took us years to master. Hosting a holiday party for a crowd requires the same dedication to long-term planning and consistently tackling the "to-do list." So, when you are planning a party during the holiday season, give yourself lots of time to enjoy the process and to prepare in advance to beat the crowds when it comes to sourcing ingredients and decor. You'll find that Ginger Snaps (page 235), Melt-in-Your-Mouth Shortbread Cookies (page 236), Scottish Shortbread Cookies (page 239), Walnut Snowballs (page 240), Reindeer Bait (page 243), and Grandma's English Fruit Cake (page 247) allow room for advance preparation, so you can relax and enjoy a slower paced holiday season by baking up a storm well in advance or over several weekends. French Canadian Tourtière (page 251), Giant Peppermint Patty Brownies (page 245), and Stollen (page 259) can be whipped up a few days before your event. Latkes (page 253) and Hanukkah Sufganiyot (page 257) are best made on the day you want to serve them. If you want a more casual approach, host a cookie swap. Invite nine guests and have each guest bake ten dozen cookies and package them in dozens. Your swap party can be spent sipping tea and sampling the extra dozen of each cookie. Then everyone leaves with nine unique packages of cookies to share over the season.

Winter Holiday

Ginger Snaps Ⓥ

DO AHEAD: Make the dough at least 1 day ahead and store it, wrapped tightly in plastic wrap, in the refrigerator for up to 3 days. Store baked cookies in an airtight container at room temperature for up to 1 month.

½ cup fancy molasses
2½ tablespoons granulated sugar
2½ tablespoons white corn syrup (or honey; not vegan)
2½ tablespoons water
2½ tablespoons vegetable shortening
2¼ cups all-purpose flour
2 teaspoons Speculoos Spice Mix (page 311)
1 teaspoon ground ginger
½ teaspoon baking soda
½ teaspoon salt

Snappy, spicy, and just the right amount of gingery goodness makes these thin cookies an absolute delight. Honing your skills to roll these out super thin will become easier as you make them more often, and we are sure they will become a much-requested holiday cookie. You can roll out the dough only twice before it tends to get dry and crack. If you need a third roll, try massaging ¼ to ½ teaspoon of shortening into the dough to help bring it back together into a rolling consistency. Conversely, the dough can be sticky to roll out at first, so do not be tempted to add more flour; you want to roll these out with as little flour as possible. Any shape will do for these cookies but avoid complex cookie cutters with lots of small angles, as the thin dough works best with relatively smooth edges. We love stars best but often do a classic scalloped circle shape too.

1. In a medium pot, stir together the molasses, sugar, corn syrup, and water and bring the mixture to a boil, stirring constantly with a wooden spoon or silicone spatula, over high heat. Once the mixture is boiling, reduce the heat to low and maintain a gentle boil, stirring frequently, for 5 minutes.

2. Remove the pot from the heat and stir in the vegetable shortening until the mixture is smooth. Set aside to cool to room temperature, about 30 minutes.

3. Sift the flour, speculoos spice mix, ginger, baking soda, and salt into a large bowl and stir together.

4. Once the molasses mixture has come to room temperature and is the same texture as molasses, mix it into the flour mixture until a dough has formed and no dry flour remains. Bring the dough together into a rough disc, then wrap it tightly in plastic wrap and refrigerate it for at least 4 hours or up to 24 hours before rolling it out.

5. Preheat the oven to 350°F (180°C). Line 4 baking sheets with parchment paper or silicone baking mats.

6. On a lightly floured work surface, roll out the dough very thin, about ¹⁄₁₆-inch thickness. Move the dough around and check underneath it frequently to make sure it is not sticking to the work surface, dusting lightly with more flour as needed. Using a 2½-inch-wide star-shaped cookie cutter, cut out the cookies and place 24 on each of the prepared baking sheets, evenly spaced.

7. If there is any flour on your cookies, brush it off with a dry pastry brush before baking. Bake for 10 to 12 minutes, or until the cookies have puffed up and appear dry. Allow the cookies to cool completely on the baking sheets.

Melt-in-Your-Mouth Shortbread Cookies

1 cup unsalted butter,
  room temperature
½ cup icing sugar
½ cup cornstarch
½ teaspoon vanilla bean paste
¼ teaspoon salt
1 cup all-purpose flour

For Josie, this childhood Christmastime favourite came from her mother's copy of *The Harrowsmith Cookbook, Volume 1*, but for Nickey it recalls the nostalgic Fleishmann's cornstarch box recipe instructions. Either way, we are sure that many families have a go-to cornstarch-based shortbread recipe; this is a quintessential winter cookie for good reason, and if you don't have a coveted recipe, we hope you make this one your own. Whether it be the simplicity or a love of anything melt-in-your-mouth and buttery, we invite you to embrace our most popular holiday decadence. We've adjusted the recipe over the years to our tastes and experimented with various additions and coatings. At home, Josie's family favourite is to dip them in melted Toblerone bars.

1. Preheat the oven to 325°F (160°C). Line 2 baking sheets with parchment paper or silicone baking mats.

2. In the bowl of a stand mixer fitted with the paddle attachment, lightly cream the butter on medium-high speed just until the butter is smooth, 2 to 3 minutes. Scrape down the sides and bottom of the bowl.

3. Add the icing sugar, cornstarch, vanilla bean paste, and salt and mix on low speed, increasing to medium-high, until the mixture is smooth and there are no chunks, 2 to 3 minutes. Scrape down the sides and bottom of the bowl.

4. Add the flour and mix on low speed, increasing to medium-high, until the flour is fully incorporated, 2 to 3 minutes.

5. Fill a 16-inch piping bag fitted with a No. 824 star tip with the cookie dough. Pipe eighteen 1½-inch-wide rosettes evenly spaced on each prepared baking sheet (see Buttercream and Whipped Cream Piping Styles, page 286, C).

6. Bake, one sheet at a time, for 20 to 24 minutes, or until very lightly browned around the edges and dry all the way through. Allow the cookies to cool completely on the baking sheets.

DO AHEAD ━━━━━━━━━━━━━━━━━━━━━━━━━━━━━

These cookies are best served within 2 days of baking but can be stored in an airtight container at room temperature for up to 3 weeks.

Scottish Shortbread Cookies

1¼ cups unsalted butter,
   room temperature
⅔ cup packed dark brown sugar
½ teaspoon salt
3 cups all-purpose flour
¼ cup granulated sugar,
   for sprinkling

If you prefer a crisp, buttery shortbread that's begging to be dipped in tea, then Scottish shortbread is for you. The brown sugar gives these a slight caramel flavour that's emphasized by the sparkly sugar crust gracing the cookie's golden caramelized surface. For years we sold these cookies stamped with "C+L" every winter, and we love that you can personalize them with your own messages.

1. Preheat the oven to 350°F (180°C). Line 2 baking sheets with parchment paper or silicone baking mats.

2. In the bowl of a stand mixer fitted with the paddle attachment, lightly cream the butter on medium-high speed just until smooth, 1 to 2 minutes. Do not incorporate air into the butter. Scrape down the sides and bottom of the bowl.

3. Add the brown sugar and salt and mix on low speed, increasing to medium-high, until the mixture is smooth and there are no chunks. Scrape down the sides and bottom of the bowl. Add the flour and mix on low speed, increasing to medium-high, until the flour is fully incorporated, without whipping air into the dough.

4. On a lightly floured work surface, roll out the dough to ¼-inch thickness. Move the dough around and check underneath it frequently to make sure it is not sticking to the work surface, dusting lightly with more flour as needed. Using a pizza cutter and ruler, cut the dough into 1- × 3-inch rectangles. First, cut the dough into 1-inch wide strips horizontally, then cut those into 3-inch long portions. Carefully transfer them to the prepared baking sheets, 27 per sheet, evenly spaced. Using letter impression cookie cutters, press a message into the cookies or simply leave them plain. Sprinkle the tops of the cookies generously with granulated sugar.

5. Bake, one sheet at a time, for 16 to 20 minutes, or until they appear dry, have puffed up a little, and are a deep golden brown. Allow the cookies to cool completely on the baking sheets.

DO AHEAD

These cookies are best served within 2 days of baking but can be stored in an airtight container at room temperature for up to 3 weeks.

Walnut Snowballs

1½ cups finely chopped toasted
   walnuts
¾ cup unsalted butter,
   room temperature
¼ cup + 1 tablespoon granulated
   sugar
1½ teaspoons pure vanilla extract
¼ teaspoon salt
1½ cups all-purpose flour
3 cups icing sugar

We aren't kidding when we call Josie's husband, Luke, a cookie monster. He is a man who loves his cookies, and because he has been in a relationship with a baker for more than twenty years, he is a bit of a cookie snob. When Josie and Luke were dating, they travelled to Cape Breton to visit Luke's family. There was never a shortage of delicious baked goods to eat around the kitchen tables of his great-aunts, but his favourite cookie was Great-great-Aunt Mary's walnut snowballs. We are still in awe of her perfectly round cookies, which we have never been able to quite replicate, but Josie did manage to leave Cape Breton with Mary's handwritten recipe. These have been a wintertime staple at the bakery since we opened, and we hope you enjoy them as much as Luke does.

1. Preheat the oven to 350°F (180°C). Line 2 baking sheets with parchment paper or silicone baking mats.

2. **Make the cookies:** In the bowl of a stand mixer fitted with the paddle attachment, lightly cream the walnuts and butter on medium-high speed just until the butter is smooth and the walnuts are evenly distributed, 1 to 2 minutes. Scrape down the sides and bottom of the bowl.

3. Add the granulated sugar, vanilla, and salt and mix on medium-high speed until light and fluffy, 2 to 3 minutes. Scrape down the sides and bottom of the bowl. Add the flour and mix on low speed, increasing to medium-high, until the flour is fully incorporated.

4. Scoop twenty-four 1-tablespoon portions of cookie dough onto each prepared baking sheet, leaving space between them. Once they are all scooped, roll each portion in your hands to make it a smooth ball, then place it back on the baking sheet, leaving 1 inch between balls. Bake, one sheet at a time, for 15 to 18 minutes, or until lightly browned at the edges.

5. **Coat the cookies:** Fill a large bowl with the icing sugar. While the cookies are still warm, toss the cookies, 4 at a time, in the icing sugar. Return the icing sugar–covered cookies to the baking sheets and allow them to cool completely. Cover the bowl of icing sugar and leave it at room temperature.

6. When the cookies are completely cool, 2 to 3 hours, toss the cookies, 4 at a time, in the icing sugar for a second time.

DO AHEAD —————————————————————

These cookies are best served within 2 days of baking but can be stored in an airtight container at room temperature for up to 3 weeks.

Reindeer Bait

5 cups hard pretzels
2 cups Shreddies cereal
2 cups corn puff cereal
2 cups green and red candy-covered
    chocolate (like M&Ms or Smarties)
⅓ cup unsalted butter
14 ounces (400 g/2 cups) white
    chocolate callets or good-quality
    chopped chocolate, divided
2 cups icing sugar
2 cups jujubes
⅓ cup Christmas sprinkles

Our version of the popular party food Puppy Chow is more white chocolate forward and is packed with salty-sweet flavours. Everyone loves a snack mix because there is something in it for everyone. This reindeer bait was created when Josie took a trip to a bulk food store with the objective of getting fun candy decorations for our Build Your Own Gingerbread House Kits. While cruising the aisles and dreaming about candy, she realized that she had never made the classic snack mix before and was inspired to create a Cake & Loaf signature version. No need to invest in full boxes of cereal here, just purchase generic brands at your local bulk food store. They don't need to be name brand cereals—just make sure they are crispy and crunchy.

1. Line 2 baking sheets with parchment paper or silicone baking mats.

2. In an extra-large bowl, mix together the pretzels, Shreddies, corn puffs, and candy-covered chocolate.

3. In a medium heat-resistant bowl, heat the butter and 1½ cups of the white chocolate in the microwave for 1 minute. Vigorously stir until the ingredients are incorporated and the mixture is smooth. If you see any lumps, heat in the microwave in 30-second intervals, stirring after each interval, until smooth.

4. Pour the white chocolate mixture over the dry ingredients and gently fold them together until the white chocolate mixture has coated about half of the dry ingredients. Add the icing sugar and very gently mix the ingredients together with your hands, separating individual pieces, until everything is evenly coated and no large lumps of the white chocolate mixture remain.

5. Using clean hands, scoop the mixture out of the bowl, leaving behind any dust or crumbs, and evenly spread the mixture in a thin layer on the prepared baking sheets. Sprinkle the jujubes evenly over the mixture.

6. In a small heat-resistant bowl, heat the remaining ½ cup white chocolate in the microwave for 30 seconds. Vigorously stir for 1 full minute until the chocolate is melted. If you see any lumps, heat in the microwave in 15-second intervals, stirring after each interval for 1 full minute, until smooth.

7. Fill a small piping bag fitted with a No. 2 round tip with the melted white chocolate. Drizzle thin lines of chocolate over the surface of the reindeer bait. While the chocolate is wet, decorate the whole surface with sprinkles. Allow the reindeer bait to dry at room temperature for 2 to 3 hours.

DO AHEAD

This mix is best served within 2 days of making it but can be stored in an airtight container at room temperature for up to 3 weeks. If you are giving it as a gift, package it in airtight containers as soon as it is dry and store it at room temperature for up to 3 weeks.

Giant Peppermint Patty Brownies

Brownie Layer

1 cup cocoa powder, sifted

2 cups granulated sugar

½ teaspoon salt

1 cup unsalted butter, melted

2 large eggs

1 tablespoon pure vanilla extract

½ cup buttermilk

1 cup all-purpose flour, sifted

12 York Peppermint Patties
  (1½ ounces/39 g each),
  unwrapped

Whipped Ganache Layers

1 batch White Chocolate Whipped
  Ganache (page 308)

½ to 1 teaspoon peppermint extract

⅛ to ¼ teaspoon leaf green gel
  food colouring

To finish

⅓ cup unsalted butter

14 ounces (400 g/2 cups)
  semi-sweet chocolate callets or
  good-quality chopped chocolate

2 candy canes, crushed

If York Peppermint Patties are your jam, you are going to love these fudgy white chocolate mint layered brownies. You only need a little square of these decadent treats with their refreshing mint kick and luscious dark chocolate. This bar is a sibling of our famous The Cream Egg Brownie (page 55), which is so popular that we created several variations of it from candy corn for Halloween to a raspberry rooibos version for Valentine's Day. They do take a couple of days to make, so read the recipe thoroughly and plan your bake days accordingly. To prepare for the holiday season in advance, you can make the brownie and whipped ganache layers of this bar and freeze it, then defrost it in the refrigerator before adding the semi-sweet chocolate layer and slicing the bar.

1. Make the brownie layer: Preheat the oven to 350°F (180°C). Line a 9- × 13-inch cake pan with parchment paper, allowing excess paper to hang over each side for easy removal.

2. In a large bowl, whisk together the cocoa, sugar, salt, and melted butter until the mixture is smooth and no oily film remains around the edges.

3. Whisk in the eggs and vanilla, adding a little air, until the mixture is smooth and has lightened slightly in colour. Whisk in the buttermilk until the mixture is smooth.

4. Stir in the flour and mix until no dry flour remains and the batter is smooth.

5. Using a small offset palette knife, evenly spread the batter into the base of the prepared pan. Press the 12 peppermint patties into the batter, evenly spaced (3 × 4 grid) so that each cut brownie will have a patty in the centre. Cover the tops of the patties by pulling some batter over them with a small offset palette knife or spoon. The brownies will level out as they bake. Bake for 30 to 35 minutes, or until a toothpick inserted into the centre of the brownie comes out clean. Allow the brownie to cool at room temperature for 1 to 2 hours.

6. Prepare the ganaches and layer on the brownie: Place 2½ cups of the white chocolate whipped ganache in a medium heat-resistant bowl. Cover and set aside at room temperature for step 8. (CONTINUES)

DO AHEAD

These brownies are best enjoyed on the day they are assembled, but you can store them in an airtight container at room temperature for up to 5 days. Or make the brownie layer and whipped ganache ahead and store the brownie, tightly wrapped with beeswax or plastic wrap, at room temperature for up to 3 days and the whipped ganache in an airtight container in the refrigerator for up to 2 weeks. Warm the refrigerated whipped ganache in the microwave for 30 seconds to make it easy to stir in the colour and pourable again.

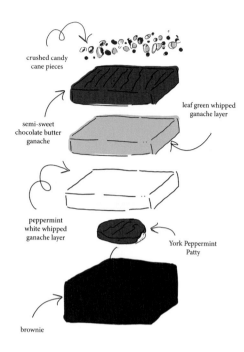

crushed candy
cane pieces

leaf green whipped
ganache layer

semi-sweet
chocolate butter
ganache

peppermint
white whipped
ganache layer

York Peppermint
Patty

brownie

7. Stir ½ to 1 teaspoon peppermint extract into the remaining 3½ cups of the white chocolate whipped ganache. Adjust the peppermint to taste. It should be fairly minty since it will balance out the rich brownie and chocolate. Using an offset palette knife, spread the white peppermint ganache evenly over the brownie base. Refrigerate the brownie for 20 to 30 minutes.

8. Stir ⅛ teaspoon of the food colouring into the reserved 2½ cups white chocolate whipped ganache. Add more food colouring, a few drops at a time, to achieve a mint green colour. If the ganache has hardened, microwave it for 30 seconds to make it easy to stir in the colour and pourable again. Pour the green ganache layer carefully over the white layer and, using a small offset palette knife, spread it out evenly. Wrap the pan in plastic wrap or cover with a tight-fitting silicone cover or lid. Refrigerate overnight or for at least 12 hours.

9. Finish the bar: In a medium heat-resistant bowl, heat the butter and semi-sweet chocolate in the microwave in 30-second intervals, stirring vigorously for 30 to 45 seconds after each interval, until the ganache is smooth and the chocolate is melted, 1 minute total. It is very important not to overheat the chocolate or it will bloom after setting so make sure you stir vigorously until all the heat is dissipated between intervals before returning the bowl to the microwave. Stir the ganache until the chocolate is smooth and silky. Spread the ganache evenly over the top of the green ganache layer. Drag a small offset palette knife horizontally back and forth across the top to shape ridges in the chocolate. Allow the chocolate to firm up in the fridge just until it has set, 15 to 20 minutes, before cutting.

10. Cut the brownie using a warm chef's knife by dipping it into hot water and drying it on a clean kitchen towel. Wipe the knife between each cut to get nice clean cuts. Trim the edges to get clean sides, then cut 12 brownies with a peppermint patty in the centre of each (3 × 4 grid). Evenly sprinkle the crushed candy canes over the bars before serving.

Grandma's English Fruit Cake

Fruit Soaker
½ cup roughly chopped glacé cherries

1 cup golden raisins

1 cup sultana raisins

¼ cup currants

⅔ cup (2 batches) Mixed Candied Peel (page 318) or store-bought (if using store-bought, add the zest of 1 lemon and 1 orange)

¼ cup sliced or slivered almonds (we prefer sliced)

¼ cup spiced rum

1 teaspoon pure vanilla extract

Cake
2¼ cups all-purpose flour, sifted

1 tablespoon cocoa powder, sifted

1 teaspoon Pumpkin Spice Mix (page 312) or English mixed spice

1 teaspoon allspice

1 teaspoon freshly grated or ground nutmeg

½ teaspoon salt

1¼ cups unsalted butter, room temperature

1½ cups packed dark brown sugar

2 tablespoons fancy molasses or golden syrup

¼ cup spiced rum

1 tablespoon pure vanilla extract

8 large eggs

For assembly
2¼ cups spiced rum (increase to 3¼ cups if you wish to "feed" the cake for 6 weeks total)

14 ounces (400 g) marzipan

½ cup icing sugar, for rolling

½ batch Royal Icing (page 295)

¼ cup sanding sugar

We call this the fruitcake that changes everything! It will change your opinion from the dramatic "Oh, I never eat that gross old fruit cake" to "Are you going to finish your piece, because I'll have it if you don't." The sweet, sparkly royal icing shell is hiding a sweet marzipan exterior that coats a boozy spiced rum–soaked dark brown sugar cake loaded with dried fruits and nuts. This is an old family recipe from Josie's grandma Mary. When we first received the recipe, we couldn't figure out how Mary had made such beautifully dark brown fruit cakes when ours kept turning out light brown. It turns out that although the original handwritten Lamb family recipe didn't include cocoa, this was the secret ingredient that you had to bake alongside grandma to discover. There's a lot of alcohol in this cake, so if rum isn't your preferred liquor, you can use any high proof liquor you enjoy with a complementary flavour, such as Grand Marnier, whisky, or brandy. The Lamb family usually uses brandy, but we prefer spiced rum at the bakery.

1. Make the fruit soaker: In a medium bowl, stir together the glacé cherries, raisins, currants, mixed candied peel, and almonds until well combined. Add the spiced rum and vanilla and stir to coat everything in liquid. Cover the bowl with a lid or beeswax wrap. Set aside to soak at room temperature for 24 hours.

2. Make the cake: Preheat the oven to 325°F (160°C). Grease an 8-inch cake pan with canola oil cooking spray and line the bottom with a parchment paper circle.

3. In a medium bowl, mix together the flour, cocoa, pumpkin spice mix, allspice, nutmeg, and salt. Set aside.

4. In the bowl of a stand mixer fitted with the paddle attachment, beat the butter and brown sugar on medium-high speed until light and fluffy, 2 to 3 minutes. Scrape down the sides and bottom of the bowl. Add the molasses, rum, and vanilla and beat on medium-high speed until thoroughly combined, 1 to 2 minutes.

5. Reduce the speed to medium and add the eggs, one at a time, beating well and scraping down the sides and bottom of the bowl after each addition, 1 minute for each egg, until the mixture is light and smooth. Scrape down the sides and bottom of the bowl.

6. Add half of the flour mixture and beat on medium speed until just combined, 1 minute. Scrape down the sides and bottom of the bowl, add the remaining flour mixture, and beat on medium speed until just combined, 1 minute. Remove the

(CONTINUES)

DO AHEAD

Since making the fruit cake is such a long-term project, you may want to mark your calendar with these key dates. You can make the cake up to 6 weeks ahead but need only 18 days to make it. Day 1, you soak the fruit.

Day 2, you bake the cake and "feed" it for the first time. Days 3, 5, 7, 9, 11, and 13, you "feed" the cake with ¼ cup of rum each session. At this point you can extend the timeline and create an even richer flavour by "feeding" the

cake once a week for 4 weeks (days 20, 27, 34, and 41). Day 15 (or day 43), you "feed" the cake for the last time and let it dry out for 2 days. Day 17 (or day 45), you ice the cake. Day 18 (or day 46), you get to eat it!

247

bowl from the stand mixer and, using a spatula, fold in the fruit soaker, including any liquid that has not been absorbed by the fruit. Mix until just combined.

7. Spread the batter evenly into the prepared pan and smooth out the top. Bake for 1 hour and 30 minutes to 2 hours, until the internal temperature reaches 205°F (96°C) or a toothpick inserted into the centre of the cake comes out clean. Lower the oven temperature to 200°F (100°C) and continue to bake the cake for 60 minutes to dry it out. Allow the cake to cool in the pan on a wire rack for 30 minutes. Remove the cake from the pan, peeling off the parchment paper circle on the bottom, and cool completely on the wire rack.

8. "Feed" the cake: Once the cake is cool, using a pastry brush, brush the entire surface of the cake with ¼ cup of the rum. Store the cake in an airtight container at room temperature for at least 2 weeks and up to 6 weeks, continuing to "feed" it regularly. For the first 2 weeks, brush the cake with ¼ cup of the rum every other day. After the first 2 weeks (7 feeding sessions), brush the cake with ¼ cup of the rum at least once a week until you ice the cake.

9. Two days before icing the cake, apply the final ¼ cup rum and then allow the cake to sit, covered, at room temperature to ensure that the liquid has fully absorbed before decorating.

10. Cover the fruit cake with marzipan: Place the cake on a 10- to 12-inch cake board or serving plate. Lightly dust a work surface with icing sugar. Roll out the marzipan into a 14-inch circle, ¼ inch thick. Move the marzipan around and check underneath it a couple of times to make sure it is not sticking to the work surface, dusting with more icing sugar as needed. Brush any icing sugar off the top of the marzipan, gently fold the circle in half, and flip it over to brush off any icing sugar from the other side. Using both of your hands, lift the marzipan circle and unfold it and centre it on top of the cake. Using pressure, smooth the top so that the marzipan adheres to the cake surface. Continue pressing down the sides of the cake until it is completely covered and there are no air pockets between the marzipan and the cake. If there are air pockets, use even pressure to push the bubble down the side of the cake. Trim off any excess marzipan at the bottom with a paring knife or pizza wheel. Brush off any excess icing sugar dust and set aside.

11. Seal the cake with royal icing: In the bowl of a stand mixer fitted with the paddle attachment, re-beat the royal icing on medium speed for 3 to 4 minutes until fluffy.

12. Fill a piping bag fitted with a No. 804 round tip with the royal icing. Place the cake in the centre of a turntable and, using even pressure, begin to coat the exterior of the cake in concentric circles starting at the bottom of the cake and working your way to the top, while turning the turntable. Using an offset palette knife, smooth out the royal icing over the top and sides of the cake. Clean the offset palette knife on a wet kitchen towel and then begin to create horizontal lines by starting at the bottom edge of the cake, placing the tip of the pallete knife against the cake horizontally. Slowly turn the turntable, pulling the palette knife up the cake to create horizontal lines on the side of the cake and ending in the centre of the top of the cake.

13. Sprinkle the sanding sugar on top of the cake while the royal icing is still wet. Allow the cake to dry, uncovered, at room temperature for at least 24 hours.

French Canadian Tourtière

Meat Filling
1 tablespoon canola oil
1½ cups chopped white onion
2 cloves garlic, crushed
1 pound (450 g) lean ground beef
1 pound (450 g) lean ground pork
1 tablespoon Worcestershire sauce
2 teaspoons ground sage
2 teaspoons dried thyme
2 teaspoons freshly grated or
    ground nutmeg
2 teaspoons ground allspice
½ teaspoon ground cloves
1 teaspoon salt, more for seasoning
1 teaspoon freshly ground black
    pepper, more for seasoning
2 cups water
1 bay leaf
2 pounds (900 g) russet potatoes,
    peeled and cubed

Butter Pastry
1 batch Butter Pastry (page 296)

Egg Wash
1 large egg
1 tablespoon water,
    room temperature

In high school, Josie participated in a cultural exchange program during which she lived in northern Quebec. There she fell in love with two Quebecois classics: sugar pie and tourtière. Tourtière is a traditional double crust meat pie with several regional variations from around the country. Some are based on cubed pork or beef (as opposed to ground meat) and often include other game animals like rabbit or venison. Many are veal or lamb based, but they all generally contain some kind of potato and are highly spiced with a blend of warm spices like allspice and cloves and herbs like sage and thyme. Melissa, a baker and chef of multiple talents, created this tourtière for us, inspired by the tourtières of Montreal, where she grew up. It's usually enjoyed with a condiment like chutney or ketchup.

1. Make the meat filling: In a large heavy pot, heat the canola oil over medium-high heat. When the oil is hot, add the onions in a single layer and sauté, stirring frequently, until soft and translucent, 5 to 7 minutes. Add the garlic and sauté for 1 more minute.

2. Add the ground beef and pork and brown the meat, stirring occasionally until cooked through, 5 to 7 minutes.

3. Deglaze the pan with the Worcestershire sauce, scraping up the browned bits from the bottom of the pan. Add the sage, thyme, nutmeg, allspice, cloves, salt, and pepper and sauté for 3 to 4 minutes until fragrant and the seasoning is thoroughly incorporated.

4. Add the water and bay leaf and bring to a boil over high heat, then reduce the heat to low and simmer, uncovered and stirring occasionally, for 1 hour until all the liquid has been absorbed. Remove and discard the bay leaf.

5. Meanwhile, add the potatoes to a large pot of salted cold water, bring to a boil over high heat, and cook for 18 to 25 minutes, or until the potatoes are fork-tender. Drain the potatoes. Spread the hot potatoes out on a baking sheet to steam and dry out as they cool. You want the potatoes to gain a chalky appearance on their surface as they cool to room temperature.

6. In the bowl of a stand mixer fitted with the paddle attachment, mix together the meat filling and cooled potatoes on low speed until the potatoes are mostly incorporated (there may be some potato chunks). Season with salt and pepper to taste. Transfer the filling to an airtight container and store in the refrigerator for at least 24 hours to allow the flavours to mingle. (CONTINUES)

DO AHEAD

You can make this pie up to 3 days ahead and store it, covered, in the refrigerator. To serve, warm in a 350°F (180°C) oven for 45 to 60 minutes. The butter pastry can be made ahead, wrapped tightly in plastic wrap, and stored in the refrigerator for up to 1 week or in the freezer for up to 6 months. If frozen, thaw in the refrigerator overnight before using.

The meat filling can be made ahead and stored in an airtight container for up to 3 days. Store leftovers in an airtight container in the refrigerator for up to 4 days.

7. The next day, assemble the pie: Preheat the oven to 375°F (190°C). On a lightly floured work surface, cut the pastry in half and cover one-half with beeswax or plastic wrap and set aside while you roll out the other half. Roll out half of the butter pastry dough into an 11- to 12-inch circle, about ⅛ inch thick (depending on the depth of the pie plate). Fold the dough in half to lift it without stretching and gently unfold it in a 9-inch pie plate. Roll out the remaining dough into a circle about 1 inch larger than the top of the pie plate. Place all the rolled trimmings in a flat layer on a plate or baking sheet and store them, uncovered, in the refrigerator to stay cool while you finish assembling the pie. You can reroll the scraps to make cutout decorations (step 11), if desired.

8. Scoop the filling into the pie shell and smooth it level with the rim of the pie plate.

9. Make the egg wash: In a small bowl, thoroughly whisk together the egg and water until combined. Using a pastry brush, brush the egg wash all around the edge of the pastry.

10. Continue assembling the pie: Using a small cookie cutter or paring knife, cut any shapes out of the second dough circle before you place it on top of the pie. Fold the circle in half to lift it without stretching and gently unfold and place it over the pie. Press the edge of the top dough firmly into the bottom crust edge all the way around the pie. Trim excess pastry and crimp the edges to seal. If the pastry is getting soft, refrigerate the pie for 10 to 15 minutes before adding pastry cutouts, if using.

11. Lightly brush the egg wash over the entire surface of the pie. To make cutout decorations (optional), reroll the scraps. If needed, you can reroll the dough, but every time you do so it will get less flaky. You can have up to 3 layers of pastry overlapping in your image but no more than that or it won't bake through fully. Use the egg wash sparingly as a paste to glue your pieces onto the crust. Lightly brush the egg wash over the whole surface of the pie one more time. Make at least 1 cut on the top of the pie to let the steam escape.

12. Bake for 50 to 60 minutes, or until the pastry is a deep golden brown. Let the pie rest for 5 to 10 minutes before serving.

Latkes

Latkes

1 pound (450 g) russet potatoes (3 medium potatoes)

1 medium white onion, peeled and root end removed

1 egg

3 tablespoons all-purpose flour

1 teaspoon baking powder

1 teaspoon salt

½ teaspoon freshly ground black pepper

1½ cups canola oil or chicken schmaltz, for frying

To serve

2 teaspoons flaky sea salt (we use Maldon)

1 cup sour cream

1 cup sweetened applesauce

Josie's family has been celebrating Hanukkah for the last several years with their friends Michael and Amy and their children. At first virtually, because they lived so far away, and now in person. Michael had to teach Josie to make all the delicious Hannukah fare over video chats and texts, and this latke recipe was the first he shared. Traditionally these are served with sour cream and sweetened applesauce, but Josie's son, Finn, loves them best with peanut butter. The key is squeezing out every last drop of moisture from the onions and potatoes and then allowing the liquid to sit for 10 minutes until the potato starch has settled to the bottom of the liquid. Drain off the watery liquid and save the starch to mix into the latkes for extra-crispy latkes. If you have access to chicken schmaltz to fry the latkes for extra flavour and authenticity, we highly suggest it, but canola oil will work just fine. Since no one taught Josie how to actually form latkes, we have a cheater's version (that's much easier) we think you will like. This recipe is small enough to make on a box grater, but if you want to double or triple the recipe, you could use the grating attachment on a food processor to grate the potatoes and onions.

1. Scrub the potatoes well to remove any dirt and cut out any blemished sections or eyes, but do not peel them. Grate the potatoes and onions on the large holes of a box grater set over a large bowl.

2. Place a large piece of cheesecloth in a mesh sieve set over a medium bowl, allowing 8 to 10 inches of cheesecloth to hang over the edges of the sieve. Scoop the grated potato and onions, as well as any liquid, into the cheesecloth.

3. Gather the edges of the cheesecloth and lift the cheesecloth-wrapped potatoes and onions above the sieve. Twist the cheesecloth and wring out any liquid from the potatoes and onions, squeezing as hard as you can, catching the liquid in the bowl.

4. Pour the liquid into a 2-cup glass measuring cup and place the squeezed potatoes and onions in a medium bowl. Allow both the potato onion mixture and the liquid to sit separately, uncovered, at room temperature for 10 minutes. (CONTINUES)

DO AHEAD

These latkes are best served immediately, but they can be stored in an airtight container in the refrigerator for up to 3 days or in the freezer for up to 2 weeks. To serve, warm them straight from the refrigerator or freezer in a 375°F (190°C) oven in a single layer on a baking sheet for 15 to 20 minutes (add 5 minutes if frozen), or until crispy again.

5. Check your potato and onion mixture and soak up any remaining liquid with a dry paper towel. Pour off all the watery liquid from the reserved potato and onion liquid and add the thick white starch that remains to the potato and onion mixture.

6. Add the egg, flour, baking powder, salt, and pepper to the potato and onion mixture and toss together with your fingers to make sure everything is evenly distributed.

7. Preheat the oven to 200°F (100°C). Line a baking sheet with paper towel.

8. In a 12-inch cast iron skillet, heat the canola oil over high heat. Once the oil reaches 375°F (190°C) on a laser or candy thermometer, reduce the heat to medium. Using a 3-tablespoon cookie scoop, carefully place 4 portions of the potato and onion mixture into the hot oil. As you scoop the portions into the oil, press them flat with the back of the scoop to shape them into latkes about ½ inch thick and 3 inches wide. Fry the latkes until deep golden brown, 2 to 3 minutes per side. Using a metal spatula, transfer the latkes to the prepared baking sheet and place in the oven to keep warm.

9. Continue to test the oil temperature as you fry the remaining latkes in batches of 4 and adjust the heat as needed to maintain 375°F (190°C). Stir the mixture a little with the scoop before scooping each round so that the mixture stays homogenous.

10. The latkes can stay warm in the oven for up to 1 hour before serving. Sprinkle them with flaky sea salt and serve with the sour cream and applesauce on the side.

Hanukkah Sufganiyot

Doughnuts

3½ cups all-purpose flour

¼ cup granulated sugar

1 tablespoon instant dry yeast

1 teaspoon baking powder

1 teaspoon salt

1 cup whole milk, warm

2 eggs, room temperature

¼ cup unsalted butter, melted
and cool

1 teaspoon pure vanilla extract

6 cups + 1 teaspoon canola oil,
divided

To finish

1½ cups Strawberry Compote
(page 309) or strawberry jam

2 cups icing sugar

Once upon a time, Nickey and Josie participated in the Food Network's *Donut Showdown*. We developed fried doughnut recipes just for the competition, and the base yeast dough is still our favourite go-to for fluffy, flavourful doughnuts. We've used it here to make our own version of sufganiyot, jam-filled fried doughnuts covered in icing sugar. You can fill them with whatever jam strikes your fancy, or even try filling them with Nutella or cookie butter. We also love them filled with our Lemon Curd (page 316). An Israeli folk tale claims that Adam and Eve were given sufganiyot as consolation after they were expelled from the Garden of Eden. It seems pretty unlikely, but we'd have to agree that these doughnuts do improve any bad mood and are best shared with loved ones. They have become a favourite part of our family traditions over the holidays.

1. Make the dough: In the bowl of a stand mixer fitted with the dough hook attachment, add the flour, sugar, instant yeast, baking powder, and salt and stir on low speed for 1 minute to evenly distribute the yeast.

2. Add the milk, eggs, melted butter, and vanilla and mix on medium speed until no dry flour remains, about 1 to 2 minutes. Mix on medium-low speed for 9 to 12 minutes, or until the dough has pulled away from the sides and bottom of the bowl and is silky smooth. If after 12 minutes the dough is still sticking to the bottom of the bowl, add 2 tablespoons of flour and mix for 3 more minutes on medium-low speed.

3. Lightly grease a large bowl with 1 teaspoon of the canola oil. Form a ball with the dough, place it in the bowl, and allow it to rise, covered, for 1 hour at room temperature, or until it has doubled in size.

4. Line 2 baking sheets with parchment paper or silicone baking mats and spray the pans and parchment paper generously with canola oil cooking spray.

5. On a lightly floured work surface, roll out the dough to about ½-inch thickness. Move the dough around and check underneath it frequently to make sure it is not sticking to the work surface, dusting lightly with more flour as needed. (CONTINUES)

DO AHEAD

These doughnuts are best enjoyed within 12 hours of frying, and unfortunately the dough doesn't stand up well to being made ahead. You can fry the doughnuts and store them, covered, at room temperature for up to 12 hours before filling them with jam and coating them in icing sugar.

6. Using a 2½-inch round cookie cutter, cut out 24 dough circles, rerolling the scraps as needed. Evenly space 12 dough circles on each of the prepared baking sheets, leaving ample space between them for the dough to rise. If there is any flour on top of the circles, brush it off with a dry pastry brush. Allow the doughnuts to rise in a warm, humid area for 30 to 45 minutes, or until they increase in volume by 50 percent. If the surface of the dough seems to be drying out, lightly spray them with warm water from a spray bottle every 10 to 15 minutes.

7. Fry the doughnuts: In a large saucepan, heat the remaining 6 cups of canola oil over high heat. When the oil reaches 350°F (180°C), measured with a laser or candy thermometer, reduce the heat to medium. Using your hands or a bench scraper, carefully transfer the doughnuts, one at a time, to the oil and fry in batches of 4 to 6 until golden brown, 90 seconds per side. Transfer the fried doughnuts to a wire cooling rack.

8. Continue to test the oil temperature as you fry the remaining doughnuts and adjust the heat as needed to maintain 350°F (180°C). Fry the remaining doughnuts in batches of 4 to 6 and transfer to the wire rack.

9. Once the doughnuts are cool enough to handle, use the handle of a small spoon to pierce the side of each doughnut, pushing the handle halfway through the doughnut and wiggling it a little inside the doughnut to create an air pocket in the centre.

10. Fill and finish the doughnuts: Fill a 16-inch piping bag fitted with a No. 804 round tip with the strawberry compote. Insert the piping tip into the air pocket of each doughnut and squeeze gently until it pushes back and feels full. Stop squeezing and remove the tip from the doughnut. Return the doughnuts to the wire rack as you fill them.

11. Place the icing sugar in a large bowl. Using your hands, toss the doughnuts in the icing sugar, 3 to 4 at a time, to completely cover the exterior of the doughnuts in sugar. Place the doughnuts on a serving platter as you finish them.

Stollen

Stollen

1½ cups Thompson raisins
2 tablespoons hot water
1 tablespoon spiced rum
⅛ teaspoon bitter almond oil
    (or 1 teaspoon almond extract)
1 batch (⅓ cup) Mixed Candied
    Peel (page 318) or store-bought
    (if using store-bought, add the
    zest of 1 lemon and 1 orange)
1¼ cups all-purpose flour,
    more for dusting
1¼ teaspoons baking powder
½ teaspoon salt
½ cup unsalted butter,
    room temperature
⅓ cup granulated sugar
1 large egg, room temperature
½ cup almond flour
½ cup sour cream

Icing Crust

3 cups icing sugar
⅔ cup unsalted butter, melted
    and warm

Starting with a traditional recipe and perfected by our bakers over the last decade, stollen has become a staff favourite at the bakery. Its thick icing sugar and butter crust helps keep it fresh for up to 2 weeks, so you can wrap it and gift it to loved ones to enjoy over the holidays or use it as a stocking stuffer. This recipe yields two loaves—one for you and one to gift in the spirit of the season. Sometimes stollen includes yeast, but our version is leavened with baking powder. The loaf itself is cake-like and buttery with an intense citrus flavour and a delightful bitter almond aroma, but most of the sweetness comes from the crust and the fruit. We think that our Mixed Candied Peel (page 318) makes all the difference, but you can certainly use store-bought in a pinch. We've deviated from the traditional shaping for simplicity, but feel free to do some research on the traditional shaping technique, which will also work with this dough.

1. Make the stollen: Preheat the oven to 350°F (180°C). Line a baking sheet with parchment paper or a silicone baking mat.

2. In a small bowl, soak the raisins with the hot water, spiced rum, bitter almond oil, and mixed candied peel. Stir together and set aside until step 6.

3. Sift the flour, baking powder, and salt into a medium bowl and stir together.

4. In the bowl of a stand mixer fitted with the paddle attachment, cream the butter and sugar on medium-high speed until light and fluffy, 2 to 3 minutes. Scrape down the sides and bottom of the bowl.

5. Add the egg and beat on medium speed until fluffy, 2 to 3 minutes. Scrape down the paddle and the sides and bottom of the bowl.

6. Add the dry mixture, almond flour, sour cream, and soaked fruit and beat on low speed, increasing to medium-high, just until the dough comes together and the fruit is evenly distributed, 1 to 2 minutes.

7. Heavily dust a work surface with flour. Turn the dough out onto the work surface. Working quickly and with as little kneading as possible, divide the dough in half and shape each portion into a tall football shape, 6 to 7 inches long. Brush any flour off the surface of the loaves using a dry pastry brush.

8. Transfer the loaves to the prepared baking sheet and, using a sharp knife, slash the dough down the centre lengthwise, making a cut about ½ inch deep along the whole length of the loaf. Bake for 35 to 45 minutes, or until the loaves are puffy and dry and the edges look crispy. Allow the loaves to cool briefly on the baking sheet, 10 to 15 minutes. (CONTINUES)

9. Make the icing crust and coat the stollen: Place the icing sugar in a 9- × 13-inch baking dish and line a baking sheet with parchment paper. Using a pastry brush and rotating a loaf in your hand, brush the entire surface of the loaf with melted butter. Transfer the buttered loaf to the icing sugar and roll the loaf in the sugar to coat it generously. Pat the icing sugar onto the loaf and into the crevices. Transfer the coated loaf to the prepared baking sheet and repeat with the second loaf. Let the loaves sit, uncovered, for 20 minutes, until they are ready for another layer of butter and icing sugar.

10. Gently brush any loose icing sugar off the loaves with your hands. Reheat the butter so that it is warm, then using a pastry brush and rotating a loaf in your hand, brush the entire surface of the loaf with melted butter, dabbing the butter-soaked brush against the icing sugar without rubbing it off. Transfer the buttered loaf to the icing sugar and roll the loaf in the sugar to coat it completely. Return the coated loaf to the prepared baking sheet and repeat with the second loaf. Let the loaves sit again, uncovered, for 20 minutes.

11. Repeat the process one last time, reheating the butter as needed. Once the loaves are coated in 3 layers of butter and icing sugar, allow them to cool on the prepared baking sheet for 2 hours.

Being surrounded by friends and family is the perfect way to start off a new year. It can be an opportunity to get all glitzed up with your favourite folks and let loose dancing the night away. For dancing, you'll need a constant flow of carbs to keep everyone's energy up. Invite guests for 8 p.m. to avoid the dinner hour and then serve them a delicious tasting menu of treats to last the whole evening. While greeting your guests, serve them some stunning Dulce de Leche Ruby Chocolate Bars (page 265) to set a tone of sophistication for the evening. By 9 p.m., set up a cookie bar with fresh fruit, Cranberry Lemon Icebox Cookies (page 266), and Sugar Cookies and Frosting Dip (page 269). Serve the Tiramisu Jars (page 271) as midnight approaches for an extra boost of energy. If your guests are likely to stay well beyond midnight, have the Roasted Vegetable Torta Rustica (page 275) ready to bake off and serve warm as a post midnight snack. If fancy outfits and crowds aren't your thing, New Year's Eve can be a chance to catch up in a small dinner party setting with friends after a busy year. Maybe with people you haven't been able to connect with meaningfully over the busy holiday season. As guests arrive, have the Pull-Apart Garlic Cheese Buns (page 277) baking in the oven for an aromatherapy experience and serve them with a signature beverage. Keep the meal vegetarian by featuring the Roasted Vegetable Torta Rustica (page 275) or serve it as a starter and add your own savoury courses to complement it. Snack on cookies and Dulce de Leche Ruby Chocolate Bars (page 265) as you while away the evening playing games and chatting.

New Year's Eve

Dulce de Leche Ruby Chocolate Bars

DO AHEAD: You can bake the shortbread crust and dulce de leche layers and store the bar wrapped in beeswax or plastic wrap at room temperature for up to 4 days before cutting and dipping them in chocolate. Store the finished bars in an airtight container at room temperature for up to 2 weeks.

Shortbread Crust

½ cup unsalted butter
¼ cup icing sugar
¼ cup cornstarch
1 tablespoon finely ground raspberry
    rooibos tea
¼ teaspoon salt
¾ cup all-purpose flour

Dulce de Leche Fudge

1 batch (1⅓ cups) Dulce de Leche
    (page 319)
12 ounces (340 g/1¾ cups) white
    chocolate callets or good-quality
    chopped chocolate

For assembly

3 pounds + 5 ounces
    (1.5 kg/7½ cups) ruby chocolate
    callets or good-quality chopped
    chocolate
4 teaspoons edible gold flake

New Year's Eve events are often a chance to get dressed up with all the trimmings, and this bar is ready to set the tone for sophistication. The buttery rooibos cookie base has a honey-like flavour and pairs beautifully with the creamy dulce de leche fudge layer. They are completely encased in the beautifully unique sweet and sour ruby chocolate. These bars require some planning since the base will need to set up overnight before you cut them up to enrobe them in chocolate.

1. Make the shortbread crust: Preheat the oven to 350°F (180°C). Grease an 8-inch square cake pan with canola oil cooking spray and line with parchment paper.

2. In the bowl of a stand mixer fitted with the paddle attachment, cream the butter on medium-high speed until smooth. Scrape down the sides and bottom of the bowl. Add the icing sugar, cornstarch, finely ground tea, and salt and continue to beat just until the tea is evenly distributed. Scrape down the sides and bottom of the bowl. Add the flour and mix on medium speed until the mixture comes together as a cookie dough, 1 to 2 minutes.

3. Press the dough into the bottom of the prepared pan. Bake for 20 to 25 minutes, or until the crust is light brown and appears dry.

4. Make the dulce de leche fudge: In a medium heat-resistant bowl, heat the dulce de leche and white chocolate in the microwave in 30-second intervals, stirring vigorously after each interval, until the chocolate is melted and the mixture is glossy and smooth, 1 to 2 minutes total. Pour the fudge over the shortbread base and let sit, covered, at room temperature for at least 8 hours or overnight to firm up.

5. Assemble the bars: Cut the bar into 16 equal squares and place them on a clean baking sheet lined with parchment paper.

6. Temper the ruby chocolate following the instructions on page 305. Place a wire rack on a clean baking sheet for your dipped bars in step 8.

7. Holding a bar firmly, dip the shortbread base of the bar ¼ inch into the tempered ruby chocolate. Gently scrape the excess chocolate off the bottom of the bar using the side of the bowl, allowing the chocolate to drip back into the bowl as you lift the bar out of the chocolate. Return the bar to the lined baking sheet so the chocolate can set. Repeat with the remaining bars.

8. Working quickly and starting with the first bar dipped, transfer the bars to the wire rack as the chocolate bases set. Reserve about ¼ cup of tempered ruby chocolate, then pour the remaining tempered ruby chocolate evenly over the tops of the bars, enrobing the bars completely in chocolate.

9. Fill a 12-inch piping bag fitted with a No. 1 round tip with the reserved ¼ cup tempered ruby chocolate. Drizzle the chocolate over the bars in a zig-zag pattern. Top each bar with ¼ teaspoon of gold flake before the chocolate hardens completely.

NEW YEAR'S EVE

Cranberry Lemon Icebox Cookies

DO AHEAD: These cookies require at least 6 hours to firm up before you slice and bake them, so you may want to make the dough a day ahead. The cookie dough logs can be wrapped and stored in the refrigerator for up to 1 week or in the freezer for up to 6 months. If frozen, thaw the dough in the refrigerator overnight, then use it cold from the fridge, coat in turbinado sugar, slice, and bake as needed. Store the baked cookies in an airtight container at room temperature for up to 2 weeks.

2½ cups all-purpose flour
¾ teaspoon baking powder
½ teaspoon salt
1 cup unsalted butter,
    room temperature
¾ cup granulated sugar
Zest of 2 lemons
1 egg
2 teaspoons vanilla bean paste
1½ cups dried cranberries,
    lightly chopped
1 cup turbinado sugar

A classic and consistent go-to cookie dough that can easily be cut up and baked on the fly. Having a couple of these cookie dough logs in the freezer or fridge during December will come in handy if you're expecting a quick visit from friends or family and are looking for a fast cookie to slip into the oven to welcome your guests. We chose this recipe as a feature for the New Year's Eve chapter because it can easily be doubled or tripled, and the flavour of bright zesty lemon and sour dried cranberries with a crisp coarse sugar edge tends to be a hit at any party. Not to mention, they are a great little party favour that can be wrapped in parchment like a party cracker and tied with festive ribbon and a tag.

1. Make and chill the cookie dough: Sift the flour, baking powder, and salt into a medium bowl and stir together. Set aside.

2. In the bowl of a stand mixer fitted with the paddle attachment, cream the butter, granulated sugar, and lemon zest on medium-high speed until pale in colour and the sugar is starting to dissolve, 2 to 3 minutes. Scrape down the sides and bottom of the bowl.

3. Add the egg and vanilla bean paste and beat on medium speed until fluffy, 2 to 3 minutes. Scrape down the paddle and the sides and bottom of the bowl.

4. Add the dry mixture and cranberries and beat on low speed, then briefly on medium-high, just until the dough comes together and the cranberries are evenly distributed, 1 to 2 minutes. Do not overmix or the cranberries may change the texture of the cookie.

5. On a lightly floured work surface, divide the dough into 3 equal portions and roll each, one at a time, into a 16-inch-long log. Wrap each log tightly in plastic wrap or parchment paper. Place the wrapped logs on a baking sheet and chill in the refrigerator until firm, 6 to 24 hours.

6. Bake the cookies: Preheat the oven to 350°F (180°C). Line 3 baking sheets with parchment paper or silicone baking mats.

7. Pour the turbinado sugar onto a clean baking sheet in a single layer. Working with one log of dough at a time, remove a log from the refrigerator and unwrap it. Using the tines of a fork, score the entire exterior of the log and then roll and press it in the turbinado sugar until completely encrusted in sugar. Cut the log into ½-inch slices and place them on one of the prepared baking sheets, evenly spaced. Repeat with the remaining logs. Bake, one sheet at a time, for 10 to 14 minutes, or until the cookies have puffed up, appear dry, and are slightly brown on the bottom. Allow the cookies to cool completely on the baking sheets.

Sugar Cookies and Frosting Dip

DO AHEAD: These cookies can be made ahead and stored in an airtight container at room temperature for 1 month. The frosting can be made ahead and stored in an airtight container in the refrigerator for up to 1 week; just don't add the sprinkles until you are ready to serve.

Ermine Frosting

5 tablespoons all-purpose flour
1 cup granulated sugar
1 cup whole milk
1 cup unsalted butter, room temperature
1 tablespoon pure vanilla extract
½ teaspoon salt
2 tablespoons rice-shaped rainbow sprinkles

Cookies

1 batch Sugar Cookie Dough (page 301)
½ cup mini semi-sweet chocolate chips
2 tablespoons rainbow nonpareil sprinkles

The playfulness of this nostalgic treat pairs well with the hopeful party atmosphere at a New Year's Eve gathering. These dunkaroo-style treats are crowd-pleasers, and the unique ermine frosting stays very stable at room temperature, so you can make it a day ahead and still keep dunking all evening. Ermine frosting is a traditional frosting from the southern United States, sometimes referred to as butter roux frosting or boiled milk frosting. It uses a cooked flour roux base to provide stability and a fluffy texture that lasts. If the frosting doesn't appeal to you, try our Dulce de Leche (page 319) or Dreamy Cream Cheese Icing (page 295) instead.

1. Prepare the ermine frosting roux base: In a medium saucepan, add the flour and sugar and cook over medium heat, whisking constantly, for 45 seconds. Slowly add the milk while whisking constantly until smooth, 1 to 2 minutes.

2. Increase the heat to medium-high and bring the mixture to a boil, whisking constantly. Once the mixture is boiling, reduce the heat to medium-low and cook, stirring frequently with a silicone spatula, for 5 to 8 minutes, to cook the starch out of the flour and until the mixture has a thick custard-like texture. Scoop the mixture into a medium bowl and cover the surface with plastic wrap to prevent a skin from forming. Allow to cool to room temperature before finishing the frosting in step 6.

3. Make the cookies: Preheat the oven to 350°F (180°C). Line 3 baking sheets with parchment paper or silicone baking mats.

4. Divide the freshly mixed sugar cookie dough into 3 portions. Working with one portion at a time and keeping the other portions covered with beeswax or plastic wrap, fold the mini chocolate chips into the first portion of dough until evenly distributed. On a lightly floured work surface, roll out the cookie dough to about ¼ inch thick. Move the dough around and check underneath it frequently to make sure it is not sticking, dusting lightly with more flour as needed. (Use a floured metal ruler to run between the counter and dough to release the dough if it does stick.) Using a metal ruler for guidance, cut the dough into 1¼-inch squares. Dust off any flour and reroll the scraps. (Only reroll the scraps once.) Place the cookies on one of the prepared baking sheets, evenly spaced (6 × 8 grid). Bake for 10 to 14 minutes, or until the bottoms are slightly brown and the top corners are slightly golden. Allow the cookies to cool completely on the baking sheet. (CONTINUES)

5. Meanwhile, working with the second portion of dough in a medium bowl, fold in the nonpareil sprinkles until evenly distributed. Repeat the instructions in step 4 to roll out, cut, and bake the sprinkle cookies, then repeat again with the third portion of dough, making plain cookies (no add-ins).

6. Finish making the ermine frosting: In the bowl of a stand mixer fitted with the paddle attachment, beat the butter, vanilla, and salt on low speed, gradually increasing to high speed as the vanilla incorporates. Mix on high speed for 6 to 8 minutes, stopping to scrape down the sides and bottom of the bowl once or twice, until the mixture is light and fluffy.

7. Reduce the speed to medium and, with the mixer running, add the room-temperature roux base, 1 tablespoon at a time, until fully incorporated, 3 to 4 minutes. Scrape down the sides and bottom of the bowl. Mix on high speed for 2 to 3 minutes, until the icing is light and fluffy and holds stiff peaks. Scoop the frosting into a serving bowl and top with the rice-shaped rainbow sprinkles just before serving to ensure that the sprinkles don't bleed.

8. Serve the cookies with the ermine frosting separately so that guests can dunk the cookies in the frosting as if it's a dip.

Tiramisu Jars

Mocha Cocoa Mixture
1½ tablespoons dark instant
    coffee granules
3 tablespoons hot water
3 tablespoons cocoa powder, sifted
1 tablespoon canola oil

Mocha Swirl Cake
½ batch Vanilla Cake Batter
    (page 282)

Coffee Simple Syrup
1¼ cups cold brewed coffee or
    cold espresso
¼ batch Simple Syrup (page 316)

Mascarpone Filling
1 batch Mascarpone Filling
    (page 317)

Whipped Cream
½ batch Whipped Cream
    (page 300)

For assembly
½ cup cocoa powder

An easy and approachable way to get that coffee infusion straight to the vein and gain that required second wind when waiting for the clock to strike midnight; after all, tiramisu roughly translates to "pick me up." These beautiful desserts look stunning all lined up on a buffet, and they are easy to carry around a party as you snack. We've decided to skip the traditional liqueur component to give this dessert more mass appeal, but you can always swap out up to ¼ cup of the coffee for a coffee liqueur or the more traditional Marsala wine.

1. Preheat the oven to 350°F (180°C). Grease a 9- × 13-inch cake pan with canola oil cooking spray and line with a parchment paper rectangle.

2. Make the mocha cocoa mixture: In a small bowl, whisk together the instant coffee and hot water until the coffee is completely dissolved. Add the sifted cocoa and canola oil and whisk to a smooth consistency.

3. Make the mocha swirl cake batter: To the mocha cocoa mixture, add 1 cup of the vanilla cake batter and whisk until smooth. Set aside.

4. Pour the remaining vanilla cake batter into the prepared cake pan and, using a small offset palette knife, smooth out the top. Pour circles of mocha cake batter on the surface of the vanilla cake batter. Using a butter knife or toothpick, swirl the 2 batters by pulling through and folding in the mocha batter. Do not over-swirl; you want the marbling to stand out. Bake for 16 to 20 minutes, or until a toothpick inserted into the centre of the cake comes out clean. Allow the cake to cool in the pan on a wire rack for 20 minutes. Remove the cake from the pan, leaving the parchment paper on the bottom, and cool completely on the wire rack.

5. Make the coffee simple syrup: In a medium bowl, stir together the coffee and simple syrup until combined.

6. Whip the mascarpone filling and assemble the tiramisu jars: Clean and dry eight 1-cup mason jars, then line them up on a clean baking sheet. In the bowl of a stand mixer fitted with the paddle attachment, whip the mascarpone filling on medium speed for 2 minutes until light and fluffy. Fill a 16-inch piping bag fitted with a No. 804 round tip with the whipped mascarpone. (CONTINUES)

DO AHEAD

The cake can be baked and stored, wrapped in beeswax or plastic wrap, at room temperature for up to 3 days. You can make the simple syrup and mascarpone filling ahead. The simple syrup can be stored in an airtight container in the refrigerator for up to 3 weeks. The mascarpone filling can be stored in an airtight container in the refrigerator for up to 1 week. The finished tiramisu jars are best enjoyed from the refrigerator on the day they are assembled but can be covered and stored in the refrigerator for up to 3 days.

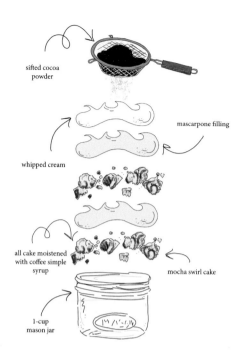

sifted cocoa
powder

mascarpone filling

whipped cream

all cake moistened
with coffee simple
syrup

mocha swirl cake

1-cup
mason jar

7. Cut the cake into cubes using a bread knife or tear the cooled cake into 1-inch pieces and transfer to a medium bowl.

8. Lay a single layer of cake pieces on the bottom of each mason jar and moisten the cake in each jar with 1½ tablespoons of the coffee simple syrup, soaking all cake pieces thoroughly. Pipe the mascarpone filling to just below the middle of each jar. Repeat the same layering sequence of cake, syrup, and mascarpone filling, leaving ¼-inch headspace.

9. Make the whipped cream and dollop about 2 tablespoons into each jar to fill to the top completely. Using a small step palette knife and with even pressure, push the palette against the top of the jar and smooth the whipped cream even with the glass rim, flat like the top of a cake. Clean the outside of the rim and exterior of the jar with a clean kitchen towel. If you have any remaining whipped cream and you are not concerned with potentially placing the lids on the jars, add a decorative flourish or rosette on top (see Buttercream and Whipped Cream Piping Styles, page 286).

10. Before serving, use a fine sifter to evenly sift cocoa on top of all the jars.

Roasted Vegetable Torta Rustica

Filling
1 small Italian eggplant,
    cut into ¼-inch rounds
2 small zucchini,
    cut into ¼-inch rounds
1 medium red onion,
    cut into ½-inch slices
6 medium portobello mushrooms,
    cut into ½-inch slices
2 tablespoons olive oil
1 teaspoon salt
½ teaspoon freshly ground
    black pepper
¼ cup panko bread crumbs
1 cup ricotta cheese
6 tablespoons basil pesto, divided
2 red, orange, or yellow bell peppers,
    roasted, peeled, seeded, and
    cut into 1-inch strips
½ cup marinara sauce, divided

Butter Pastry Dough
1 batch Butter Pastry (page 296)

Egg Wash
1 large egg
1 tablespoon water,
    room temperature

This layered beauty packed with veggie goodness and Mediterranean flavours is as delicious as it is stunning to slice. It's almost like a lasagna minus the pasta, all wrapped up in flaky buttery pastry. We love this as a vegetarian main, or for a vegan version, use our Vegan Pastry (page 297), swap out vegan cheese for the ricotta, and make sure your pesto is vegan. This pie has a rustic elegance we think works so well at a New Year's Eve party. It's not too heavy and provides everyone with a hearty serving of vegetables so that you can leave lots of room for desserts.

1. Preheat the oven to 400°F (200°C). Line a baking sheet with parchment paper or a silicone baking mat.

2. Make the filling: Toss together the eggplant, zucchini, red onions, mushrooms, olive oil, salt, and pepper on the prepared baking sheet and spread out evenly. Roast the vegetables for 15 to 20 minutes, tossing halfway through, until tender, the eggplant is cooked through, and the onions are nicely caramelized. Remove from the oven and allow the vegetables to cool to room temperature.

3. Reduce the oven temperature to 375°F (190°C).

4. Roll out the butter pastry dough: On a lightly floured work surface, roll out half of the prepared pastry dough, keeping the other portion covered with beeswax or plastic wrap, into an 11- to 12-inch circle, about ⅛ inch thick (depending on the depth of the pie plate). Fold the dough in half to lift it without stretching and gently unfold it into a 9-inch pie plate. Roll out the other half of the dough into a circle about 1 inch larger than the top of the pie plate. Place all the rolled trimmings and the pastry top in a flat layer on a plate or baking sheet and store them, uncovered, in the refrigerator to stay cool while you finish assembling the pie.

5. Assemble the pie: Sprinkle the panko evenly over the bottom of the pie shell. Spread the roasted onions and mushrooms over the panko, packing them together to form an even layer. Using a spoon, press the ricotta into an even layer over the mushrooms and onions.

6. Spoon 3 tablespoons of the pesto over the ricotta and spread it out into an even layer. Place the roasted pepper strips in an even layer over the pesto.

(CONTINUES)

DO AHEAD

The butter pastry can be made ahead, wrapped tightly in plastic wrap, and stored in the refrigerator for up to 1 week or in the freezer for up to 6 months. If frozen, thaw in the refrigerator overnight before using. The filling can be made ahead and stored in an airtight container in the refrigerator for up to 2 days. This dish is best enjoyed on the day of baking. Store leftovers in an airtight container in the refrigerator for up to 4 days.

7. Spoon ¼ cup of the marinara sauce evenly over the roasted peppers. Place the roasted zucchini rounds on top, overlapping them slightly to form an even layer.

8. Spoon the remaining ¼ cup marinara sauce evenly over the zucchini. Place the roasted eggplant rounds on top, overlapping them slightly to form an even layer. Spoon the remaining 3 tablespoons of pesto over the eggplant and spread it out into an even layer.

9. Make the egg wash and finish the pie: In a small bowl, thoroughly whisk together the egg and water until well combined. Brush the egg wash around the outer edge of the pie crust. Remove the pastry top from the refrigerator. Fold the rolled-out dough in half to lift it without stretching and gently unfold it over the pie plate. Using your fingertips, gently press the edges together around the tart, trim the excess pastry, and crimp the edges with your fingers to seal the top and bottom together. If the pastry is getting soft, refrigerate the pie for 10 to 15 minutes before adding your pastry details.

10. Lightly brush the egg wash over the entire surface of the pie. To make cutout decorations (optional), reroll the trimmings. If needed, you can reroll the dough, but every time you do so it will get less flaky. You can have up to 3 layers of pastry overlapping in your image but no more than that or it won't bake through fully. Use the egg wash sparingly as a paste to glue your pieces onto the crust. Lightly brush the egg wash over the whole surface of the pie one more time. Using a paring knife, make at least 1 cut on the top of the pie to let the steam escape.

11. Bake for 50 to 60 minutes, or until the pastry is a deep golden brown. Allow the pie to rest for 5 to 10 minutes before serving.

Pull-Apart Garlic Cheese Buns

1 batch Enriched Dough (page 304)
¾ cup unsalted butter, melted
4 green onions, thinly sliced
4 cloves garlic, crushed
1 teaspoon garlic powder
1 teaspoon salt
½ teaspoon freshly ground
   black pepper
½ cup shredded old cheddar cheese

Bake these buns as people are arriving for a mouthwatering aromatherapy experience, and make sure you enjoy them warm from the oven for the ideal pull-apart experience. Garlic bread and its variations have been around for centuries, and these familiar flavours should please most guests.

1. Generously grease a 12-cup muffin pan with canola oil cooking spray.

2. On a lightly floured work surface, roll out the enriched dough into a 14-inch square. Move the dough around and check underneath it a couple of times to make sure it is not sticking to the work surface, dusting lightly with more flour as needed. Brush any flour off the top of the dough with a dry pastry brush. Let the dough rest on the counter for 5 minutes. If it shrinks while resting, roll it out again to a 14-inch square and let rest again for 5 minutes.

3. In a small bowl, stir together the melted butter, green onions, garlic, garlic powder, salt, and pepper.

4. Using a pizza cutter, cut the square of dough into 4 even strips, 14 inches long × 3½ inches wide. Spoon 3 tablespoons of the melted butter mixture over the first strip and use the back of the spoon to spread the butter evenly over the entire surface of the dough. Stack a second strip of dough directly on top of the buttered dough, lining up the edges and pressing down gently. Spoon 3 tablespoons of the melted butter mixture over the second strip and use the back of the spoon to spread the butter evenly over the entire surface of the dough. Stack a third strip of dough and repeat with the melted butter. Stack the final piece of dough on top but do not butter it.

5. Cut the stacked dough in half so that you have two rectangles, each 7 inches long × 3½ inches wide. Spoon 2 tablespoons of the melted butter mixture over one of the rectangles and use the back of the spoon to spread the butter evenly over the entire surface of the dough. Stack the second rectangle of dough directly on top of the buttered dough, lining up the edges and pressing down gently. Set aside the remaining butter mixture at room temperature for step 7. (CONTINUES)

DO AHEAD

You can prepare these buns up to 3 hours in advance and allow them to rise slowly in their well-greased muffin pan (step 6), covered, in the refrigerator instead of at room temperature. If refrigerated, allow 30 minutes for the buns to come to room temperature before baking. The dough can be made ahead and stored, covered with beeswax or plastic wrap, in the refrigerator for up to 36 hours or in the freezer for up to 1 month. If frozen, thaw in the refrigerator overnight. Allow refrigerated or previously frozen dough to come up to room temperature for 45 to 60 minutes before rolling it out. These buns are best enjoyed warm on the day of baking. Store leftovers in an airtight container at room temperature for up to 2 days.

6. Using a large chef's knife or a sharp pizza cutter, cut the rectangle into 12 equal pieces, each about 1¾ × 1¼ inches. Place the pieces in the prepared muffin cups with the longer cut side facing up so that you can see the layers of dough. Allow the buns to rise in a warm, humid area for 30 to 45 minutes, or until they increase in size by 50 percent. If the surface of the buns seems to be drying out, lightly spray them with warm water from a spray bottle.

7. Meanwhile, preheat the oven to 325°F (160°C). Bake the buns for 18 to 22 minutes, or until they have puffed up and are golden brown around the edges. Sprinkle the shredded cheddar over the buns and bake for 3 to 5 more minutes until the cheese is melted and bubbly. While the buns are warm, use a pastry brush to brush a layer of the reserved melted butter mixture over each bun.

The backbone of any good cookbook and baker is your building blocks—the pieces you know you can exchange to completely transform a dish or adjust it to your preference. These reference recipes are just a small portion of the basic recipes we have developed over the years, and we encourage you to make your own binder or file full of various base doughs, curds, compotes, ganaches, and cake fillings to enrich your baking experience. Having these recipes at your fingertips reduces food waste since you will always have a quick way to use up any fruit about to expire or other surplus ingredients. With a freezer full of butter pastry or sugar cookie dough, you can whip up a snack for guests in less than an hour and impress everyone with your from-scratch baking skills.

Basic Recipes

Cakes and Cake Decorating

Vanilla Cake Batter

PREP: 25 minutes

This oil-based cake stays moist longer than butter-based cakes and comes together with very little effort. The combination of vanilla extract and vanilla bean paste gives this cake a deep, rich vanilla flavour that tastes great all on its own.

1. Sift the flour, baking powder, and salt into a medium bowl and, using a whisk, blend until thoroughly combined.

2. In the bowl of a stand mixer fitted with the whisk attachment, combine the canola oil, sugar, eggs, and vanilla extract and paste. Whip on high speed until the mixture is pale in colour and has reached the ribbon stage, 12 to 15 minutes. You will know the mixture has reached the ribbon stage when you lift the whisk and the mixture drops back into the bowl in long ribbons.

3. Add half of the dry ingredients to the wet ingredients and whip on medium speed until almost fully incorporated, less than 1 minute. Scrape down the sides and bottom of the bowl. Add the buttermilk and whip on medium-high speed just until combined. Scrape down the sides and bottom of the bowl.

4. Add the remaining dry ingredients and whip just until combined. Scrape down the sides and bottom of the bowl. Whip a final time on medium-high speed until smooth, about 1 minute. Do not overmix, as doing so may deflate the air bubbles.

DO AHEAD: Bake this batter immediately after mixing, following the instructions in the recipe you are making.

Full Batch
2½ cups all-purpose flour
2¼ teaspoons baking powder
1 teaspoon salt
¾ cup canola oil
2 cups granulated sugar
4 large eggs, room temperature
1 tablespoon pure vanilla extract
1 tablespoon vanilla bean paste
1 cup buttermilk, room temperature

Half Batch
1¼ cups all-purpose flour
1 teaspoon baking powder
½ teaspoon salt
¼ cup + 2 tablespoons canola oil
1 cup granulated sugar
2 large eggs, room temperature
½ tablespoon pure vanilla extract
½ tablespoon vanilla bean paste
½ cup buttermilk, room temperature

One and a Half Batches
3¾ cups all-purpose flour
1 tablespoon + ½ teaspoon
 baking powder
1½ teaspoons salt
1 cup + 2 tablespoons canola oil
3 cups granulated sugar
6 large eggs, room temperature
1½ tablespoons pure vanilla extract
1½ tablespoons vanilla bean paste
1½ cups buttermilk,
 room temperature

How to Assemble and Decorate a Cake

Use these instructions as a guide to assemble and decorate the Mini Egg Cake (page 71), Raspberry Lemon Poke Cake (page 85), Strawberries and Cream Celebration Cake (page 183), and Pumpkin Spice Monster Cake (page 225). Practice definitely makes perfect when stacking and masking cakes, and the process can be a little challenging at first. We hope these step-by-step instructions will demystify the process and help you realize that it's not as difficult as it initially appears.

Tools:
- 12-inch cake turntable
- 8-inch or 10-inch cake board or platter
- Offset palette knife
- Silicone spatula
- Pastry brush
- Serrated knife
- Two 16-inch piping bags
- No. 804 round tip
- Two clean kitchen towels

Prepare the Cake Layers

1. When the cake layers have fully cooled, remove the parchment paper from the bottoms. Using a serrated knife, trim the domes off the top of the cake layers to make them flat and level with the bottom of the layers. Keep your knife level while cutting. Save the cake domes to use for the Summer Berry Trifle (page 147). Cut the cake layers in half horizontally, making four layers of cake total (see photo A). Use the cake halves with a flat-baked bottom for the bottom and top layers of your cake and the halves with two cut sides for the centre layers. If the cake recipe has four separate cakes, only remove the domes.

Stack the Cake

2. We will be using our simple stacking method, so stack as you go. To start, in the bowl of a stand mixer fitted with the paddle attachment, beat the room-temperature buttercream on medium-high speed for about 10 minutes to remove any large bubbles, creating a light and fluffy texture. You will re-beat the buttercream several times during cake assembly, so keep your mixer and paddle attachment handy. Fill a 16-inch piping bag fitted with a No. 804 round tip with buttercream. Place the bottom cake layer, cut side up, on a round cake board or serving plate that is 2 inches larger than the diameter of your cake and moisten it with simple syrup (see photo B). Using even pressure, pipe a buttercream dam around the top edge of the cake layer (see photo C). As indicated in the recipe, evenly spoon any fillings onto the cake layer. Using an offset palette knife, spread semi-solid fillings outward until they meet the edge of the buttercream dam. If the recipe indicates, place ½ cup of buttercream over the toppings and/or fillings in the well. Using an offset palette knife, spread out and smooth the buttercream, fillings, or icings just until they meet the edge and are level with the top of the dam (see photos D and E). Repeat this process for the second and third cake layers using the fillings or buttercreams indicated in the recipe. Place the remaining flat-baked bottom cake layer, cut side down, so you have a smooth, flat surface for the top of your cake.

Crumb Coat the Cake

3. Use a pastry brush to moisten the entire surface of the top cake layer with up to 4 tablespoons of Simple Syrup (page 285; see photo F). Clean the edge of the cake board with a damp kitchen towel to remove excess crumbs. Place the cake on a turntable. In the bowl of a stand mixer fitted with the paddle attachment, beat the buttercream on medium-high speed for about 10 minutes, until light and fluffy. Scoop about ¼ cup of buttercream on top of the cake. Using a step palette knife, with even pressure, spread out and lightly coat the top of the cake with a layer of buttercream (see photo G). Begin to cover the sides of the cake in a thin, flat coating of buttercream while turning the turntable, flattening and removing excess buttercream. You will have a thin coating with some exposed cake areas; you should be able to see some of the cake through the icing. Clean the cake board, removing any buttercream splatter and crumbs. This crumb coat captures all the crumbs and will give the cake a nice clean finish when the second layer of buttercream is applied. Place the cake in the refrigerator to harden for at least 15 minutes.

Mask the Cake

4. In the bowl of a stand mixer fitted with the paddle attachment, beat the remaining buttercream on medium-high speed until light and fluffy, about 10 minutes. This will release large bubbles, while aerating finer bubbles, which makes it easier to achieve a smooth buttercream finish. Remove the cake from the refrigerator and place it on a turntable. Place ¼ cup of buttercream on top of the cake. Using a step palette knife, spread and smooth the icing ¼-inch thick over the top surface of the cake (see photo H). Cover the sides of the cake with additional buttercream, flattening it to ¼-inch thick while turning the turntable to create smooth sides. The icing from the sides will peak and push over the top of your cake, creating a wall (see photo I). Wipe the palette knife clean on a damp kitchen towel and complete the sides by creating horizontal lines like on the Mini Egg Cake (page 71) or a rustic finish as seen here. A rustic finish is intentionally a little messy and unrefined and is the easiest way to finish the sides of a cake. Use the tip of a palette knife to push the buttercream back and forth in different directions to create a rough and patchy, textured buttercream finish (see photo J).

Finish the Cake

5. To finish the top of the cake, flatten the wall of buttercream creating a sharp edge by pulling a palette knife from the outside in toward the centre of the cake. Continue with this technique until you have a smooth, level top, cleaning the palette knife between each pass (see photo K). Continue with the rustic finish technique for the top (see photo L). Clean the edges of the cake board with a clean, damp kitchen towel, removing any buttercream splatter and crumbs.

Piping Styles

You will find a variety of piping styles adorning some of our favourite baked goods throughout this book. Below, you will see examples of all the ones we love! Feel free to experiment and change it up. No matter if it's buttercream or whipped cream, we tend to use a large No. 804 round tip, a slightly wider No. 806 round tip, or a No. 825 star tip. For small details like writing on cakes or for finer decorative pieces, we use smaller tips ranging from No. 1 to No. 10 round tips and various star, leaf, and basket weave tips. However, do not limit yourself to these tips—let your imagination play! Build a collection of different tips. We highly recommend adding at least three large and six small couplers to your collection so that you can easily swap out tips without emptying your piping bags.

Buttercream and Whipped Cream Piping Styles

A. Writing and Flourishes (No. 4 round tip): used for writing and fine details

B. Round Reverse Shell Border (No. 804 round tip): used for cakes

C. Star Swirl Border, Classic Small Rossette, and Star Drop (No. 824 or No. 825 star tip): used for cakes or pies

D. Classic Large Rosette (No. 827 star tip) and Flat Whisp (No. 126 petal icing tip): used for cupcakes, doughnuts, or bars

E. Fine Star Rossette and Fine Star Rosette (No. 199 fine star tip): used for cakes

F. Textured Fur Finish (No. 288 grass tip): used for cakes to create texture

G. Floral Accents (assortment of Russian flower tips): used for cakes

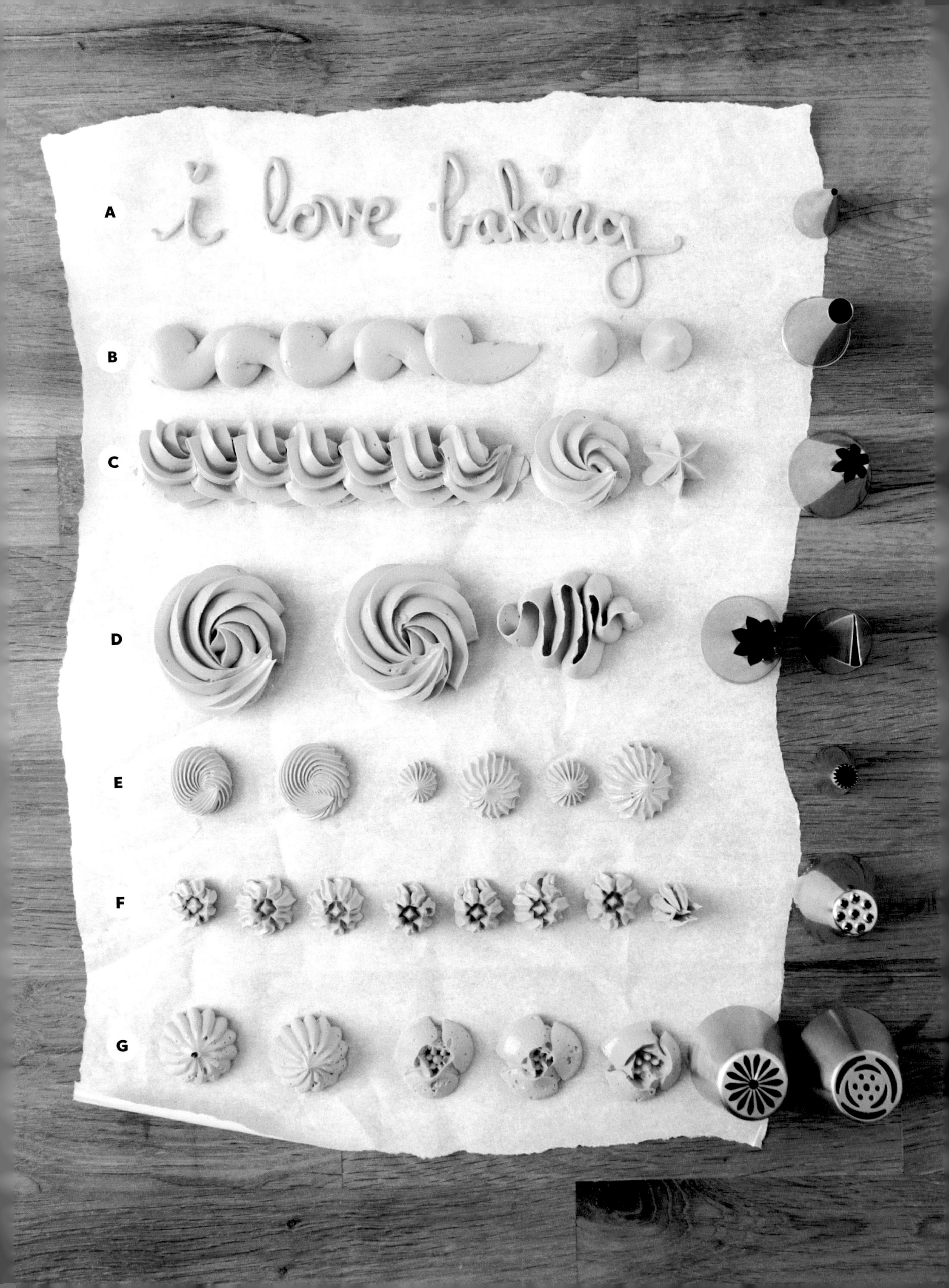
A
i love baking
B
C
D
E
F
G

Royal Icing Piping Styles

STIFF TEXTURE

H. Writing and Borders (No. 1 to No. 4 round tips): used for writing, outlining cookies, and fine details

I. Basket Weave (No. 46 basket weave tip): used to create basket patterns or bandages like for for Chocolate Dipped Brownie Mummies (page 213) and cakes

J. Classic Rosette and Kisses (No. 824 and No. 825 star tips): used for Sugar Dot Cookies (page 177)

STABLE FLOODING TEXTURE

K. Eyes or Flat Rounds (No. 4 round tip): used to make eyeballs for Monster Krispies (page 219) and for Sugar Dot Cookies (page 177)

FLOODING TEXTURE

L. Flooding Centers of Cookies (No. 2 round tip or spoon): used for "flooding" decorated cookies like We Belong Together Iced Sugar Cookies (page 35)

Fondant Cake Details

Fondant is an edible, pliable, dough-like icing that can be transformed into anything you can imagine with a little ingenuity and creativity. By adding colours and flavours, you can create decorative pieces and even sculptures to adorn and elevate pastries, cakes, pies, and cookies. Fondant is a wonderfully creative tool but can be frustrating if it is new to you. To ensure success, here are a few of our secrets.

Helpful Tools: cornstarch (for rolling), marble rolling pin, fondant smoothing tool, metal pin (sewing pins), plastic wrap, pizza cutter, ruler, plastic gloves (when tinting with colours), cutting board, and general gum paste tool set.

Storage and Working: Keep fondant that isn't being used covered, whether in a container or tightly wrapped in plastic wrap. Wrap everything up as you work.

Colouring: Colour all your fondant before you start to craft your details, wrapping colours tightly in plastic wrap individually as you go and using gloves to save your hands from staining. If you knead colours in with your hands, you can use baking soda as an exfoliant when it's time to wash up. Also, if you are using your bare hands, wash them in between each colour.

Flavouring: Choose complementary flavours and remember that you'll need only a small amount. Almond flavouring is a classic addition but try using different flavours like cotton candy, cinnamon, or peppermint. Take into consideration what the fondant will be covering and if it will complement the flavour in the interior. A variety of flavours can be found at your local grocery store or bulk food store. Oils are also much better for this application than extracts, as they are more concentrated and a few drops go a very long way.

Rolling: A light dusting of sifted cornstarch is always recommended when rolling fondant to ensure that it doesn't stick to your rolling surface or rolling pin. You can fill a small overlapping square of cheesecloth with cornstarch and tie it with string or elastic so that you can dab the surface and control the amount you use. The cheesecloth method is great for dusting an even layer inside moulds before pressing in the fondant.

Crafting: Use water as your glue; a small amount will make the surface tacky and easily sticky. Toothpicks and skewer sticks can also be used to attach or to stick into cakes. Cover your creation as you work because you may want to add items, and if the surface begins to dry and you want to make an addition, it may crack.

Drying: A metal cooling rack works well or if you have something that must remain propped up, such as the monster horns (page 291), pierce the end of the skewer inside the horn into a styrofoam cake covered with some parchment paper to ensure that it doesn't stick to the styrofoam. Tylose powder can be used as an additive; this acts as a drying agent in combination with fondant. If you are creating a topper, such as monster horns (page 291) or a spider (page 292) and you would like to ensure that it holds its form and integrity, follow the package instructions for amounts of fondant and tylose powder and knead them together thoroughly. Be sure to cover and wrap your dough as you work. Allow the items you create to air-dry for 2 to 3 days until completely hardened.

Pumpkin Spice Monster Cake Fondant Eyes and Horns

MAKES 12 to 16 eyes and 2 horns • **PREP:** 25 minutes, plus drying time

These fondant eyes and horns decorate the Pumpkin Spice Monster Cake (page 225), one of our seasonal favourites at Halloween. See opposite page for tips before getting started.

1. Make the eyes: On a work surface lightly dusted with cornstarch, roll out 2 ounces (50 g) of the white fondant to about ¼-inch thickness. Move the dough around and check underneath it frequently to make sure it is not sticking to the work surface. Place a piece of plastic wrap on top of the fondant before cutting. Using the circle cookie cutters and large ends of the round piping tips, cut out 12 to 16 different-sized circles (eyes). Use even pressure and push down, twisting to ensure that the cut is through the fondant to the bottom, but don't cut or tear the plastic. The plastic wrap will give the eyeballs a rounded edge. Remove the plastic wrap and transfer the circles to a wire cooling rack.

2. On a work surface lightly dusted with cornstarch, knead 5 drops of black food colouring into ½ ounce (10 g) of the white fondant, using plastic gloves if you want to avoid dyeing your hands. Add additional drops of black food colouring and continue to knead until you are happy with the colour. Roll out the black fondant to about ¼-inch thickness. Move the dough around and check underneath it frequently to make sure it is not sticking to the work surface. Place a piece of plastic wrap on top of the fondant before cutting. Using the small and large ends of the round piping tips, cut out 12 to 16 different-sized circles (pupils) smaller than your white eyes. Use even pressure and push down, twisting to ensure that the cut is through the fondant to the bottom, but don't cut or tear the plastic. Remove the plastic wrap and transfer the circles to a wire cooling rack. Using water and a small paintbrush, attach the black pupils to the white eyes.

3. Pinch a tiny amount of white fondant, roll it into very small balls, and attach 1 ball to the top right edge of each pupil, leaving a 1/16-inch border, to create highlights on the pupils. Place the finished eyeballs on a wire cooling rack to stiffen up for 2 to 3 days.

4. Make the horns: On a work surface lightly dusted with cornstarch, knead 5 drops of orange food colouring into 6½ ounces (190 g) of the white fondant, using plastic gloves if you want to avoid dyeing your hands. Add additional drops of orange food colouring and continue to knead until you are happy with the colour. Divide the ball in half and cover one-half with plastic wrap while you work with the other half. Working with the first ball, roll into a short 4-inch cylinder with a tapered, pinched end (the horn's point). Roll the tapered end of the horn into a small spiral. Repeat with the second ball. (CONTINUES)

DO AHEAD: Make the fondant pieces at least 3 days ahead and allow them to dry, uncovered, at room temperature in a dry area for 3 days. Once completely dry, you can store them in an airtight container at room temperature for up to 6 months.

You'll need:
Rolling pin
Plastic wrap
1-inch and 2-inch round cookie cutter
No. 804 and No. 806 round piping tips
Two 6-inch-long wooden skewers
Small paint brush and water (for attaching items)
Drying/cooling rack

Fondant Eyes and Horns
8 ounces (250 g) white vanilla fondant (we use Satin Ice)
½ cup cornstarch, for rolling
5 to 8 drops black gel food colouring
5 to 8 drops orange gel food colouring

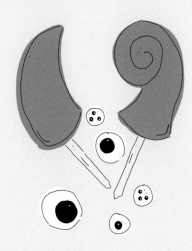

5. Pierce the base of each horn with a skewer's flat end (not the sharp end), right through the centre of the horn. Leave 3½ inches of skewer hanging out and make sure you don't go through the top of the horns. Place the horns on a flat surface with a ball of paper towel keeping the skewer end level with the insertion point. Or, if you have a styrofoam cake round, place parchment paper on top and pierce both horns through the surface, standing them up to dry. Allow the horns to dry, uncovered, at room temperature in a dry area for 2 to 3 days.

DO AHEAD: Make the fondant spider at least 2 days ahead and allow it to dry, uncovered, at room temperature in a dry area for 2 to 3 days. Once completely dry, you can store the spider in an airtight container at room temperature for up to 6 months.

You'll need:
Small paint brush and water
   (for attaching items)
Drying/cooling rack

Fondant Spider
2 ounces (50 g) white vanilla
   fondant (we use Satin Ice)
½ cup cornstarch, for rolling
5 to 8 drops black gel
   food colouring

PB&J Crunch Pie Fondant Spider

MAKES one 2-inch spider • **PREP:** 15 minutes, plus drying time

This adorable fondant spider tops our PB&J Crunch Pie (page 223). The pie is just as delicious without the spider but definitely scarier and more fun for trick-or-treaters with it! See page 290 for tips before getting started.

1. Before tinting all the white fondant, pinch off ¼ teaspoon of the white fondant to be the eyes of the spider. Wrap in plastic wrap and set aside.

2. Make the body and head: On a work surface lightly dusted with cornstarch, knead 5 drops of black food colouring into the remaining white fondant, using plastic gloves if you want to avoid dyeing your hands. Add additional drops of black food colouring and continue to knead until you are happy with the colour. Divide the dough into 3 equal portions and wrap one portion in plastic wrap for step 4.

3. Take one portion and divide it in half, then add one half to the second portion, which you will use to make the spider's body. Set aside the smaller portion of fondant, which you will use to make the spider's head. Shape the larger portion of fondant into a ball and set it on a flat work surface. Next, take the smaller portion of fondant and roll it into a ball. Using a small paint brush, brush water on one side of the small ball and press the wet side gently into the larger ball to attach the head to the body so that they are both resting on the flat work surface.

4. Make the legs: Divide the last portion of fondant into 4 equal-sized balls. Roll each ball into short 4-inch ropes with tapered, pinched ends. Lay them out parallel to one another and pinch the centre of all of them together. This will cause the legs to jump out to the sides. Organize the legs with 2 sets on either side, pointing inwards at the front and back of the body (see illustration). Using water and a small paintbrush, wet the centre of the legs where they are pinched and place the spider's body on top.

5. Use the reserved white fondant to pinch off 2 very small portions and roll them into tiny balls. Gently press the white balls onto the top section of the spider's head to form eyeballs. Transfer the spider to a wire cooling rack and allow it to dry, uncovered, at room temperature in a dry area for 2 to 3 days.

Buttercreams and Icings

Vanilla Bean Buttercream

MAKES about 6 cups • **PREP:** 30 minutes

This is a very stable icing and easy to make in big batches to keep around for last-minute cupcakes. Don't be shocked if it breaks and appears curdled when you are re-beating it for use. It just wasn't the right temperature. Keep beating the icing on high speed and it will come back together within 15 minutes. Just like a quality cheese, never serve this buttercream chilled but always at room temperature. Since it contains so much butter, it is essentially solid when cold and will make your baked goods seem dry and flavourless unless it is allowed to come to room temperature. Consider trying this buttercream for icing cakes and cupcakes, filling sandwich cookies, topping coffee cakes or bars, piping on top of shortbread, or using as a dip for cookies or fruit. See page 286 for Buttercream and Whipped Cream Piping Styles.

1. Fill a medium saucepan with 2 to 3 inches of hot water as part of a double boiler and bring to a boil over high heat. Once boiling, reduce the heat to low to maintain a simmer.

2. In a medium glass or stainless steel bowl that will fit nicely over the pan of hot water but not touch the simmering water below, whisk together the egg whites, sugar, and salt. Place the bowl over the simmering water bath. Whisk constantly until the sugar has dissolved and the mixture has a sticky, tacky-looking texture. As it is heating, you will notice the mixture becoming more fluid; keep whisking until it reaches 140°F (60°C) on a candy thermometer, or until the mixture is body temperature to the touch and the sugar is dissolved.

3. Transfer the meringue mixture to the bowl of a stand mixer fitted with the whisk attachment. Whisk on high speed for 10 to 15 minutes, or until stiff peaks have formed and you can no longer feel any heat coming from the bottom of the mixing bowl.

4. Reduce the speed to medium-high and start adding the butter pieces, waiting until each addition is fully incorporated before adding the next. Scrape down the sides of the bowl at least twice while making your additions.

5. Once all the butter is incorporated and the buttercream is smooth, beat for 5 minutes on high speed. Give the bowl one final scrape, then add the vanilla extract and paste and continue to beat on high speed for 2 more minutes.

6. Use immediately or keep covered at room temperature for up to 1 day until ready to use. When ready to use, in the bowl of a stand mixer fitted with the paddle attachment, beat on high speed for 5 to 10 minutes.

DO AHEAD: Store in an airtight container in the refrigerator for up to 2 months or in the freezer for up to 6 months. If refrigerated, let soften at room temperature. If frozen, thaw in the refrigerator overnight. When ready to use, in the bowl of a stand mixer fitted with the paddle attachment, beat on high speed for 5 to 10 minutes.

8 large egg whites (about 1 cup)
1¼ cups granulated sugar
⅛ teaspoon salt
2 cups unsalted butter, cut into
    1-inch pieces, room temperature
1 tablespoon pure vanilla extract
1 tablespoon vanilla bean paste

2¼ cups icing sugar
⅔ cup unsalted butter, cut into
  1-inch cubes, room temperature
2 teaspoons vanilla bean paste
1 to 2 tablespoons whipping (35%)
  cream, divided

Vanilla Bean American Buttercream

MAKES about 2 cups • **PREP:** 12 minutes

Sweet and fluffy, this buttercream is the most basic combination of butter and icing sugar with just a touch of cream to lighten it up and vanilla for flavour. Many consider this classic birthday cake frosting. Although it will never have the beautiful smooth finish of a Swiss meringue buttercream, it stands up well for extended periods at room temperature and can be used interchangeably with Vanilla Bean Buttercream (page 293).

1. In the bowl of a stand mixer fitted with the paddle attachment, beat the icing sugar, butter, vanilla bean paste, and 1 tablespoon of the cream, starting on low speed and increasing to high speed as the icing sugar incorporates. Mix on high speed for 6 to 8 minutes, stopping to scrape down the sides and bottom of the bowl once or twice, until the icing is light and fluffy. This can take up to 10 minutes, depending on the temperature of the butter.

2. Add up to 1 tablespoon of the remaining cream, mixing well after each addition, to adjust the consistency, if needed.

2 cups icing sugar, sifted
¼ cup soft vegan margarine
  (we use Crystal), room
  temperature
¼ cup vegan butter (we use
  Earth Balance Buttery Sticks),
  room temperature
1½ teaspoons vanilla bean paste

Vegan Vanilla Bean Buttercream ⓥ

MAKES 2 cups • **PREP:** 12 minutes

A vegan version of our sweet and fluffy Vanilla Bean American Buttercream (above). Use our recommended brands, as margarines and vegan butters can vary greatly in flavour and moisture content. If you cannot find these brands, look for a margarine that is soft and spreadable even when refrigerated and a vegan butter that's firm and salted and has a subtle butter flavour.

1. In the bowl of a stand mixer fitted with the paddle attachment, beat the icing sugar, vegan margarine and butter, and vanilla bean paste on low speed until combined. Scrape down the sides and bottom of the bowl. With the mixer on high speed, beat until light and fluffy, about 10 minutes.

Dreamy Cream Cheese Icing

MAKES about 6 cups • **PREP:** 15 minutes

It is essential to use soft, room-temperature cream cheese to avoid lumps and achieve perfectly smooth icing. If your kitchen is cool, you may want to microwave the cream cheese for 30 seconds to remove the chill. This sweet but slightly tart versatile icing is great to have on hand to spread on cakes, swap out for buttercream in cake fillings, fill sandwich cookies, or use as a dip for cookies or fruit platters.

1. In the bowl of a stand mixer fitted with the paddle attachment, combine the icing sugar and butter. Starting with the mixer on low speed and slowly increasing to high speed to avoid creating an icing powder storm, mix until combined. Then beat on high speed until light and fluffy, about 10 minutes. Scrape down the sides and bottom of the bowl.

2. With the mixer on medium-high speed, add the cream cheese in 3 additions, scraping down the sides and bottom of the bowl after each addition.

3. When the cream cheese has been fully incorporated, scrape down the sides and bottom of the bowl, then beat the icing for just 1 more minute.

DO AHEAD: Store in an airtight container in the refrigerator for up to 1 month or in the freezer for up to 2 months. If refrigerated, let soften at room temperature. If frozen, thaw in the refrigerator overnight. When ready to use, in the bowl of a stand mixer fitted with the paddle attachment, beat on high speed for 5 to 10 minutes.

3½ cups icing sugar
1 cup unsalted butter,
    room temperature
1¾ pounds (790 g/3½ cups)
    cream cheese, cut into 1-inch
    cubes, room temperature

Royal Icing

MAKES about 3 cups • **PREP:** 18 minutes

Great for icing fruitcakes or cookies, this icing transforms from pillowy clouds to crunchy candy as it dries and hardens. It's excellent for baked goods intended to last for weeks, as it's super stable at room temperature. You can tint royal icing any colour imaginable with gel food colouring to add creative flair to any baking project. See page 288 for Royal Icing Piping Styles.

1. In a stand mixer fitted with the whisk attachment, whisk the egg whites, lemon juice, and vanilla on medium-high speed until the egg whites have quadrupled in volume and soft, frothy white peaks have formed, 2 to 3 minutes.

2. Add the icing sugar, 1 cup at a time, and whip thoroughly after each addition on medium-low speed until all the icing sugar is incorporated, 1 minute per addition. Scrape down the sides and bottom of the bowl after each addition.

3. Increase the speed to medium-high and continue to whisk until the icing is thick and luxurious and no grit remains from the icing sugar, about 6 to 7 minutes. Test the thickness by pulling the whisk out of the mixer and looking for a soft serve ice cream curl when you turn the whisk upside down. It should hold this shape when the icing is the correct consistency.

4. Scrape down the sides and bottom of the bowl. Place a wet clean kitchen towel over the bowl so that the icing does not dry out. Keep covered at all times when not using.

DO AHEAD: Store in an airtight container in the refrigerator for up to 1 month. When ready to use, in the bowl of a stand mixer fitted with the paddle attachment, beat on high speed for 5 to 7 minutes.

¼ cup + 2 tablespoons egg whites
    (3 large eggs)
½ teaspoon fresh lemon juice
1 teaspoon pure vanilla extract
4 cups icing sugar, sifted

Crusts, Toppings, and Doughs

Butter Pastry

MAKES enough for 12 Creamy Garlic Kale and Prosciutto Tarts (page 89), 12 Quiche Two Ways (page 111), 15 Raspberry Pop Tarts (page 163), 1 Rainbow Pie (page 165), or 1 Turkey and Wild Rice Pie with Mashed Potato Topping (page 207); 1½ batches required for 12 Mini Chicken Pot Pies (page 91), the Mile-High Pulled Pork Mac and Cheese Pie (page 149), French Canadian Tourtière (page 251), or Roasted Vegetable Torta Rustica (page 275) • **PREP:** 10 minutes, plus chilling time

Great for sweet and savoury pies and tarts of all varieties, this is classic flaky butter pastry at its best. If you tend to have hot hands, wash them in cold water before you touch your pastry to keep it flaky. There's often a little pastry left over, so try baking pastry scraps in a 400°F (200°C) oven until deep golden brown and dusting them with cinnamon sugar or herbs and Parmesan cheese just as they come out of the oven. Let kids play with pastry scraps to make their own unique pastries or wrap them around your favourite butcher sausage and bake at 400°F (200°C) for 30 to 35 minutes for sausage rolls. We like to double the recipe and freeze half, tightly wrapped (your future self will thank you). Just defrost in the fridge before using.

1. Grate the frozen butter on the large holes of a box grater into a large bowl. Place in the freezer for 10 to 15 minutes to make sure the butter remains frozen.

2. In a liquid measuring cup, mix the cold water, sugar, and salt until the solids are fully dissolved. Place in the refrigerator until ready to use.

3. Remove the bowl from the freezer and toss the flour with the grated butter to distribute the butter evenly throughout the flour.

4. Using a fork, mix the cold water mixture into the flour mixture, causing as little friction as possible, until you have a shaggy dough. You want to try to maintain those butter pieces. Resist the urge to add more water unless absolutely necessary to bring the pastry together into a shaggy dough with just a little dry flour. If needed, add 2 to 3 more tablespoons of cold water to the dough, 1 tablespoon at a time.

5. Bring the pastry together by gently folding it into a rough disc, then wrap it tightly in plastic wrap and refrigerate for at least 1 hour before rolling it out.

DO AHEAD: Store pastry wrapped tightly in plastic wrap in the refrigerator for up to 1 week or in the freezer for up to 6 months. If frozen, thaw in the refrigerator overnight before using.

1 cup unsalted butter, frozen
½ cup cold water, more if needed
1½ teaspoons sugar
1 teaspoon salt
2½ cups all-purpose flour

Vegan Pastry Ⓥ

MAKES enough for 12 Creamy Garlic Kale and Prosciutto Tarts (page 89), 12 Quiche Two Ways (page 111), 15 Raspberry Pop Tarts (page 163), 1 Rainbow Pie (page 165), or 1 Turkey and Wild Rice Pie with Mashed Potato Topping (page 207); 1½ batches required for 12 Mini Chicken Pot Pies (page 91), the Mile-High Pulled Pork Mac and Cheese Pie (page 149), French Canadian Tourtière (page 251), or Roasted Vegetable Torta Rustica (page 275) • **PREP:** 10 minutes, plus chilling time

This pastry can be used interchangeably with the butter pastry in any recipe found in this book.

1. Grate the frozen vegan butter on the large holes of a box grater into a large bowl. Place the bowl in the freezer for 10 to 15 minutes to make sure the vegan butter remains frozen.

2. In a liquid measuring cup, mix the apple cider vinegar, cold water, sugar, and salt until the solids are fully dissolved. Place in the refrigerator until ready to use.

3. Remove the bowl from the freezer and toss the flour with the grated vegan butter to distribute the butter evenly throughout the flour.

4. Using a fork, mix the cold water mixture into the flour mixture, causing as little friction as possible, until you have a shaggy dough. You want to try to maintain those vegan butter pieces. Resist the urge to add more water unless absolutely necessary to bring the pastry together into a shaggy dough with just a little dry flour. If needed, add 2 to 3 more tablespoons of cold water to the dough, 1 tablespoon at a time.

5. Bring the pastry together by gently folding it into a rough disc, then wrap it tightly in plastic wrap and refrigerate for at least 1 hour before rolling it out.

DO AHEAD: Store pastry wrapped tightly in plastic wrap in the refrigerator for up to 1 week or in the freezer for up to 6 months. If frozen, thaw in the refrigerator overnight before using.

1 cup vegan butter, frozen (we use Earth Balance Buttery Sticks)
2 tablespoons apple cider vinegar
⅓ cup cold water, more if needed
1½ teaspoons sugar
½ teaspoon salt
2½ cups all-purpose flour

DO AHEAD: Mix the pastry dough and allow it to rest in the refrigerator for at least 12 and up to 24 hours before continuing the layering process in step 4. The pastry dough can be made ahead, wrapped tightly in plastic wrap, and stored in the refrigerator for up to 3 days or in the freezer for up to 6 months. If frozen, thaw in the refrigerator overnight before using.

1¾ cups all-purpose flour
1 cup unsalted butter, cold and cut into ¾-inch cubes
½ teaspoon salt
½ cup ice cold water

Blitz Puff Pastry

MAKES enough for 9 Fresh Fruit Passion Puffs (page 141) or one 18- × 13-inch Fresh Vegetable Pizza base (page 189) • **PREP:** 25 minutes, plus chilling time

This cheater's puff pastry is so straightforward to mix and skips the complications of forming a butter block and incorporating it into the dough. This is laminated dough at its easiest. Make sure all your ingredients are cold and be aware that the dough will need to rest overnight before you layer and fold it.

1. Mix and chill the dough: In the bowl of a stand mixer fitted with the paddle attachment, add the flour, butter cubes, and salt. Mix on medium-low speed for 30 seconds to 1 minute just to coat all the butter in flour. You do not want to break up the butter chunks.

2. With the mixer running on low speed, in a steady stream add the cold water. Mix as little as possible to wet all the flour and bring the ingredients together into a shaggy dough while keeping the butter chunks intact. Briefly pulse at medium speed to bring the dough together.

3. Using your hands, bring the pastry together by gently folding it into a rough disc, then wrap it tightly in plastic wrap and refrigerate overnight or at least 12 hours.

4. Roll out the dough and make the first fold: On a lightly floured surface, roll out the pastry dough into a 9- × 18-inch rectangle. Using a dry pastry brush, brush any flour off the surface of the dough. With a short side facing you, fold the 2 short sides into the centre of the dough, leaving about ½ inch of space between them. You will have about a 9-inch square of pastry dough. Brush off any flour on the surface of the dough and then fold the dough again along the centre as if closing a thick book. If you look at the pastry from the side, you should be able to see 4 distinct layers. Wrap the pastry lightly in plastic wrap or parchment paper and place it in the refrigerator for 30 minutes.

5. Roll out the dough and make the second fold: On a lightly floured surface, roll out the pastry into a 9- × 18-inch rectangle. Make a second book fold following the instructions in step 4, making sure to brush any flour off the pastry surface with a dry pastry brush before folding it. Wrap the pastry lightly in plastic wrap or parchment paper and place it in the refrigerator for 30 minutes.

6. Roll out the dough and make the third fold: On a lightly floured surface, roll out the pastry into a 9- × 18-inch rectangle and make a third and final book fold following the instructions in step 4. Wrap the pastry lightly in plastic wrap or parchment paper and place it in the refrigerator for at least 2 hours.

Graham Crumb Crust

MAKES enough for one 9-inch pie base for Mini Egg Cream Pie (page 66) or Pumpkin Cheesecake Pie with Pecan Praline (page 203) or bases for 20 Mini Chocolate Chili Heat Cheesecakes (page 45) • **PREP:** 5 minutes

Definitely the fastest way to make a pie crust, you can use this crust instead of butter pastry for any custard- or pudding-based pies. Avoid using it for moist pies like apple or mixed berry. Depending on the humidity of your kitchen and the graham cracker crumbs you use, you might need to adjust this recipe slightly. To test that your crumb base is the right texture, squeeze some in the palm of your hand. It should stay in large clumps once you open your palm. If it crumbles, add another tablespoon of melted butter.

1. In a medium bowl, mix together the graham cracker crumbs, melted butter, and brown sugar until well combined.

DO AHEAD: Store graham crumb in an airtight container in the refrigerator for up to 1 month or in the freezer for up to 6 months. If frozen, thaw in the refrigerator overnight before using.

2 cups graham cracker crumbs
6 tablespoons unsalted butter, melted and warm
½ cup lightly packed dark brown sugar

Chocolate Graham Crumb Crust

MAKES enough for one 9-inch pie base for PB Chocolate Cream Pie (page 123) or alternative bases for 20 Mini Chocolate Chili Heat Cheesecakes (page 45) • **PREP:** 5 minutes

If you would like to add a little chocolate kick to any of our graham crust recipes, swap in this rich chocolate base for the regular graham base; they can be used interchangeably. We find that the salt makes all the difference in this graham base to elevate the chocolate flavour.

1. In a medium bowl, mix together the graham cracker crumbs, melted butter, cocoa, sugar, and salt until well combined.

DO AHEAD: Use immediately and bake according to recipe instructions or store in an airtight container in the refrigerator for up to 1 month or in the freezer for up to 6 months. If frozen, thaw in the refrigerator overnight before using.

2 cups graham cracker crumbs
½ cup unsalted butter, melted and warm
¼ cup cocoa powder
2 tablespoons granulated sugar
½ teaspoon salt

2 pounds (900 g) russet potatoes, peeled and quartered (6 cups)
½ cup buttermilk, warm
⅓ cup unsalted butter, melted and warm
2 teaspoons salt, more for seasoning
½ teaspoon freshly ground black pepper, more for seasoning

Mashed Potato Topping

MAKES about 6 cups • **PREP:** 10 minutes • **COOK:** 25 minutes

Mashed potatoes are one of our ultimate comfort foods, and what better way to enjoy them than on top of pie? You can use this topping in lieu of a pastry top for any of the savoury pies in this book. Any potato will work here, but the starch in russets will give you the best results for creamy but stable mashed potatoes.

1. Place the potatoes in a large pot of salted cold water and bring to a boil over high heat, then reduce the heat to medium and boil until fork-tender, 20 to 25 minutes. Drain and return the potatoes to the warm pot to dry out for 5 minutes. You will see the edges of the potatoes become white and a little flaky.

2. In the bowl of a stand mixer fitted with the paddle attachment, add the warm potatoes, buttermilk, butter, salt, and pepper. Mix on medium speed until no lumps remain. Taste the mixture and season with more salt and pepper, if desired. Use hot as a topping for savoury pies as instructed.

1 cup whipping (35%) cream, cold
1 tablespoon icing sugar
1 teaspoon pure vanilla extract

Whipped Cream

MAKES 2 cups • **PREP:** 5 minutes

It's simple but often overlooked, and you won't regret whipping your own fresh cream and skipping the store-bought. The whipping cream also can be whipped by hand in a bowl with a whisk, but maybe spread the workload out over a couple of helpers, as your arm may get sore.

1. Pour the cream, icing sugar, and vanilla into the bowl of a stand mixer fitted with the whisk attachment and whip on medium speed. The cream will start to get frothy and begin to thicken after 2 to 3 minutes. Increase the speed to high and whip for another 30 seconds to 1 minute, or until the cream looks fluffy and the whisk leaves deep markings in the whipped cream.

Meringue

MAKES about 2 cups • **PREP:** 15 minutes • **COOK:** 5 minutes

This is a Swiss meringue, which we find the easier of the two standards: Swiss and Italian meringue. It's almost impossible to overmix but commonly is undermixed, so if you aren't sure, give it another minute or two on the mixer.

1. Select a medium saucepan that fits the bottom of your stand mixer bowl. You will be using the bowl and pan to create a double boiler. Fill the pan with 2 inches of water and bring to a boil over high heat. Once the water has come to a boil, reduce the heat to a simmer.

2. In the bowl of the stand mixer, add the sugar and egg whites and gently whisk by hand just to wet all the sugar. Place the bowl over the simmering water and whisk constantly until the mixture reaches 140°F (60°C) on a candy thermometer, about 5 minutes. (Whisking keeps the egg whites moving so that you do not end up cooking them by accident.) If testing by hand, rub a bit of the mixture between 2 fingertips. It should feel smooth, not gritty, and warm to the touch.

3. Place the bowl on the stand mixer fitted with the whisk attachment. Whip on high speed until opaque, glossy white, stiff peaks form and you can no longer feel heat coming from the bottom of the bowl, 7 to 10 minutes.

DO AHEAD: Use immediately as instructed in the recipe. Prepared meringue cannot be stored.

½ cup + 1 tablespoon granulated sugar
¼ cup egg whites, room temperature (from about 2 large eggs)

Sugar Cookie Dough

MAKES enough for 20 We Belong Together Iced Sugar Cookies (page 35), 2½ dozen Belgium Cookies (page 103), 24 Nut-Free Mini Linzer Tarts (page 181), 12 dozen Sugar Dot Cookies (page 177), 12 dozen Sugar Cookies and Frosting Dip (page 269), or two 9-inch pie crusts (½ batch for the Peach Custard Pie crust, page 145) • **PREP:** 10 minutes

This versatile dough is great for cookies, iced cookies, and pie crusts. We love its shortbread-like texture and buttery flavour. It was one of the first recipes we developed at the bakery, and it remains a staple in all seasons for us.

1. In the bowl of a stand mixer fitted with the paddle attachment, cream the butter, sugar, and vanilla extract and paste on medium speed until pale in colour, 2 to 3 minutes. Do not overmix. You don't want this to be light and fluffy, as too much aeration will dry out the dough and cause it to crumble after baking. Scrape down the sides and bottom of the bowl.

2. Add the egg and beat until fully incorporated, 1 to 2 minutes. Scrape down the sides and bottom of the bowl. Remove the paddle and scrape it down, then return it to the stand mixer.

3. Add the flour and salt and mix on low speed to start for 30 seconds, then increase to medium-high speed, just until the mixture has formed a dough, about 1 minute. Do not overmix.

4. The dough should be rolled immediately after mixing according to the directions in the recipe.

1½ cups unsalted butter, room temperature
¾ cup + 2 tablespoons granulated sugar
1 tablespoon pure vanilla extract
1 teaspoon vanilla bean paste
1 large egg, room temperature
4¼ cups all-purpose flour, more for dusting
½ teaspoon salt

Yeast Doughs

We have been teaching bakers to make bread for more than a decade, and one thing is clear—even the most experienced bread bakers have bad days when the bread just doesn't turn out right. Sometimes there is a reason you can point to and a way to improve, but sometimes you have no idea what happened, and you have to just shrug it off and try another time. Here, we introduce you to some basic but flexible bread doughs. They are a great starting point to exploring yeast-raised doughs, but they are just the tip of the bread-baking iceberg. Yeast-raised doughs are very sensitive to the humidity and temperature in your kitchen, so rising times often vary. Keep an eye on your dough as it rises and use your senses, not the clock, to evaluate when something is ready to shape or go in the oven. The humidity of your kitchen can also affect your ingredients—for example, you may find that you need slightly more water to mix the same recipe in dry winter weather than during the humid summer months. Flour absorbs humidity from the air and therefore might be higher in moisture depending on the weather or season. To adjust for this, don't be afraid to add a couple of extra tablespoons of water or hold back a few tablespoons to get the right supple texture while mixing. Always store flour and other ingredients in a dry, room-temperature area and never in the fridge. When using a stand mixer for dough, never mix above medium-low speed (3 on a KitchenAid mixer) or you can easily burn out your motor with the torque required. The bread doughs in this book generally freeze well; simply defrost them in the refrigerator overnight before bringing them to room temperature. It's important to remember that yeast is a living thing, and you need to treat it gently. Always use fresh yeast and check the expiry date. Never put salt or sugar directly on yeast. We use instant yeast in all our recipes, which you add right into the mixture and do not bloom in advance. If you are concerned that the yeast is old or might have been improperly stored, the instant yeast can still bloom by adding it to the liquid in the recipe with 1 teaspoon of sugar and letting it sit for 10 minutes. It should bubble up and expand within that time, letting you know it's ready to work.

Pizza Dough

MAKES enough for 6 Heart-Shaped Pizzas (page 51), 2 giant Flatbread Seed Crackers (page 95), 1 Pierogi Pizza (page 230), or 2 dozen Ghost Bread Dippers (page 229) • **PREP:** 15 minutes, plus rising time

This basic bread dough is excellent for pizza, breadsticks or dippers, and crackers. The poolish starter helps the bread develop flavour and aroma. You'll never order takeout pizza again once you have mastered this recipe.

1. Make the poolish: In a large container (at least 12 cups) with a tight-fitting lid, mix the bread flour, whole wheat flour, water, and instant yeast until no dry flour remains and the yeast is evenly distributed. You will need enough room in the container for the poolish to triple in size.

2. Put the lid on the container and allow the mixture to sit at room temperature for 30 minutes. Then place the container in the refrigerator and allow the poolish to develop for at least 24 hours, up to 48 hours.

3. Make the dough: Remove the poolish from the refrigerator 30 minutes before making the dough so that it can come to room temperature.

4. In the bowl of a stand mixer fitted with the dough hook attachment, add the flour, salt, and instant yeast and stir on low speed for 1 minute to evenly distribute the yeast.

5. Add the poolish, water, and ⅓ cup of the olive oil and mix on medium speed until no wet flour remains, about 1 minute. If there is still dry flour in the bowl, scrape down the sides and bottom of the bowl, add 1 to 2 tablespoons of water, and mix on medium speed for 1 minute until no dry flour remains. Mix on medium-low speed for 8 to 12 minutes, or until the dough has pulled away from the sides and bottom of the bowl. If after 12 minutes the dough is still sticking to the bottom of the bowl, add 2 tablespoons of flour and mix for 3 more minutes on medium-low speed.

6. Lightly grease a large bowl with the remaining 1 tablespoon olive oil. Form a ball with the dough, place it in the bowl, cover with beeswax or plastic wrap, and allow it to rise at room temperature until it has doubled in size, about 1 hour.

DO AHEAD: Mix the poolish, a pre-ferment, at least 24 hours and up to 48 hours before you want to mix your dough. The pizza dough can be made ahead and stored, covered with beeswax or plastic wrap, in the refrigerator for up to 36 hours. Allow the chilled dough to come to room temperature for 30 to 45 minutes before using.

Poolish

1¾ cups bread flour
⅓ cup whole wheat flour
1¼ cups water, room temperature
1 teaspoon dried instant dry yeast

Dough

2⅓ cups bread flour
2 teaspoons salt
1 teaspoon instant dry yeast
⅓ cup water, room temperature
⅓ cup + 1 tablespoon olive oil, divided

DO AHEAD: This dough can be made ahead and stored, covered with beeswax or plastic wrap, in the refrigerator for up to 36 hours or in the freezer for up to 1 month. If frozen, thaw in the refrigerator overnight. Allow refrigerated or previously frozen dough to sit at room temperature for 45 to 60 minutes before rolling it out.

2 cups all-purpose flour
2 tablespoons granulated sugar
2 teaspoons instant dry yeast
1 teaspoon salt
¾ cup whole milk, warm
¼ cup unsalted butter
1 teaspoon pure vanilla extract

Enriched Dough

MAKES enough for 6 large Nutella Twists (page 47), 12 Mini-Cinny Buns (page 113), or 12 Pull-Apart Garlic Cheese Buns (page 277) • **PREP:** 15 minutes, plus rising time

Enriched doughs contain a higher percentage of fats, sugar, and dairy than lean doughs. They are more tender and fluffier than their lean counterparts and are flexible in both sweet and savoury recipes.

1. In the bowl of a stand mixer fitted with the dough hook attachment, add the flour, sugar, instant yeast, and salt and stir on low speed for 1 minute to evenly distribute the yeast.

2. Add the milk, butter, and vanilla and mix on medium speed until no wet flour remains, about 1 minute. Mix on medium-low speed for 8 to 12 minutes, or until the dough has pulled away from the sides and bottom of the bowl and the dough is silky smooth. If after 12 minutes the dough is still sticking to the bottom of the bowl, add 2 tablespoons of flour and mix for 3 more minutes on medium-low speed.

3. Lightly grease a large bowl with canola oil. Form a ball with the dough, place it in the bowl, and allow it to rise, covered, for 1 hour at room temperature or until it has doubled in size. (If you are using the dough the next day and wish to refrigerate it overnight, allow the dough to rise for only 30 minutes, then place it in the fridge, covered, with room to double in size, for up to 36 hours.)

Chocolate

How to Temper Chocolate

Tempering chocolate is the act of heating and cooling chocolate to form beta crystals that stabilize the chocolate, giving it a glossy, smooth finish that won't melt on your hands or discolour as it cools. Properly tempered chocolate has a lovely snap to it when it breaks and melts smoothly on the tongue. The simplest way to explain this process is that when you melt the chocolate, all the crystals in the cocoa butter relax and start floating around freely. When you add the seeding chocolate (small pieces of chocolate that are already properly tempered) to your melted chocolate and stir vigorously, you are cooling the chocolate, and at the same time the seeding chocolate is "teaching" the melted chocolate how to form proper crystals again. Once you return the chocolate to below 89°F (32°C) by continuing to stir, it should be tempered. Tempered chocolate hardens quickly at room temperature, so you will need to work quickly. You can always re-temper the chocolate if it firms up before you complete the project.

1. Tempered chocolate is time sensitive and will firm up quickly once properly tempered, so make sure you have prepared all your tools and have the items you wish to dip or coat within reach. We are using the seeding method of tempering chocolate. It is the easiest way to temper at home. Set up a double boiler by first filling a medium pot with 2 to 3 inches of water and bringing it to a boil. Select the largest glass or metal bowl you have that will fit over your pot but won't touch the water. Once the water has boiled, reduce the heat to maintain a low simmer and place the bowl over the pot. Add two-thirds of the total chocolate to the bowl, setting the remaining one-third aside. It is important that no steam gets into the bowl. Any moisture can seize the chocolate and make it impossible to temper. Stir the chocolate frequently with a silicone spatula until it has all melted and reaches 125°F to 130°F (52°C to 55°C) on a candy thermometer. Do not heat the chocolate over 130°F (55°C) (see page 306 photo A).

2. Once the melted chocolate has reached 125°F to 130°F (52°C to 55°C), remove it from the heat and place the bowl on a damp kitchen towel to keep it from shifting while you stir. Add most of the remaining chocolate, reserving about one-quarter. Stir vigorously in one direction until all the seeding chocolate is melted (see page 306 photo B). The goal is to have all the chocolate melted and the temperature reduced to 89°F (32°C).

3. Check the temperature of your chocolate. If it is still above 93°F (34°C), add the reserved chocolate and stir vigorously in the same direction until all the seeding chocolate is melted (see page 306 photo C). If your arm gets sore, switch hands but maintain the same direction while stirring.

4. Check the temperature of your chocolate again. If it is still above 93°F (34°C), add the remaining 1 to 2 ounces (28 to 57 g) chocolate and stir vigorously in the same direction until all the seeding chocolate is melted (see below, photo D). If the chocolate is still not at 89°F (32°C), continue to stir vigorously until it is.

5. Once your chocolate is below 89°F (32°C), check your temper by drizzling chocolate over the back of a metal spoon or palette knife (see photo E). Let sit for 3 to 4 minutes. The chocolate on the tester should harden and be glossy within 4 minutes (see photo F). If your chocolate does not harden or is cloudy or streaky, stir as hard as you can for 60 to 120 seconds and test again.

DO AHEAD: This ganache can be made ahead and stored in an airtight container in the refrigerator for up to 2 weeks or in the freezer for up to 6 months. When ready to use, in a small heat-resistant bowl, reheat in the microwave in 15-second intervals, stirring after each interval, until a pourable consistency is achieved. If frozen, thaw in the refrigerator overnight before reheating.

3½ ounces (100 g/½ cup)
   semi-sweet chocolate callets or
   good-quality chopped chocolate
¼ cup whipping (35%) cream
3 tablespoons white corn syrup

Dark Chocolate Ganache

MAKES ½ cup • **PREP:** 5 minutes

Use your favourite eating chocolate, whatever that is, to make ganache! For chocolates with higher cocoa contents, you may need to add a tablespoon or two of extra cream. For very sweet chocolates, reduce the corn syrup to 2 tablespoons. We like to triple or quadruple this recipe and freeze ½-cup portions of chocolate ganache to make it easy to ice a cake or create a sundae bar at the last minute.

1. Combine all the ingredients in a small heat-resistant bowl and heat in the microwave for 30 seconds. Vigorously stir until the ingredients are incorporated and the mixture is glossy and smooth. If you see any lumps, heat in the microwave in 15-second intervals, stirring after each interval, until smooth.

DO AHEAD: This ganache can be made ahead and stored in an airtight container in the refrigerator for up to 2 weeks or in the freezer for up to 6 months. When ready to use, in a small heat-resistant bowl, reheat in the microwave in 15-second intervals, stirring after each interval, until a pourable consistency is achieved. If frozen, thaw in the refrigerator overnight before reheating.

3½ ounces (100 g/½ cup) milk
   chocolate callets or good-quality
   chopped chocolate
3 tablespoons whipping (35%)
   cream
3 tablespoons white corn syrup

Milk Chocolate Ganache

MAKES about ½ cup • **PREP:** 5 minutes

Ganache is a flexible addition to many recipes and very common around the bakery. This is a very straightforward recipe that requires only that you start with good-quality chocolate and cream for great results. After that, you just need to avoid overheating and scorching the chocolate. Thirty seconds might seem like nothing, but in most microwaves it is usually enough time to get the mixture warm enough that it will continue to melt as you stir.

1. Combine all the ingredients in a small heat-resistant bowl and heat in the microwave for 30 seconds. Vigorously stir until the ingredients are incorporated and the mixture is glossy and smooth. If you see any lumps, heat in the microwave in 15-second intervals, stirring after each interval, until smooth.

White Chocolate Ganache

MAKES about ⅓ cup • **PREP:** 5 minutes

This ganache is used mostly to add a punch of colour to our baked goods. However, just like in our other ganaches, good-quality chocolate is the key here. Pick a chocolate you enjoy eating, but you do not need to buy the most expensive one.

1. Combine the ingredients in a small heat-resistant bowl and heat in the microwave for 30 seconds. Vigorously stir until the ingredients are incorporated and the mixture is glossy and smooth. If you see any lumps, heat in the microwave in 15-second intervals, stirring after each interval, until smooth.

DO AHEAD: This ganache can be made ahead and stored in an airtight container in the refrigerator for up to 2 weeks or in the freezer for up to 6 months. When ready to use, in a small heat-resistant bowl, reheat in the microwave in 15-second intervals, stirring after each interval, until a pourable consistency is achieved. If frozen, thaw in the refrigerator overnight before reheating.

3 ounces (85 g/½ cup) white chocolate callets or good-quality chopped chocolate
2 tablespoons whipping (35%) cream
3 tablespoons white corn syrup

White Chocolate Whipped Ganache

MAKES about 6 cups • **PREP:** 30 minutes

It took us years to develop just the right texture for this melt-in-your-mouth but stable whipped ganache. We now use it to make chocolate-covered Easter eggs, as layers in bars, and even in stuffed cookies. It mixes for a very long time, so if your mixer seems to be getting too warm, reduce the speed and mix for a longer period, or take a few 3-minute breaks during mixing to cool down your mixer.

1. In a medium heat-resistant bowl, heat the cream and white chocolate in the microwave in 30-second intervals, stirring vigorously after each interval, until the ganache is smooth and the chocolate is melted. Stir the ganache until silky smooth.

2. In the bowl of a stand mixer fitted with the paddle attachment, start mixing the warm white chocolate ganache with the icing sugar on low speed, gradually increasing the speed to high. Mix on high speed until all the icing sugar is incorporated, about 2 minutes. Reduce the speed to medium-high and continue to mix for 20 to 25 minutes until the mixture is smooth and fluffy and the bowl is cool. Use immediately while the ganache is still fairly liquid.

DO AHEAD: This ganache can be made ahead and stored in an airtight container at room temperature for up to 2 days or in the refrigerator for up to 2 weeks. When ready to use, warm it in the microwave in 30-second intervals, stirring after each interval, until a pourable consistency is achieved.

¾ cup + 2½ teaspoons whipping (35%) cream
17½ ounces (500 g/3 cups) white chocolate callets or good-quality chopped chocolate
4¼ cups icing sugar

Compotes and Jams

Strawberry Compote Ⓥ

MAKES 2 cups • **PREP:** 5 minutes • **COOK:** 30 minutes

Depending on the size of your strawberries, you may want to quarter the fruit, but we love a chunky compote with big pieces of fruit that burst in your mouth. Compotes freeze really well, so always make a double batch so you can have some on hand.

1. Place the ingredients in a heavy medium pot over medium-high heat. Using a wooden spoon, stir together to coat the strawberries evenly in the sugar and lemon juice. Stir occasionally, breaking up any larger berries with the spoon, until the mixture comes to a boil, and then reduce the heat to low. Keep the mixture at a low rolling boil, stirring occasionally, for 15 to 20 minutes until the strawberries start to soften and lose their shape. You will notice that the juices evaporate and thicken. Depending on your desired final thickness, you can simmer the compote for up to 30 minutes. The compote will thicken more as it cools. Remove from the heat and allow to cool completely.

DO AHEAD: This compote can be made ahead and stored in an airtight container in the refrigerator for up to 2 weeks or in the freezer for up to 4 months. If frozen, thaw in the refrigerator overnight before using.

3 cups fresh or frozen strawberries, hulled
¼ cup granulated sugar
1 tablespoon lemon juice

Mixed Berry Compote Ⓥ

MAKES 2 cups • **PREP:** 5 minutes • **COOK:** 30 minutes

Enjoy this compote on toast as a jam, as a topping for yogurt or ice cream, as a filling for sandwich cookies or cakes, to flavour buttercreams, or as a topping for mini cheesecakes. Any combination of strawberries, blueberries, raspberries, or blackberries will work if you can't find a mixed berry blend or want to use what you have on hand.

1. Place the ingredients in a heavy medium pot over medium-high heat. Using a wooden spoon, stir together to coat the berries evenly in the sugar and lemon juice. Stir occasionally, breaking up any larger berries with the spoon, until the mixture comes to a boil, and then reduce the heat to low. Keep the mixture at a low rolling boil, stirring occasionally, for 15 to 20 minutes until the berries start to soften and lose their shape. You will notice that the juices evaporate and thicken. Depending on your desired final thickness, you can simmer the compote for up to 30 minutes. The compote will thicken more as it cools. Remove from the heat and allow to cool completely.

DO AHEAD: This compote can be made ahead and stored in an airtight container in the refrigerator for up to 2 weeks or in the freezer for up to 4 months. If frozen, thaw in the refrigerator overnight before using.

3 cups fresh or frozen mixed berries
¼ cup granulated sugar
1 tablespoon lemon juice

Sour Cherry Compote ⓥ

MAKES about 3 cups • **PREP:** 5 minutes • **COOK:** 12 minutes boiling

This compote is delicious served over ice cream or yogurt and as a filling for cakes or tarts. It's not overly sweet and the touch of orange makes the cherry flavour shine.

DO AHEAD: This compote can be made ahead and stored in an airtight container in the refrigerator for up to 1 month or in the freezer for up to 6 months. If frozen, thaw in the refrigerator overnight before using.

2 cups jarred pitted red sour cherries in light syrup
2 tablespoons fresh orange juice, freshly squeezed
Zest of ½ orange

1. Using a fine-mesh strainer, drain the cherries over a small bowl. Reserve ½ cup of the cherry juice. Check the cherries to ensure that there are no pits.

2. Place the drained cherries, orange juice, orange zest, and reserved ½ cup cherry juice in a heavy medium pot over medium-high heat. Using a silicone spatula, stir and scrape down the sides and bottom of the pot until the mixture comes to a boil, then reduce the heat to low, maintaining a gentle boil, and cook, stirring occasionally, for 8 to 12 minutes until the cherries have burst and the liquid is reduced by half. The sauce will thicken considerably as it cools. Remove from the heat and allow to cool completely.

Raspberry Jam ⓥ

MAKES about 2 cups • **PREP:** 5 minutes • **COOK:** 15 minutes boiling

Our bakers first developed this jam to fill pop tarts, but it is so delicious we quickly started using it as our standard raspberry jam. The raspberry flavour is the star here, so seek out good-quality berries.

DO AHEAD: This jam can be made ahead and stored in an airtight container in the refrigerator for up to 1 month or in the freezer for up to 4 months. If frozen, thaw in the refrigerator overnight before using.

2 cups frozen or fresh raspberries
1¼ cups granulated sugar

1. Place a small plate in the refrigerator.

2. Place the raspberries and sugar in a heavy medium pot over medium-high heat. Using a wooden spoon, stir together to coat the raspberries evenly in the sugar. Cook, stirring occasionally, breaking up the berries a little with the spoon, until the mixture comes to a boil, and then reduce the heat to medium. Keep the mixture at a rolling boil and continue to cook, stirring occasionally, for 10 to 15 minutes until the jam starts to thicken.

3. Continue to boil the jam until it reaches 220°F (105°C) on a candy thermometer, then test for set point by spooning a small amount of jam on the refrigerated plate. Let sit for 30 seconds and then push the jam with a spoon. The surface of the jam should wrinkle like jelly, not move like a liquid. Remove from the heat and allow to cool completely.

Cranberry Sauce Ⓥ

MAKES about 2 cups • **PREP:** 5 minutes • **COOK:** 7 minutes boiling

Obviously this is the go-to side for roasted turkey, but we also love this sauce served with brie cheese, mixed with mayonnaise as a sandwich spread, or added to pre-made BBQ sauce or glazes for meat.

1. Place the ingredients in a heavy medium pot over medium-high heat. Use a silicone spatula to stir and scrape down the sides and bottom of the pot until the mixture comes to a boil, and then reduce the heat to low. Keep the mixture at a low rolling boil and continue to cook, stirring occasionally, for 5 to 7 minutes until the cranberries have burst and the liquid is reduced by half. The sauce will thicken considerably as it cools. Remove from the heat and allow to cool completely.

DO AHEAD: This sauce can be made ahead and stored in an airtight container in the refrigerator for up to 1 month or in the freezer for up to 6 months. If frozen, thaw in the refrigerator overnight before using.

2 cups fresh or frozen cranberries
½ cup granulated sugar
½ cup water

Dry Mixes

Speculoos Spice Mix Ⓥ

MAKES ⅓ cup • **PREP:** 3 minutes

Traditionally a cookie spice mix used in Belgium and the Netherlands, our speculoos spice mix was developed to give our Ginger Snaps (page 235) a unique twist. For the best flavour and aroma, use whole spices and grind them in a coffee grinder yourself. Use a fine-mesh metal sieve to sift out any large pieces. This batch size should be perfect to get you through six months of use. Avoid overstocking spices since they taste best fresh. Try it as a substitute for pumpkin spice mix, add a teaspoon to a batch of chocolate chip or oatmeal cookies, stir ¼ teaspoon into a mug of your favourite coffee or black tea, or add a teaspoon to a batch of Pastry Cream (page 315).

1. In a medium bowl, whisk together the ingredients until fully combined.

DO AHEAD: This dry mix can be made ahead and stored in an airtight container at room temperature for up to 6 months.

3 tablespoons + 1 teaspoon cinnamon
1 tablespoon freshly grated or ground nutmeg
1 tablespoon ground cloves
2 teaspoons ground ginger
1 teaspoon ground white pepper
1 teaspoon ground black pepper
1 teaspoon ground cardamom

Pumpkin Spice Mix Ⓥ

MAKES about ¾ cup • **PREP:** 3 minutes

We make our own special pumpkin spice blend at the bakery that evolved from a whole spice, chai tea mix that Josie has been making for more than two decades, influenced by her time in high school as a waitress at an Indian restaurant where she fell in love with cardamom. We think it really rounds out our pumpkin spice and gives it a distinctive flavour.

1. In a medium bowl, whisk together the ingredients until fully combined.

> **DO AHEAD:** This dry mix can be made ahead and stored in an airtight container at room temperature for up to 6 months.

¼ cup cinnamon
¼ cup ground ginger
1 tablespoon ground allspice
1 tablespoon ground cardamom
1 tablespoon freshly grated or
    ground nutmeg
1½ teaspoons ground cloves

Ranch Spice Mix Ⓥ

MAKES about ¼ cup • **PREP:** 3 minutes

Not a traditional mix for ranch, but one of our multi-talented bakers, Melissa, whipped it up to create a dip for veggies one day and everyone loved it so much it became a bakery staple.

1. In a medium bowl, whisk together the ingredients until fully combined.

> **DO AHEAD:** This dry mix can be made ahead and stored in an airtight container at room temperature for up to 6 months.

2 tablespoons Italiano seasoning
    (we use Club House)
1 tablespoon dried dill
1 tablespoon onion powder
1½ teaspoons garlic powder

Barbecue Spice Mix

MAKES about ½ cup • **PREP:** 3 minutes

This flexible spice mix is delicious on pork, poultry, fish, or seafood. It's not sweet like a lot of BBQ spice mixes, it has more of an earthy citrus quality from the cumin and coriander. We love it as a rub for pulled pork in our Mile-High Pulled Pork Mac and Cheese Pie (page 149), but it is also an easy way to flavour chicken or fish for the grill. Mix a ratio of 1 tablespoon of spice mix with 1 teaspoon of salt and sprinkle it liberally on your protein of choice just before grilling.

1. In a medium bowl, whisk together the ingredients until fully combined.

DO AHEAD: This dry mix can be made ahead and stored in an airtight container at room temperature for up to 6 months.

2 tablespoons onion powder
2 tablespoons paprika
2 tablespoons chili powder
2 teaspoons ground coriander
2 teaspoons ground cumin

Vegan Egg Replacer Ⓥ

MAKES about 6 tablespoons, enough to replace 12 eggs • **PREP:** 3 minutes

Great for replacing eggs in cookies or bars, this is an excellent alternative to have on hand for last-minute vegan guests or when a baking urge strikes and you are out of eggs. Avoid using it as an egg replacer in aerated products like cakes, though, as it just doesn't provide the volume you need.

1. In a medium bowl, whisk together the ingredients until fully combined.

DO AHEAD: This egg replacer can be made ahead and stored in an airtight container at room temperature for up to 6 months. When ready to use, for the equivalent of 1 egg, stir together 2 tablespoons of water and 1½ teaspoons of egg replacer.

6 tablespoons cornstarch
1 teaspoon xanthan gum
½ teaspoon baking powder

Miscellaneous Basic Recipes

Marshmallows

MAKES 4 dozen 1½-inch square marshmallows (about 2 pounds/900 g)
• **PREP:** 30 minutes, plus setting time

DO AHEAD: These marshmallows can be made ahead and stored in an airtight container at room temperature for up to 2 months.

13 ounces (370 g/1⅓ cups + 2 tablespoons) water, room temperature, divided
1½ ounces (40 g/¼ cup) gelatin powder
1⅓ pounds (600 g/3 cups) granulated sugar
15 ounces (425 g/1⅓ cups) liquid glucose
1 tablespoon vanilla bean paste
¼ teaspoon salt
3⅓ cups (455 g) icing sugar, sifted and divided, more for dusting the knife

Once you have made these fluffy, melt-in-your-mouth, real vanilla cubes of sugary goodness, you will never eat a stale store-bought marshmallow again. Glucose is not a common home baking ingredient, but it can be found at most bulk stores or online. It is not the same as light corn syrup but is much thicker and acts as a stabilizer in this recipe. This is a sticky recipe! When working with the glucose, coat your tools with water or canola oil cooking spray to avoid sticking. We suggest you use a kitchen scale, as this is a recipe easier made by weight instead of cups, but we have included both measures here in case you do not have a scale.

1. Generously spray a 13- × 9-inch baking dish with canola oil cooking spray. Line the bottom (not the sides) of the pan with parchment paper and generously spray the parchment with cooking spray.

2. In the bowl of a 6-quart or larger stand mixer, combine half of the water and all the gelatin powder and set aside to bloom. It will take 2 to 3 minutes for the gelatin to swell with the water and form a gel.

3. Pour the remaining water into a large pot. Pour the granulated sugar and glucose over the water. Do not stir. Bring the mixture to a boil over high heat and boil, without stirring, until the temperature reaches 238°F (114°C) on a candy thermometer, 8 to 12 minutes.

4. Place the bowl with the bloomed gelatin on a stand mixer fitted with the whisk attachment. Carefully pour the hot sugar mixture into the bowl and immediately start mixing on low speed, gradually increasing the speed to high. The mixture will foam and steam. Whip on high speed for 6 to 7 minutes. The whipped marshmallow will continue to increase in volume until it has almost filled the bowl. It is done when you can see the marshmallow forming stretchy bands like chewing gum as it whips and the mixture is opaque and glossy white. The marshmallow should still be warm when done. In the last minute of whipping, add the vanilla bean paste and salt.

5. Using a silicone spatula coated in canola oil cooking spray, heap the marshmallow into the prepared baking dish, scraping the bowl clean. Spread out the marshmallow evenly, then tap the bottom of the dish on the counter to settle the marshmallow. Sprinkle ⅓ cup of the icing sugar over the entire surface to prevent the marshmallow from forming a hard crust. Cover the dish with plastic wrap and let sit at room temperature overnight to firm up.

(CONTINUES)

6. The next day, dust the countertop generously with 1 cup of the icing sugar and turn out the marshmallow slab onto the counter so that the bottom is facing up. Remove the parchment paper and sprinkle 1 cup of the icing sugar over the bottom of the marshmallow slab.

7. Place the remaining 1 cup icing sugar in a medium bowl to use for cutting and dusting the marshmallows. Using a 10-inch or longer chef's knife with the blade dusted with icing sugar, slice the marshmallow into forty-eight 1½-inch square pieces by first cutting it into eight 9-inch-long strips. Then cut each strip into 6 equal pieces. Dust the knife with icing sugar as you make each cut and dust all sides of the marshmallows as you cut them. This will prevent them from sticking together.

Pastry Cream

MAKES 2½ cups • **PREP:** 10 minutes, plus chilling time

Pastry cream, or thick vanilla custard, is one of those incredibly versatile and useful basic recipes that once you have made it, you will use all the time. Our version is very vanilla forward in flavour, just lightly sweet, and not too heavy since it uses just milk and no cream.

1. In a heavy medium pot, combine the milk and ¼ cup of the sugar and bring to a simmer over medium heat, 2 to 3 minutes.

2. In a medium heat-resistant bowl, whisk together the remaining ⅓ cup sugar and the cornstarch to remove any lumps from the cornstarch. Add the egg yolks and whole egg to the mixture, whisking to a smooth consistency. Roll a clean kitchen towel into a tube and place it in a circle on the countertop. Place the bowl inside this nest to keep it in place.

3. When the milk comes to a simmer, carefully pour it into the bowl in a steady, slow stream while mixing vigorously with a whisk to prevent overheating the eggs. After you have tempered the mixture, pour it back into the pot and bring to a boil over medium-high heat, stirring constantly so that the eggs do not curdle or scorch on the bottom. When the mixture comes to a boil and thickens with fierce bubbles rising to the top, reduce the heat to medium-low and cook out the cornstarch, stirring constantly, for 1 minute.

4. Remove from the heat and stir in the butter, vanilla paste and extract, and salt, mixing until the butter is completely melted and the pastry cream is smooth. Pour into a heat-resistant container and place a piece of plastic wrap directly on the surface to prevent a skin from forming. Refrigerate in an airtight container for 4 to 6 hours to thicken before use.

DO AHEAD: This pastry cream can be made ahead and stored in an airtight container in the refrigerator for up to 2 weeks. When ready to use, place the chilled pastry cream in the bowl of a stand mixer fitted with the paddle attachment and beat on medium speed to return it to a smooth consistency, about 2 minutes.

2 cups whole milk
¼ cup + ⅓ cup granulated sugar, divided
¼ cup cornstarch
2 large egg yolks
1 large egg
2 tablespoons unsalted butter
1 tablespoon vanilla bean paste
1 teaspoon pure vanilla extract
½ teaspoon salt

DO AHEAD: This lemon curd can be made ahead and stored in an airtight container in the refrigerator for up to 1 month or in the freezer for up to 6 months. If frozen, thaw in the refrigerator overnight before using.

2½ cups granulated sugar
1¼ cups freshly squeezed lemon juice (about 6 lemons)
1 cup unsalted butter
Pinch of salt
4 eggs
8 egg yolks

Lemon Curd

MAKES about 4 cups • **PREP:** 5 minutes • **COOK:** 15 minutes

Our curd is more butter-heavy than other lemon curds, which gives it an extra-thick, creamy texture and helps it stand up well to freezing. If you are new to making curds or custards, watch the heat carefully and make sure you are scraping all the way to the bottom and corners of the saucepan when you stir to make sure you do not end up with scrambled eggs.

1. In a medium saucepan, heat the sugar, lemon juice, butter, and salt over medium heat, stirring occasionally with a wooden spoon until the butter has melted and the sugar has dissolved, about 3 minutes.

2. In a medium bowl, whisk together the eggs and egg yolks. While whisking, very slowly pour in the hot lemon mixture. It is important to keep whisking while you do this to avoid curdling the mixture.

3. After you have tempered the mixture, pour it back into the saucepan and cook, stirring constantly, over medium-low heat until it has thickened and coats the back of the wooden spoon, up to 10 minutes. Be careful not to overheat the mixture or you will end up with lemon-flavoured scrambled eggs.

4. When the mixture has thickened, remove from the heat and carefully strain the mixture through a fine-mesh sieve into a clean medium bowl to remove any eggy bits. Allow the mixture to cool completely.

DO AHEAD: This simple syrup can be made ahead and stored in an airtight container in the refrigerator for up to 3 weeks.

1 cup water
1 cup sugar
1 teaspoon lemon juice

Simple Syrup

MAKES 1 cup • **PREP:** 3 minutes • **COOK:** 3 minutes

Simple syrup is the baker's secret weapon that will transform your cakes from amateur to professional. Use it to moisten cakes and trifles or use the variations to add flavour to baked goods. Simple syrup is also a common cocktail ingredient, so maybe double the recipe and whip up some mojitos to go with your baking.

1. Place the ingredients in a heavy medium saucepan over high heat and stir to dissolve the sugar completely. Bring the mixture to a boil without stirring and let boil for 3 minutes. Allow to cool completely.

VARIATIONS

Raspberry Flavour: Add 2 tablespoons raspberry jam after the simple syrup has cooled. Strain out any seeds using a fine-mesh sieve.

Lemon Flavour: Add the juice of 2 lemons.

Caramel

MAKES 1½ cups • **PREP:** 3 minutes • **COOK:** 12 minutes, plus cooling time

If you do not have a candy thermometer, you can still make this caramel; at the bakery we always make it by look, not by temperature. As the caramel starts to darken and go from clear to light brown to amber brown, be observant. When smaller, more condensed bubbles form on the surface of the sugar, the caramel is close to done. The bubbles themselves will be dark amber. To test, carefully dip a spoon into the mixture, drip a drop on a plate, and check the colour. If it's ready, move on to the next step; if it requires more time, let it bubble some more. However, do not walk away! Medium brown caramel can shift to burnt caramel faster than you think.

DO AHEAD: This caramel can be made ahead and stored in an airtight container at room temperature for up to 1 month.

1½ cups granulated sugar

⅓ cup water

1 teaspoon lemon juice

½ cup whipping (35%) cream, room temperature

1 teaspoon vanilla bean paste

½ teaspoon salt

1. In a heavy medium saucepan, stir together the sugar, water, and lemon juice until the sugar is dissolved. When the sugar is mostly dissolved, bring to a boil over high heat without stirring. The lemon juice is acidic and will help keep the sugar from crystallizing. Boil on high heat, without stirring, until the temperature reaches at least 345°F (174°C) on a candy thermometer, about 10 minutes. Watch for a dark amber tone (not too dark, though; if it is black or the mixture smokes, you have gone too far).

2. When the caramel is a rich amber colour, carefully remove the pot from the heat and place it on a heat-resistant surface. Slowly pour the cream into the mixture in small additions, stirring carefully after each addition and backing away once it begins to climb the sides of the pot. Stir in the vanilla bean paste and salt. Leave the caramel in the pot and cool to room temperature. The cooling process may take 3 to 4 hours.

Mascarpone Filling

MAKES 2 cups • **PREP:** 8 minutes, plus setting time

As delicious as this filling is in tiramisu, it might be even better as a dip for fresh fruit or cookies. It is creamy, sweet, and surprisingly light and fresh.

DO AHEAD: This filling can be made ahead and stored in an airtight container in the refrigerator for up to 1 week.

1 pound (450 g) mascarpone cheese, room temperature

½ cup icing sugar

½ cup whipping (35%) cream

1. In the bowl of a stand mixer fitted with the paddle attachment, add the mascarpone cheese and beat on medium speed to a silky-smooth consistency, 2 to 3 minutes. Scrape down the sides and bottom of the bowl.

2. Sift the icing sugar into the bowl and beat on medium-high speed until smooth and combined, 2 to 3 minutes. Do not overmix. Scrape down the sides and bottom of the bowl.

3. Add the cream and beat on high speed until the mixture is light and fluffy, 1 minute.

4. Transfer to an airtight container and chill in the refrigerator for 4 to 6 hours to thicken before using.

Pecan Praline

MAKES 2 cups • **PREP:** 3 minutes • **COOK:** 10 minutes

An excellent addition to cheese platters or a snack spread, these aren't just for topping desserts! You can easily double the recipe but be sure if you go any bigger that your saucepan is big enough to handle the bubbling sugar.

DO AHEAD: This praline can be made ahead. Once completely cool, store in an airtight container at room temperature for up to 2 months.

½ cup granulated sugar
½ cup packed dark brown sugar
¼ cup water
1 tablespoon honey
1½ teaspoons pure vanilla extract
2 cups whole pecan halves

1. Line a baking sheet with parchment paper or a silicone baking mat.

2. In a heavy medium saucepan, add the granulated sugar, brown sugar, water, honey, and vanilla and stir together until the sugar is dissolved. When the sugar is mostly dissolved, bring to a boil and cook, without stirring, over high heat until the temperature reaches at least 240°F (115°C) on a candy thermometer, about 5 minutes.

3. Reduce the heat to medium-high and add the pecans. Stir the mixture until the liquid comes back to a boil and cook, stirring frequently, for 1 minute. Remove from the heat and continue stirring the pecans until the coating becomes whitish and opaque, almost like fudge, 3 to 5 minutes. The pecans will break up a little as you stir. Scrape the pecan mixture onto the prepared baking sheet and spread out the pecans into a single layer to cool completely.

Mixed Candied Peel ⓥ

MAKES ⅓ cup • **PREP:** 30 minutes, plus cooling time

To achieve the long and wide zest strips needed for this recipe, remove the zest from the citrus with a vegetable peeler or very carefully with a paring knife, removing as little pith as possible. These will be sticky, and don't worry if they get even stickier with time if they cannot be stored in a dry environment. If your home is very warm or humid, store these in the refrigerator to help them last longer.

DO AHEAD: If you would like to keep the candied peel soft, you can store it submerged in the syrup instead of straining it. Store the peel submerged in syrup in an airtight container in the refrigerator for up to 6 months. If you would like dry strips, strain as instructed and store in an airtight container at room temperature for up to 2 months.

1 cup granulated sugar
1 cup water
2 medium lemons, peeled in long strips lengthwise, white pith removed
1 large orange, peeled in long strips lengthwise, white pith removed

1. In a medium saucepan, add the sugar, water, and lemon and orange peel strips and bring to a boil, without stirring, over high heat. Reduce the heat to medium, maintaining a boil, and continue to cook, stirring occasionally, until the peel is translucent, 15 to 25 minutes. Remove from the heat, strain the zest and, using metal tongs, lay the pieces out in a single layer on a wire rack, using a heat-resistant spatula to separate the zest strands as best as you can. Allow to cool, uncovered, in a dry area. The peel is ready to use as soon as it comes to room temperature.

Dulce de Leche

MAKES 1⅓ cups • **PREP:** 3 minutes • **COOK:** 3 hours

We love how easy it is to make a cheater's dulce de leche with just one ingredient—right in a convenient can! Be sure that the water remains at least 2 inches over the tops of the cans as you boil them or the cans may pop open and are potentially dangerous. The longer you boil the cans, the deeper the caramelization of the condensed milk and the firmer the dulce de leche will be.

1. Remove the paper label and place the can of sweetened condensed milk in a heavy medium saucepan. Cover the can with warm water at least 2 inches above the can. (You can boil multiple cans at a time as long as there is an inch of room around each can for the water to circulate.)

2. Bring the water to a boil over high heat. Once the water is boiling, reduce the heat to low and maintain a simmer, covered, for up to 3 hours. If the water level drops, top it up with boiling water to maintain the 2-inch headspace.

3. Using metal tongs, remove the can from the water and allow it to cool for 10 to 15 minutes before opening it. Use a kitchen towel when opening the can to prevent burns.

DO AHEAD: This caramelized milk can be made ahead and stored in an airtight container at room temperature for up to 1 day or in the refrigerator for up to 2 weeks.

1 can (14 ounces/300 mL) sweetened condensed milk

Poultry Stock

MAKES 8 cups • **PREP:** 5 minutes • **COOK:** 8 hours

In any sustainably minded kitchen, you will want to minimize your waste by making stock from any bones left from roasted meats. You can even collect clean kitchen scraps like carrot tops or trimmings from onions and celery and store them in the freezer until you have enough to make a stock. Just make sure that they have been washed well to avoid dirt hiding in the stems. We've used whole vegetables here, but the equivalent amount of scraps will work too.

1. In a large pot, combine the ingredients over high heat and cook, stirring occasionally, until the mixture comes to a boil, then reduce the heat to low. Skim off any foam that rises to the surface with a ladle or large spoon and discard. Simmer, covered, for 6 to 8 hours, ensuring that it stays at a simmer.

2. Strain the stock through a fine-mesh sieve and discard the solids. As the stock cools, skim off any fat that rises to the surface with a ladle or large spoon and discard.

DO AHEAD: Once fully cooled, store this stock in an airtight container in the refrigerator for up to 1 week or in the freezer for up to 6 months. If frozen, thaw in the refrigerator overnight before using.

12 cups water
1½ pounds (675 g) cooked chicken, turkey, or other poultry bones
1 large carrot, roughly chopped
3 ribs celery, roughly chopped
1 large white onion, roughly chopped
3 cloves garlic, peeled and cut in half
2 sprigs fresh rosemary
2 sprigs fresh thyme
1 bay leaf
½ teaspoon whole black peppercorns

Acknowledgments

Thank you, Braedon and Neil, for supporting (financially and otherwise) all my early party endeavours and making me believe I could be a chef. And thank you to your parents: Mark, Barb, Paul, and Michelle, who provided us with their homes, whether they knew it or not, for us to flex our culinary muscles.

Thank you, Emma, Steve, Duncan, Willa, and Flora, for letting us use your beautiful home for photographs and for the years of recipe development feedback at parties.

Thank you, Mum and Katie, for your continuing support and love. I am so grateful for all your help and encouragement during our move and beyond.

Thank you, the Rudderhams, for their constant support and for making a family move to Nova Scotia a possibility in the midst of writing this book.

Thank you, Grandma, for all your baking advice and shared recipes over the years. You might not find the joy in baking that I do, but your cooking was foundational to my love of good food and your hosting standards have spoiled me for life. Thank you, Grandma and Grandpa, for always making me feel like I could succeed at anything.

Thank you to the whole Lamb family, but especially Steve and Lyann, for exposing me to so many culinary adventures, supporting my dreams, and letting me learn to cook for a crowd long before I knew what I was doing.

My dad would have been very proud to see this book. He was the consummate host and he instilled a strong sense of hospitality in me that flows through his whole family. Thank you for the generous welcome, loving atmosphere, and inspiring foods the extended McCrindle clan has always enthusiastically provided.

Thank you, Luke, Lily, and Finn, for tolerating another round of super-early mornings, testing all the recipes with me, and feeding me while I was chained to a desk. This mama bear would be lost without you.

Thank you, Amanda and Erica, for being my best friends through all the chaos and life-altering disruptions. Thank you for all the parties and hours of cleanup that made me a chef.

Thank you, Michael, Amy, Evie, and Abby, for sharing your family recipes and your family with us. You are the other half we never knew we needed.

—**Josie**

Thank you to everyone who inspired, encouraged, and saw the baking passion burning within me all these years. It's certainly been a wild ride, and I am thankful that you joined me on this journey. From baking mishaps during childhood with friends (moms, you sure were brave to leave me unattended in your kitchens), to baking attempts in my own mom's kitchen developing the skills needed to later side-hustle custom cakes, to passing out cinnamon buns during the holidays in high school, to chancing a jump into the bustling hospitality industry through co-ops, apprenticeships, and beyond—you all helped play a part in the past, present, and future of Cake & Loaf! Much love to you all.

Most importantly, to my partner, Alex—you have supported me through all of these ups and downs, and as difficult as it's been sometimes, you've always been there for hugs and reassurance, shaping a positive approach and celebrating the wins!

To everyone who gave friendly support throughout this whole process or helped me with small inquiries; answered my illustration, design, or Photoshop queries; and loaned equipment—thank you for helping me broaden my skills and finish this massive body of work.

A thank you to everyone who stopped by for porch pickups of all the delicious baked goods post–photo shoots.

If you're reading any of the above and think it may be you, it is, and I will be sure to thank you in person, too!

—Nickey

Thank you Ruth Mar Tam, Ashley Kosowan, Jenna Hutinson, and Duff Goldman for generously praising our first book. Especially to Duff, who gave our young imaginations flight to dream of owning a bakery in the first place.

Thank you to all our staff past and present, but especially to our current crew: Mikayla, Tristan, Sarah, Kyle, Helen, Huong, Quinn, Melissa, Erin, Kristin, and Zoie. Special thanks to Erin and Sarah—we are so proud of your leadership and growth over the past couple of years.

Thank you to our editor, Andrea, for her patience and to all of Penguin Random House Canada for believing in us and giving us another chance.

Thank you Kate Sinclair for taking our words and pictures and transforming them into a piece of art.

A big warm hug to all our small business buddies in Hamilton and beyond who supported our first book. We are forever grateful.

—Josie and Nickey

Index

LAND ACKNOWLEDGMENT

We recognize and acknowledge that this book was written on and our bakery resides on the traditional territories of the Erie, Neutral, Huron-Wendat, Haudenosaunee, and Mississauga. This land is covered by the Dish With One Spoon wampum belt covenant, which was an agreement between the Haudenosaunee and Anishinaabek to share and care for the resources around the Great Lakes. Subsequent newcomers have been invited into this treaty in the spirit of peace, friendship, and respect. We further acknowledge that this land is covered by the Between the Lakes Treaty No. 3 (1792) between the Crown and the Mississaugas of the Credit First Nation.

Without this unique land, our bakery would not have been possible. We acknowledge that our privileges have been achieved at the expense of the original inhabitants of Turtle Island. We believe we must all work to educate ourselves about the history and continuing effects of colonialism, to increase our understanding of the treatment of Indigenous peoples on Turtle Island in both the past and the present, and to move forward sharing privilege and supporting justice.

~Nickey and Josie